PART III. PRACTICAL APPLICATIONS

PART IV. FUTURE PROSPECTS

I

Overviews

1

The Structure of the Argument

This book is about systems methodology, and therefore it might be well to start by saying something about the meaning of the terms *methodology* and *systems*.

The word *methodology* in the social sciences refers to the procedures used by a theorist in seeking to find out about social reality. In addition, in describing a particular methodology, reference will usually be made to the theoretical assumptions adopted in that methodology. So, for example, Durkheim (1938) describes the steps in his sociological methodology, and the theory underpinning it, in the book *The Rules of Sociological Method*. In the systems movement, also, the word *methodology* is sometimes used to refer to methods for exploring and gaining knowledge about systems. Because of a more practical orientation, however, the more normal usage is to describe the organized set of methods an analyst employs to intervene in and change real-world problem situations. Whichever is the case, it is not normally felt to be necessary for the advocate of a systems methodology to delve into its theoretical presuppositions.

The two meanings given to *methodology* in the social sciences and systems thinking suggest a different emphasis rather than a real distinction, and point to the respective strengths of the two traditions. The social sciences are strong on theory, on thinking about the ontological and epistemological assumptions that go into gaining knowledge, but they are weak on practice. It is quite obvious that the theoretical presuppositions that guide a methodology used for studying the social world will also have implications for how one might intervene in social reality. However, social scientists rarely seem to draw out these implications in terms of *specific* guidance for what should be done in changing organizations and society. Systems thinkers, on the other hand, are dedicated to practice, but often neglect theory. It is equally obvious that any attempt to change the world rests upon taken-for-granted assumptions about the nature of that world. Hidden in the commonsense or craft knowledge of the systems analyst are ontological and epistemological presuppositions. In not exploring these, systems thinking has failed to take full advantage of opportunities to learn from practice and to develop as a discipline.

In this book the word *methodology* will be used in the very broadest sense, to conjure up the best aspects of both the social scientist's and systems practitioner's meanings. It will refer to theoretically grounded sets of methods, whether the theory is explicit or implicit, and whether these are used to learn about the world or to intervene in it. I shall concentrate on systems intervention methodologies, because my main concern is with the practical task of managing problems and bringing about change. Systems methodologies are particularly strong in this area. It is clear, however, that in order to understand fully and to make the best use of systems methodologies, we shall have to learn about the theoretical assumptions on which they rest. Because systems thinking is weak in this respect, we have little option but to turn to ideas developed in the social sciences for the purpose of probing the theoretical underpinnings of methodologies. I shall not entirely neglect learning about systems. As has been said, some systems methodologies are oriented in this direction. It is also arguable, from the action-research point of view, that intervening in social systems *is* the best way of learning about them.

Examining the word *methodology* has helped to reveal some of the contributions this book hopes to make. Part I of the volume, as well as introducing the structure of the argument (which I am doing now), contains Chapter 2, "Theoretical Considerations." This deals, in summary form, with the background knowledge of theory that systems practitioners need before they can embark on the proper choice and use of a systems methodology. Part I acts, therefore, as an introduction to some highly relevant social science knowledge for *systems thinkers*. The following three parts of the book cover a variety of systems methodologies, tackle the practical application of systems approaches in the management context, and explore the future prospects facing systems thinking as a discipline. All three parts constantly refer back to the theoretical considerations of Chapter 2. Thus Parts II through IV offer to social scientists an examination of the applied world of systems thinking in terms they will understand. The book provides *social scientists* with access to modern systems approaches.

I have now outlined my broad usage of the word *methodology*, and explained why Part I of the book must provide the background theory that will enable the presuppositions made by systems methodologies to be unearthed. I can best elucidate the term *systems* while considering the structure of the argument in Part II of the book.

Until the 1970s, there was considerable agreement in the systems movement about how the notion of *system* should be understood and applied. The same could be said of the other key concepts in the systems dictionary—concepts such as *element, relationship, boundary, input, transformation, output, environment, feedback, attribute, purpose, open system, homeostasis, emergence, communication, control, identity,* and *hierarchy.* Some systems people (those of the general system persuasion) put more emphasis on learning about the nature of real-world systems, while others concentrated on developing methodologies, based on systems ideas and principles, to intervene and change systems. Nevertheless, there was a shared set of assumptions about the nature of systems and about the meaning and use of systems terms.

Systems people, whether theorists or practitioners, operated from within the same paradigm. Summarizing greatly, it was assumed that systems of all types could be identified by empirical observation of reality, and could be analyzed by essentially the same methods that had brought success in the natural sciences. Systems could then, if the interest was in practice, be manipulated the better to achieve whatever purposes they were designed to serve. Systems thinking until the 1970s, therefore, was dominated by the positivism and functionalism characteristic of the traditional version of the scientific method. We can call this type of systems thinking the *traditional* systems approach. It embraces strands of work such as "organizations as systems," general system theory, contingency theory, operational research, systems analysis, systems engineering, and management cybernetics.

During the 1970s and 1980s, however, traditional systems thinking became subject to increasing criticism, particularly from those who felt that it was proving unable to deal with ill-structured and strategic problems, and so was holding back the development and influence of the discipline. As a result of the obvious failings of traditional thinking, and the critical assault, alternative systems approaches were born and began to flourish. So, for example, in the late 1970s and early 1980s "soft systems thinking" and "organizational cybernetics" came to the fore, and in the late 1980s "critical systems thinking" was born. These new tendencies in systems thinking found themselves at war not only with the traditional approach but also with each other, for they were often opposed on fundamental matters concerning the nature and purpose of the discipline. They attracted different groups of adherents, put different emphases on the subject matter and key concepts of the field, and sometimes even harbored different interpretations of the role of the discipline. They rested upon different philosophical/sociological assumptions. In essence, they were based on different paradigms.

Inevitably, given the fundamental differences in orientation between the competing strands of the systems movement in the 1980s, even the notion of "system" came to acquire different uses and meanings. Nowhere is this more evident than in the shift achieved by Checkland in breaking from systems engineering and establishing soft systems methodology. In soft systems methodology, systems are seen as the mental constructs of observers rather than as entities with an objective existence in the world; systemicity is transferred "from the world to the process of inquiry into the world" (Checkland, 1983). Obviously, if the idea of "system" could be affected in this way, so could all the other systems concepts. This often led to considerable difficulties for systems writers, especially if they were sensitive enough to worry about whether terms tainted with positivist and functionalist implications could carry the new meanings that they were trying to give to those terms. Thus Flood (1988) attests to the difficulty he found, after his own conversion from hard to soft systems thinking, in translating a manuscript written using traditional systems concepts—with their functionalist overtones—into a book privileging soft systems meanings and intentions.

It must be accepted, then, that the different strands that now make up the systems movement will use the concept "system," and all the other important systems ideas, in different ways. Part II of the book picks out and investigates cases where systems ideas have been brought together in unique ways and invested with peculiarly powerful meaning for the purpose of understanding or intervening in the real world. In the terms of this book, that means setting out and critically examining the most significant systems methodologies. In fact, five such unique, distinct, and efficacious ways of employing systems concepts are identified. These are the organizations-as-systems tradition, hard systems thinking, organizational cybernetics, soft systems thinking, and critical systems thinking. A chapter is devoted to each, with the main contributors being identified, the general orientation of the type of systems thinking considered, and a thorough critique of the approach provided. It goes without saying that each kind of systems methodology is interrogated as to its theoretical assumptions according to the schemata provided by Chapter 2. Among other things, the sociological paradigm to which each systems approach relates is revealed. Overall, an understanding should be gained by the reader of the theoretical reasons behind the different uses of systems concepts in each systems methodology.

Given the variety of uses of systems concepts identified in Part II, the skeptical reader might be wondering what, if anything, is left of the notion of "system" that might lead anyone to want to construct a discipline around it. What core ideas are retained and held in common by the different tendencies in systems thinking? This is a difficult question to answer at the philosophical level, and an introductory chapter is probably not the best place to try. Nevertheless I will offer two possible answers.

First, all systems approaches are committed to *holism*—to looking at the world in terms of "wholes" that exhibit emergent properties, rather than believing, in a reductionist fashion, that understanding is best obtained by breaking wholes down into their fundamental elements. The strength of this commitment varies from seeing holism as a replacement for reductionism to regarding it as simply complementary. And the meaning attached varies from the call (in hard approaches) to take into account and model all relevant aspects of the whole system to the injunction in Ulrich's "critical systems heuristics" (1983) to reflect continually on the inevitable lack of comprehensiveness in our systems designs. Holism is, though, a distinct feature of the systems approach, and systems thinkers' advocacy of holism should be praised at least as a useful antidote to the prevailing emphasis upon reductionism.

Second, it might be argued along with Rescher (1979) that human beings inevitably organize their knowledge in "cognitive systems." These cognitive systems are structured frameworks linking various elements of our knowledge into cohesive wholes. They express certain intellectual norms—simplicity, regularity, uniformity, comprehensiveness, unity, harmony, economy—that people have found useful in thinking about and acting in the world. Rescher wants to argue that cognitive systems lie at the very heart of the scientific method itself, with a hypothesis becoming a scientific law not because of repeated observation and experiment but only when it can be integrated into a systematic body of scientific knowledge—that is, a cognitive system. From this it would follow that the scientific enterprise and the systems enterprise are the same.

Rescher also suggests that the success of the systematizing endeavor that is science in predicting and controlling the real world must mean that the world itself is orderly. With the continuing development of cognitive systems we should, therefore, get a growing conformity between our systems-based theories and the real world. It is not surprising to Rescher that this should be so, because he believes that there are evolutionary pressures that tend to assure a correspondence between our cognitive systems and the world. We do not have to follow Rescher in these later, somewhat "hard" systems conclusions. It is enough that his work provides some justification for using the concept of a system as the fundamental element in ordering one's cognitive endeavors. That alone supplies another powerful rationale for all the different types of systems approaches.

My argument for taking time to study systems methodologies rests partially, therefore, on the need for holism and the inevitability of cognitive systematization; things that all systems approaches respect. The more developed argument in favor of systems methodologies (as opposed to any other kind of methodology) will, however, rest upon the diversity, range, effectiveness, and efficiency of the methodologies themselves. Part

II of this volume explores the diversity and range of available methodologies and provides some examples of their use. It is in Part III, however, that I turn full attention to the practical application of the methodologies.

In Part III I devote one chapter to providing illustrative examples of the use of each of the five types of systems methodologies introduced and examined in Part II. These case studies are drawn sometimes from the available literature, sometimes from my own consulting experiences. As well as showing different methodologies being used, the chapter provides the opportunity to demonstrate further how the theoretical contributions introduced in Chapter 2 can shed light on the strengths and weaknesses, and domain of effective operation, of each methodology.

The second chapter in Part III looks at a recent development in management science—the area of work known as community operational research (COR). COR was born as an attempt to broaden the range of clients in receipt of operational research advice and, at the same time, to help develop management science methodology by confronting it with new kinds of problem situations such as those faced by community clients. It is argued in this chapter that the use of an integrated set of systems methodologies, with an awareness of the strengths and weaknesses of the different approaches, is the best way to pursue COR. Some common problems encountered by community clients and the responses that can be made by choosing appropriate systems methodologies are outlined. Thus the two chapters of Part III complement one another by providing examples of each type of systems methodology at work and showing how the integrated use of the methodologies can support COR practice.

Part IV takes up some unresolved theoretical and methodological issues related to the future prospects for systems thinking as a discipline. The orthodoxy within the systems approach and management science has clearly broken down. There is competition between advocates of alternative approaches. Extradisciplinary considerations (of career and politics) play a significant part in motivating participants in the debate and are likely to influence its outcome. To some—for example, Dando and Bennett (1981)—this indicates that there is "Kuhnian" crisis in management science. The analysis of this book, however, points to a different interpretation. It is possible to argue that the development of different versions of the systems approach is related to recognition of the existence of varying kinds of problem situations. This obviously places a different perspective on the crisis debate: There is no crisis. As systems thinking has matured, a variety of different approaches has been developed; these allow the practitioner to work, with a good chance of success, in a wide variety of problem situations.

Of course, to sustain this position, an argument has to be advanced for the existence of a coherent set of distinct, yet complementary, systems methodologies serving different management tasks and human interests. This "complementarist" vision of the future of systems thinking is put forward on the basis of evidence from Parts I–III and defended against the alternatives of isolationism, imperialism, and pragmatism. It is argued that complementarism fits hand in glove with critical systems thinking to provide a basis for systems as a discipline. Thus systems thinking, which has seemingly split into opposing tendencies, can be reconstituted on the much firmer foundations (as compared to the positivism and functionalism of traditional systems thinking) provided by complementarism and critical systems thinking. Systems thinking, in this guise, can again occupy a role at the leading edge of the development of the management sciences in general.

One chapter in Part IV is devoted to the theoretical matters set out above. Another considers the implications of the conclusions reached about these theoretical matters for the future of systems intervention and problem management. A "total systems intervention" approach to combining systems methods in order to promote creativity, choice of appropriate methodology, and implementation is outlined. Thus Part IV rounds

TABLE 1.1. *The Structure of the Argument*

Part I: "Overviews," in which there are 2 chapters	Chapter 1, setting out the structure of the argument of the book
	Chapter 2, dealing with necessary theoretical considerations
Part II: "Methodological Approaches," in which there are 5 chapters outlining distinct kinds of systems methodology, and relating them to the theoretical considerations of Chapter 2	Chapter 3, discussing the organizations-as-systems tradition
	Chapter 4, discussing hard systems thinking
	Chapter 5, discussing organizational cybernetics
	Chapter 6, discussing soft systems thinking
	Chapter 7, discussing critical systems thinking
Part III: "Practical Applications," in which there are 2 chapters	Chapter 8, providing illustrative case studies of the practical use of each type of methodology in the managerial context
	Chapter 9, showing the practical use of the methodologies in community OR
Part IV: "Future Prospects," in which there are 3 chapters on the future of systems thinking	Chapter 10, arguing for a complementarist approach to systems methodology grounded on a version of critical systems thinking
	Chapter 11, arguing for a total systems intervention approach to intervention and practical problem management
	Chapter 12, which is a short conclusion

off the book by considering the future prospects both for the theoretical development of systems thinking and for the practical use of systems ideas. There is also a short conclusion.

This introductory chapter has set out the structure of the argument in the context of some of the recurring themes that will appear in the book. In the next chapter, I pass on to the theoretical concerns upon which a proper understanding of the role and usefulness of systems methodologies depends. Table 1.1 outlines, in summary form, the structure of this volume.

2

Theoretical Considerations

Introduction

The attempt in this chapter to provide the background social theory that will enable the presuppositions made by systems methodologies to be revealed and discussed is conducted at a number of levels. At the most fundamental level, there is reference to Habermas's theory of human cognitive interests and to his later reflections on how these have become rationalized and institutionalized in the subsystems of modern society. Then there is a categorization of basic sociological orientations, drawing upon Burrell and Morgan's well-known classification of sociological paradigms but introducing a corrective to allow proper consideration of structuralism. Moving from the societal to the organizational level, the key metaphors that have influenced the way researchers have studied and sought to change organizations are set out. This is followed by the elaboration of a schema deliberately constructed to classify systems methodologies, and unearth their theoretical assumptions, in a manner suited to the language, concerns, and internal development of management science—Jackson and Keys's "system of systems methodologies." Finally, and moving back up the levels of generality, the issue of modernism versus postmodernism is addressed. This is one of the hottest debates currently absorbing time and space in the human sciences.

The ideas set out in this chapter have been selected for attention because they are central to current areas of sociological debate and concern. Even more importantly, they provide a highly relevant background against which the later discussion of systems methodologies can proceed. Some indication of this relevance is given in the following sections. As the various schemata (for classifying interests, sociological paradigms, organizations, etc.) are set out, reference will be made to the benefits to be obtained from considering systems methodologies in terms of each of them.

Knowledge and Interest and Social Evolution

In this section, I consider some aspects of Habermas's grand socio-logical theorizing that are relevant to systems methodologies. Habermas is a prolific and wide-ranging writer and, being very open to comment and criticism, is constantly adjusting and refining his arguments. It goes without saying that I cannot do justice to the complexity and sophistication of his thought in this brief exposition. But to this I must add the further apology that I will sometimes mix earlier with later formulations of ideas if this helps make a point more clearly.

A number of important themes emerged in Habermas's inaugural lecture at the University of Frankfurt in 1965 (Habermas, 1970) and continued to be developed later (Habermas, 1974). According to Habermas, human beings possess two fundamental cognitive interests that direct their attempts to acquire knowledge: a *technical* interest and a *practical* interest. The two interests are "quasi-transcendental" because they necessarily derive from the sociocultural form of life of the human species, which is dependent on "work" and "interaction." Work enables human beings to achieve goals and to bring about material well-being. Its success depends upon achieving technical mastery over the environment of action. The importance of work for the human species directs knowledge toward a technical interest in the prediction and control of natural and social systems. Interaction requires human beings to secure and expand the possibilities for intersubjective understanding among those involved in social systems. Disagreement between different individuals and groups can be just as much a threat to the reproduction of the sociocultural form of life as a failure to predict and control natural and social processes. The importance of interaction leads the human species to have a practical interest in the progress of mutual understanding.

While work and interaction have, for Habermas, preeminent anthropological status, the analysis of power and the way it is exercised are equally important, he argues, if we are to understand past and present social arrangements. The exercise of power in the social process can prevent the open and free discussion necessary for the success of work and interaction. Human beings have, therefore, a third cognitive interest: an *emancipatory* interest in freeing themselves from constraints imposed by power relations and in learning, through a process of genuine participatory democracy, to control their own destinies. This interest is subordinate to the other two because it stems from derivative types of action— exploitation and systematically distorted communication. It aims at liberating people from these historically contingent constraints.

Corresponding to the three cognitive interests are three types of knowledge. First are the "empirical analytic" sciences linked to the cognitive interest concerned with the technical control of objectified processes. They aim to produce theoretical statements about the covariance of observable events from which can be derived lawlike hypotheses. These sciences enable us, from given initial conditions, to make predictions about future events. Second are the "historical hermeneutic" sciences that correspond to the practical interest. These sciences seek to access meaning and to gain an understanding of the creation of the intersubjective life world. They aim at maintaining and improving mutual understanding among human beings. Tied to the emancipatory interest are the "critical" sciences. These recognize the limitations of the other two types of knowledge (and the dangers when they are inappropriately applied) and attempt to synthesize and go beyond them in order to provide knowledge that will enable people to reflect on their situations and liberate themselves from domination by forces that they are involved in creating but that they cannot understand or control.

If we move now to Habermas's (1975) social theory, we find him arguing that, in advanced capitalist societies, the technical interest has come to dominate at the expense of the practical interest. The knowledge produced by the empirical analytic sciences (instrumental reason) has come to be regarded as the prototype of all knowledge, and the subsystems of society concerned with the development of the forces of production and oriented to the development of the "steering" capacities of society—the subsystems served by instrumental reason—have gained primary significance. The state apparatus in particular has increased its powers and sees its function as that of "steering" society and overcoming the periodic crises to which all capitalist systems are prone. The result is that practical problems about what ought to be done are defined as administrative problems, beyond the realm of public discussion, and tackled by experts from the scientific subsystem. Politics is defined as the task of ensuring that the social system runs smoothly. Luhmann's systems theory is taken by Habermas (1976a) as the prime ideological reflection of the predominance of instrumental reason:

> This theory represents the advanced form of a technocratic consciousness, which today permits practical questions to be defined from the outset as technical ones, and thereby withholds them from public and unconstrained discussion. (p. xxxii)

Luhmann sees social evolution as determined solely by the developing steering capacities of the societal system, as it seeks to manage environmental complexity by expanding system complexity at the same time as controlling that system complexity. Thus, for Luhmann, social integration (the development of understanding and shared norms and values among individuals) is wholly secondary and, indeed, is a product of system integration.

To Habermas, this dominance of the technical interest is anathema. The knowledge produced by the empirical analytic sciences is very necessary to the development of modern societies. It can guide "instrumental action" oriented to the development of the forces of production and "strategic action" oriented to the development of steering capacities. But social evolution depends as well upon "communicative action" (Habermas, 1984) related to the practical and emancipatory interests in the creation of mutual understanding free from domination, and supported by the historical hermeneutic and critical sciences. The institutional framework of society has its own logic of "rationalization" different from that governing the subsystems of instrumental action (the economy, the state apparatus) that are embedded in the institutional framework. Rationalization in the domain of instrumental action concerns control over the forces of production and over the organizational forms that promote the steering capacity of society. Rationalization in the domain of social interaction, in the institutional realm of society, requires the development of communication free from domination. Questions of what norms should govern interaction (of what we should do, or might do) are logically independent of questions about the development of productive forces or about system integration and cannot be reduced to them.

Habermas, therefore, wants to set proper limits to the sphere of applicability of the knowledge produced by the empirical analytic sciences. At the same time, he is also careful to reject the claim of the historical hermeneutic sciences to be the sole method appropriate to studying human and social phenomena. Hermeneutics can only be universal if people make their history as knowing subjects free from the play of unconscious forces, and if their actions have only intended consequences. However, because of the existence of power relationships that make mutual understanding based on genuine consensus difficult to achieve, and because of the complexity of modern societal arrangements, the results of human actions will often be different from what was intended by human actors. So they cannot be grasped, in the manner of hermeneutics, solely in terms of subjective intention.

Both the empirical analytic and historical hermeneutic approaches must be complemented by a third type of inquiry—critical theory. To explain the relationship among the three kinds of knowledge, Habermas (1974) turns to the psychoanalytic encounter. Psychoanalysis is primarily hermeneutic. It attempts to understand what subjects say and to explicate the hidden meaning of what is said. But to achieve this the analyst cannot remain at the hermeneutic level. The analyst must get below the explanations offered by the subjects, to explain causally why they are distorted and conceal matters the subjects cannot bring to consciousness. This requires an empirical analytic study of the systematic process through which patients deceive themselves about their conditions. The hermeneutic and empirical analytic elements of the psychoanalytic method are mediated by critical theory, for the whole stimulus behind the psychoanalytic encounter should be emancipatory. If successful, the analyst liberates subjects from unconscious forces that they could not control and increases the area over which they have rational mastery. Success is measured by the extent to which the patients recognize themselves in the explanations offered and become equal partners in the dialogue with the analyst.

This psychoanalytic model can, with care, be seen as relevant to society as a whole. Where possible, Habermas wants to reduce the area of social life where people act as things (and are therefore subject to instrumental reason), and to increase the realm of the hermeneutic (where rational intentions are realized in history). To this end, he needs to develop theory that can ground the process of critique at the societal level. Here Habermas is at his most original. His elaborate theory of social evolution, forged in debate with Luhmann and linking the development of the forces of production, the organizational forms necessary to enhance the steering capacity of societies, and the institutional sector of society (the arena of politics and ethics), is one manifestation of this. Such a theory enables Habermas to argue for restricting instrumental reason to appropriate subsystems of society and for the need to pay separate attention to the creation of mutual understanding in the institutional sphere. His most famous contribution, however, is his attempt to provide a rational basis for a critique of the state of development of the institutional realm itself, through his theory of "communicative competence." This is the last part of Habermas's work we need to consider.

The theory of communicative competence was constructed to be set alongside Marx's critique of political economy, which Habermas regards as the exemplar for critical social science in the area of economics. In the modern era, the growing importance of the institutional framework of society (the sociocultural life-world) means that Marx's critique of alienated labor has to be complemented with a critique of "distorted communication," of alienation in the institutional sphere. This can be built on a study of the normative assumptions entering into communication itself, since the commitment to mutual understanding through free and open debate seems to be prefigured in all speech and discourse:

> The idea of autonomy is given to us with the structure of language. With the very first sentence the intention of a common and uncompelled consensus is unequivocally stated. (Habermas, 1970, p. 50)

I will follow McCarthy (1973) in detailing Habermas's theory. In normal linguistic interaction, Habermas argues, participants naturally accept at least four different types of validity claims. These are that the utterance is intelligible; that its propositional content is true; that the speaker is sincere in uttering it; and that it is right or appropriate for the speaker to be performing the "speech act." If any of these claims is called into question, it is necessary to enter into "discourse" to judge the truth of a problematic fact or the correctness of a disputed norm. Proper discourse is only enacted if it is conducted solely with a willingness to come to agreement through mutual understanding. This agreement must, in turn, be based on a true and genuine consensus. Habermas argues that it is a normal expectation in language games that participants are willing to enter into discourse to defend their positions, and that the outcome should reflect the better argument and not any constraints on discussion.

It is now necessary to specify the conditions for such an "ideal speech situation." According to Habermas, the structure of communication is free from constraint when all participants have equal chances to select and perform speech acts, and there is an effective equality of chances for the assumption of dialogue roles. This general requirement is further specified into demands designed to ensure unlimited discussion and demands that insist that discussion is free from constraints of domination—whether their source is conscious strategic behavior by one or more of the parties or communication barriers secured through ideology or neurosis. So all participants must have the same chance to initiate and perpetuate discourse and to put forward, call into question, and give reasons for or against statements, explanations, interpretations, and justifications. And all participants must have the same chance to express their attitudes, feelings, and intentions and to command and to oppose, to permit and to forbid, and so forth. Where these conditions are met, an ideal speech situation pertains and any consensus emerging will be rationally motivated and genuine. Obviously such circumstances will be rare, but this does not detract from the usefulness of Habermas's conceptualization, since it can equally be used to unmask "systematically distorted communication" in situations where unequal chances to participate in dialogue or an unequal distribution of power determines the nature of the false consensus reached.

The amount of distortion present in communication in a society is closely related to the development of the economic sphere and steering mechanisms of that society. It follows that communicative competence depends very much on the establishment of certain social conditions relating to freedom and justice. This, then, is the link back to Marx. Marx analyzed the development of society in terms of the forms taken by alienated labor. Habermas reinforces this with an "ideology critique" of the forms taken by distorted communication. And just as there is anticipated in actual labor an as-yet-unrealized form of free labor, so there is prefigured in discourse an as-yet-unrealized ideal speech situation. Historical materialism can therefore be reconstructed with communicative competence as the basis for its critical theory of society. For Habermas, then, our progress toward a rational society is measured by the extent to which communicative competence is realized in society. Only with the achievement of communicative competence can the power for domination inherent in instrumental reason be made subject to full public control.

I have begun this discussion of the background social theory necessary to understand systems methodologies at quite a high level of generality—with Habermas's sociological theorizing. Nevertheless, it is not difficult to see the relevance of this work both for organizations and for systems methodologies seeking to intervene in organizations and societies. Organizations as well as societies have subsystems concerned with production and with "steering" (management), and they possess an institutional framework in which issues of what should be done and what ought to be done are discussed. We all have technical, practical, and emancipatory interests in their functioning. Systems methodologies will be needed that are grounded upon all three types of knowledge, and might usefully be classified according to whether they can guide instrumental action oriented to the development of the forces of production, strategic action oriented to the development of steering capacities, or communicative action interested in the creation of mutual understanding free from domination. From the critical perspective it will be important to check that methodologies supporting the technical interest and based upon instrumental reason are self-reflective about their own limitations, and recognize their proper sphere of applicability. Methodologies that purport to serve the practical interest in intersubjective understanding by facilitating debate about purposes must pay attention to the possibility that systematically distorted communication might jeopardize the emergence of genuinely shared purposes.

Sociological Paradigms

Systems methodologies are not social theories. They are not accounts of what the "real world" is like, but are attempts to set out principles of method for systems researchers to follow when they seek to learn about and (especially) to intervene in the real world. Nevertheless, any principles of method for intervening in the real world must contain certain assumptions about how we can and should learn about reality and about the nature of that reality. This is true whether these assumptions are stated explicitly or remain hidden. The designers of systems methodologies will have either consciously or unconsciously incorporated into their methodologies assumptions about the nature of systems thinking and the nature of social systems. It would be insightful, and extremely illuminating, if we could find some means of unearthing the implied theoretical assumptions of different systems methodologies.

A useful working tool that should enable us to do this is the map of sociological paradigms developed by Burrell and Morgan (1979). This framework was constituted in order to relate work in the field of organizational analysis to a wider sociological context, and its success in that enterprise offers sufficient encouragement for anyone wishing to take up Burrell and Morgan's suggestion and apply this particular analytical scheme to some other discipline. I shall describe the framework in this section and in Parts II and III of the book relate the theoretical assumptions of different systems methodologies to it.

It is Burrell and Morgan's thesis that theories about the social world can be conceived of in terms of four key paradigms, according to the assumptions these theories make about the nature of social science and about the nature of society.

Assumptions about the nature of social science can be seen as either *objective* or *subjective* in kind. If a theory is underpinned by objective assumptions about the nature of social science, it will have certain distinguishing characteristics. Social reality will be perceived as having a hard, objective existence, external to the individual (i.e., the theory adheres to a "realist" ontology). The theory will seek to establish the existence of regularities and causal relationships in the social world ("positivist" epistemology). Human behavior will be seen as being determined by external circumstances ("determinist"). Scientific tests and quantitative analyses will be the preferred techniques for acquiring detailed knowledge ("nomothetic" methodology).

If a theory is underpinned by subjective assumptions about the nature of social science, it will have quite other distinguishing characteristics. Social reality will be perceived as having a more subjective existence as the product of individual and/or shared consciousness ("nominalist" ontology). The theory will seek knowledge by attempting to understand the point of view of the people involved in creating social reality ("antipositivist" epistemology). Human beings will be seen to possess free will ("voluntarist"). Getting as close as possible to the subject under investigation will be the preferred method of acquiring detailed knowledge ("ideographic" methodology). This distinction between objective and subjective assumptions about the nature of social science makes up the first dimension of Burrell and Morgan's framework.

Assumptions about the nature of society can be seen as emphasizing either *regulation* or *radical change*. The "sociology of regulation" concerns itself with understanding the status quo. Society is seen as being basically consensual, and the mechanisms by which social order is maintained are studied. The "sociology of radical change" concerns itself with finding explanations for radical change in social systems. Society is seen as being riven by contradictions and by structural conflict. Some groups in society benefit at the expense of others; any cohesion that exists is achieved by the domination of some groups over others. The sociology of radical change looks beyond the status quo. The distinction between these two sociologies makes up the second dimension of Burrell and Morgan's grid.

If we now combine the objective–subjective and regulation–radical change dimensions, we can produce a matrix defining the four key sociological paradigms. These four paradigms are labeled *functionalist, interpretive, radical structuralist,* and *radical humanist,* as indicated in Figure 2.1. These paradigms, according to Burrell and Morgan (1979), are founded upon mutually exclusive views of the social world. Each stands in its own right and generates its own distinctive analyses of social life (p. x).

I am arguing that systems methodologies are inevitably built upon assumptions about the nature of systems thinking (or social science) and social systems (or society). The Burrell and Morgan grid will enable us, in Parts II and III of the book, to relate systems methodologies to different sociological paradigms, and to learn much about what they take for granted about social science and society. That should put us in a position to ask whether we agree with the assumptions being made or, perhaps, whether the presuppositions underlying a particular systems methodology might be appropriate in some problem situations but not in others. To assist further with that analysis, I shall now briefly explore the ways in which adopting the perspective of each paradigm affects the way we perceive systems and problem situations.

If we view systems from within the functionalist paradigm (objective, sociology of regulation), they seem to have a hard, easily identifiable existence independent of us as observers. We understand the workings of such systems if we can find regularities in the relationships between subsystems and the whole. The human beings in the system present no more problems than do other component parts. It is possible to construct a quantitative model of the system. The purpose of studying such systems

THE SOCIOLOGY OF RADICAL CHANGE

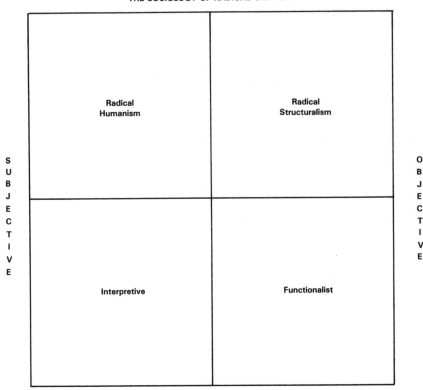

FIGURE 2.1. Burrell and Morgan's Four Paradigms for the Analysis of Social Theory

is to understand the status quo better; this facilitates the prediction and control of the system.

If we view systems from within the interpretive paradigm (subjective, sociology of regulation) they seem to be much "softer," to elude easy identification and to possess a precarious existence only as the creative constructions of human beings. We can understand such systems only by trying to understand subjectively the points of view and the intentions of the human beings who construct them. The presence in the system of human beings possessing free will makes a profound difference to the kind of analysis undertaken. It will not normally be possible to construct a quantitative model of such a system. We must acquire detailed information about it by getting involved in its activities; by "getting inside" it. The purpose of studying such systems is still to understand the status quo better so that prediction and control are facilitated.

If we view systems from within the radical structuralist paradigm (objective, sociology of radical change), they seem to have a hard existence external to us. We can discover causal regularities governing their behavior. We do not have to pay much attention, we believe, to human intentions. It is possible to develop quantitative models. However, the purpose of such study is to understand radical change. Emphasis is placed upon contradictions in the system and on conflict between different groups in the system. This facilitates the emancipation of people from presently existing social structures.

If we view systems from within the radical humanist paradigm (subjective, sociology of radical change), they seem to be the creative constructions of human beings. In order to analyze such systems, we have to understand the intentions of the human beings who construct them. The ability of people to transform the systems they have created will be apparent. The way to learn about these systems is to involve ourselves in their activities. Emphasis is placed upon gaining understanding of the current social arrangements that are seen as constraining human development. This facilitates the emancipation of people from presently existing social structures.

The purpose of studying the Burrell and Morgan framework will now be clear in terms of the overall intention of this volume. Before leaving this framework, however, it is necessary to draw attention to one problem with their dichotomies that could otherwise frustrate our efforts, later, to relate systems methodologies to the wider sociological perspective. The trouble is that Burrell and Morgan's grid prevents us from identifying the nature, and appreciating the significance, of the distinct structuralist approach in social theory (only "radical structuralism" is dealt with). This has important consequences for any analysis of systems thinking, because it can be argued that organizational cybernetics, for example, differs from hard systems thinking precisely in that it possesses structuralist rather than functionalist underpinnings. We need to pursue this matter briefly in order to get clear the main characteristics of structuralism.

According to Burrell and Morgan, as we have seen, any objectivist approach to social science is likely to be realist in its ontology; that is, it is likely to accept the existence of a constraining social world external to the individual. And it is likely to be positivist in its epistemology, seeking to discover patterns and regularities in the social world. Others, however, do not accept that all objectivists need be positivists. Keat and Urry (1975) argue, for example, that there are very significant differences among objectivists based on the epistemologies they employ—differences that, in many ways, are more important than whether the objective knowledge of the social world is incorporated into a regulative or radical-change perspective. Burrell and Morgan hide these differences by the vague way they use the phrase "positivist epistemology." For example, one might ask whether the patterns and regularities they discuss are at the surface of the social world (at the level of social facts) or whether we have to dig beneath the surface to discover "structures" (the patterns and regularities) that determine the arrangement of the social facts. And one can wonder whether understanding of patterns and regularities is to be based upon empirical observation of "well-established regularities" or whether it is to involve a theoretical description of the causal mechanisms producing the observable patterns and regularities. Important differences emerge, according to Keat and Urry, from the ways in which these questions are answered.

To bring these differences out, Keat and Urry employ a distinction between two different epistemologies they see objectivists using; these two epistemologies are called "positivist" and "realist" (not to be confused with Burrell and Morgan's ontological realism). The following quotation highlights the difference:

> For the realist, unlike the positivist, there is an important difference between explanation and prediction. And it is explanation which must be pursued as the primary objective of science. To explain phenomena is not merely to show that they are instances of well-established regularities. Instead, we must discover the necessary connections between phenomena, by acquiring knowledge of the underlying structures and mechanisms at work. Often, this will mean postulating the existence of types of unobservable entities and processes that are unfamiliar to us: but it is only by doing this that we get beyond the 'mere appearances' of things, to their natures and essences. Thus, for the realist, a scientific theory is a description of structures and mechanisms which causally generate the observable phenomena, a description which enables us to explain them. (Keat and Urry, 1975, p. 5)

It is interesting, for our purposes, to observe that the "realist" approach to the social sciences mirrors very closely what most contemporary structuralists try to do. Because Burrell and Morgan play down the epistemological distinction between positivism and realism (in Keat and Urry's sense) and stress the "political" distinction between social theories as supporting regulation or radical change, they give little attention to structuralism as a unified approach in the social sciences. Some theorists close to structuralism—such as the mature Marx and Althusser—receive attention because they are deemed to be radical. But others not so regarded, and who differ profoundly in their approach to social theory from people in the functionalist tradition, get hardly a mention—for example, Chomsky, Levi-Strauss, and Piaget.

The convergence in approach between structuralism and, for example, cybernetics has long been apparent to structuralist writers. Levi-Strauss (1968) regards Wiener as having made an outstanding contribution to structural studies. Piaget (1973) is very complimentary about the achievement of cybernetics in synthesizing information and communication theories with guiding and regulatory theories. It will be productive in Parts II and III of the book, therefore, when relating systems methodologies to sociological theory, to make reference to structuralism as well as to the sociological paradigms included in Burrell and Morgan's typology.

To be clear: *Structuralism* (as I shall employ the term) refers to a particular theoretical orientation based upon a realist epistemology. This is the most common form of structuralism. Structuralism can take on other than realist forms, but these are not significant for our purposes. Structuralism, in the realist form, is concerned with uncovering and understanding the underlying structures or systems of relationships that generate the surface phenomena perceived in the world. It demands explanation of the phenomena available to our senses in terms of the underlying, unobservable mechanisms that generate them. Structuralists attempt to provide models of the causal processes at work at the deep structural level that produce observable phenomena and the relationships between surface elements.

Metaphors of Organization

As the organization-theory literature constantly reminds us, there are many different metaphors that can be used to look at organizations, each of which yields an alternative understanding of their character and functioning. Morgan (1986), discussing different "images of organization," considers them as "machines," "organisms," "brains," "cultures," "political systems," "psychic prisons," "flux and transformation," and "instruments of domination," while making the point that these eight are only a selection of those possible. Choosing to see an organization in any of these ways will obviously affect the approach adopted to studying it or seeking to change it.

Systems methodologies, too, rest upon metaphorical understandings of the nature of systems, the most common being the "adaptive whole system" metaphor (Atkinson, 1984). And, because systems methodologies are very often used in the organizational context to bring about changes in structures, processes, and attitudes, it will obviously provide further insight into their nature, and relative strengths and weaknesses, if we can uncover the image or images of organization embedded in each systems methodology. To facilitate this process later, I take here five possible views of organization for closer study—organizations as machines, organisms, brains, cultures, and coercive systems.

Various strands of organization theory unite in treating organizations as if they were *machines*. The three most influential are administrative management theory, scientific management and a reading of Weber's bureaucracy theory. Henri Fayol (1949) can be credited with the creation of administrative management theory. In his book, first published in French in 1916, he advises managers to forecast and plan, to organize, to command, to coordinate and to control, and sets out 14 principles designed to guide managerial action; the most important of these being division of work, authority, scalar chain, and unity of command. Frederick Taylor, the founder of scientific management, believed that the best way of doing each task in an organization could be established, and that on this basis a fair day's pay for a fair day's work could be calculated (Taylor, 1947). Taylor's ideas, where adopted, tend to lead to an extreme division of labor and the shifting of control away from the point at which the task is carried out. Max Weber (Gerth and Mills, 1970) argued that bureaucracy is the most technically advanced organizational form, because it is based upon an advanced division of labor, a strict hierarchy, government by rules, and staffing by trained officials.

By putting together these three strands, it is possible to give a general account of the machine model. The organization is viewed as an instrument designed to achieve the purposes of the people who set it up or who now control it. It is constructed of parts combined according to management principles in a way that should enable maximum efficiency to be achieved. Decision making is assumed to be rational. Control is exercised through rules and a strict hierarchy of authority. Information is processed according to the arrangement of tasks and by exception reporting up the hierarchy.

The tendency to treat organizations as if they were *organisms* has been especially pronounced among advocates of the systems perspective in organization theory. This view portrays organizations as complex systems made up of parts existing in close interrelationship. Because they are like this, organizations can only be studied as wholes. The primary aim of organizations as systems is to ensure their own survival. Selznick (1948), Parsons (1956, 1957) and Katz and Kahn (1966) provide lists of needs that must be met by subsystems if organizations are to survive and be effective. Both formal and informal aspects of organizations are granted attention in the organismic model. Moreover, organizations are seen as open systems, having to take action in response to environmental changes if they want to maintain a steady state. If organizations are like organisms, it is clear what must be done to correct any malfunctions. The subsystems must be examined to ensure that they are meeting the needs of the organization, and the organization examined to see that it is well adjusted to its environment. A managerial subsystem is charged with this task.

Another strand of organization theory takes a neurocybernetic perspective and pictures organizations as being like *brains*. This metaphor emphasizes active learning rather than the somewhat passive adaptability that characterizes the organismic view. It has led to attention being focused on decision making and on information processing. The forerunner of the brain model was Herbert Simon (1947), who argued that individuals in organizations inevitably acted according to "bounded rationality," but that this could be compensated for to some extent by paying proper attention to organizational design and decision support. Later, J. R. Galbraith (1977) developed his view of organizations as information-processing systems. The best design of an organization was seen as contingent upon the uncertainty and diversity surrounding the basic task undertaken by that organization—since this determined the amount of information that would have to be processed. If task uncertainty was low, bureaucratic structures with their low information-processing capacities were adequate. But if task uncertainty was high, alternative structures would be required, based on strategies either to reduce the need for information processing or to increase the capacity for it.

To those who see organizations as *cultures*, managers who seek to promote the efficiency and effectiveness of their enterprises by concentrating their best efforts on the logical design of appropriate structures (as recommended by proponents of the machine, organism, and brain metaphors) are seriously misplacing their energies. Social organizations can exist with and perform well while employing a host of apparently illogical structures. A far more important role for managers to play is as "engineers" of their organizations' corporate cultures. According to this cultural perspective, the essential character of organizations is conditioned by the fact that their component parts are human beings, who can attribute meaning to their situation and can therefore see in organizations whatever purposes they wish and make of organizations whatever they will. Organizations are processes in which different perceptions of reality are continuously negotiated and renegotiated. Their long-term survival depends therefore upon the achievement of shared values and beliefs.

This cultural view is a relatively modern approach spurred on by the popularizing efforts of authors such as Peters and Waterman (1982). The gist of the perspective is well captured by Thomas Watson, Jr., writing about his experiences with IBM:

> Consider any great organization, one that has lasted over the years—I think you will find that it owes its resiliency not to its form of organization or administrative skills, but to the power of what we call *beliefs* and the appeal these beliefs have for its people . . . In other words, the basic philosophy, spirit, and drive of an organization have far more to do with its relative achievements than do technological or economic resources, organizational structure, innovation and timing. All these things weigh heavily in success. But they are, I think, transcended by how strongly the people in the organization believe in its basic precepts and how faithfully they carry them out. (quoted in Peters and Waterman, 1982, p. 280)

The view of organizations as *coercive systems* is based upon Marx's (1961) account of the capitalist labor process, as brought up to date by Braverman (1974) and others. According to this frame of reference, organizations are hierarchical systems made up of different class and status groups whose interests are unbridgeable given the present structure of organizations and society. Organizations only hold together at all because of the power of some group(s) to control the activities of others. Relationships between the different classes are essentially exploitative. For example, in capitalist enterprises, workers receive wages, but the amount they receive does not represent an equivalent exchange for the labor power they expend. There is always some surplus value creamed off by the capitalist. Of course, it is always likely that conflict will break out, given that the only consensus that exists is an enforced consensus. It is the job of managers to keep such conflict in check and to control the labor process so that the powerful group(s) maximize their benefits. Using some ideas of Burrell and Morgan (1979), as considered earlier, one can say that those who see organizations as coercive systems concern themselves with issues of structural conflict, modes of domination, contradiction, and emancipation (radical change). This contrasts with those of a machine, organism, brain, or cultural bent, all of whom emphasize the status quo, social order, consensus, social integration, and cohesion (regulation).

In this section, we have moved down from the societal to the organizational level and considered some of the key metaphors that researchers have employed to study organizations. As we shall see in Parts II and III of the book, systems methodologies are heavily influenced by metaphors of organization. We can use our analysis to consider how this affects the recommendations the methodologies make about how best to intervene in organizations to change them. Just as there exists knowledge on the strengths and limitations of different images of organization (Morgan, 1986), so shall we be able to build knowledge about the relative capabilities of different systems methodologies.

A System of Systems Methodologies

When interest first developed in examining the theoretical underpinnings of systems methodologies, it was Burrell and Morgan's grid of sociological paradigms that was used as the point of reference (Checkland, 1981a; Jackson, 1982). However, any way of seeing is also a way of not seeing, and that framework did not always cast the clearest light over some points of interest in the systems field. The language was foreign to management-science ears, and a job of translation always needed to be done to make the analysis clear. The action orientation and problem centeredness of systems and management science posed additional complications in carrying over ideas. The failure of Burrell and Morgan to distinguish a functionalist from a structuralist approach to social science, and the consequences of this for an analysis of systems thinking, has already been noted. For all these reasons, Jackson and Keys (1984) sought to provide a "system of systems methodologies"—an alternative framework that would serve a similar purpose to Burrell and Morgan's grid in organizational analysis but would be more suited to the language, concerns, and internal development of management science. It was designed to relate different systems methodologies to each other on the basis of the assumptions they made about the nature of problem situations or "problem contexts." Since 1984, this "system of systems methodologies" has undergone a number of modifications (Jackson 1987c, 1988b, 1990a, 1990b); it is the most modern version that is detailed here.

The formative idea of the system of systems methodologies is that it is possible to construct an ideal-type grid of problem contexts that can be used to classify systems methodologies according to their assumptions about problem situations. A problem context can be defined to include the individual or group of individuals who are the would-be problem solvers, the system(s) within which the problems lie, and the set of relevant participants. This set contains all those who can make decisions that affect the behavior of the system(s). From this definition it is reasonable to suggest that there are two aspects of problem contexts that might have a particularly important effect on the character of the problems found within them. These two aspects are the nature of the *system(s)* in which the problems are located and the nature of the relationship between the *participants*. These are two key variables that, as they change in character, would seem to result in qualitative changes in problem contexts, affecting the problems therein and thereby demanding a significant reorientation in problem-solving approach. A grid of types of problem contexts can now be drawn up by taking these two key variables and asking in each case what significant forms they take.

Systems can be classified in a variety of ways. Very generally, however, a continuum of system types may be usefully identified. At one end of the continuum will be systems that are relatively simple and are characterized by having a small number of elements with few, or at least regular, interactions between them. Such systems are likely to be governed by well-defined laws of behavior, to be largely closed to the environment, to be static over time, to be unaffected by behavioral influences, and to have subsystems that are passive and do not pursue their own goals. At the other end of the continuum of system types will be systems that are very complex and are characterized by having a large number of elements that are highly interrelated. Such systems are probabilistic, open to the environment, evolve over time, are subject to behavioral influences, and have purposeful parts. Ackoff (1974a) has used the terms *machine age* and *systems age* to refer to eras characterized by a dominant concern with understanding these two different types of systems. Applying Ackoff's terminology, reference is made in the system of systems methodologies to *mechanical* problem contexts, which contain relatively simple systems, and *systemic* problem contexts, which contain very complex systems (naturally manifesting more difficult problems).

The nature of the relationship between participants is the other factor that can greatly affect the character of a problem context. If the participants associated with a particular problem context are in genuine agreement on objectives, share common interests, have compatible values and beliefs, and all participate in decision making, then the problem context will be less difficult to handle than if, for example, their objectives conflict. Where there is, in general, genuine agreement among the relevant participants, then the problem context is called *unitary*. If the participants have divergent values and beliefs and, to some extent, differing interests and objectives, but a genuine accommodation or compromise can be reached upon which all agree (because their fundamental interests are not irreconcilable), then the problem context is *pluralist*. If, however, there is little common interest between the participants, there is fundamental conflict, and the only consensus that can be achieved is through the exercise of power and through domination (overt or more or less concealed) of one or more groups of participants over others, then the problem context is called *coercive*. Participants can therefore, in this ideal-type classification, be in a unitary, pluralist, or coercive relationship to each other, with problem contexts similarly labeled. The terms *unitary, pluralist,* and *coercive* (or *radical)* are common in the industrial-relations literature for describing the relationship between the various stakeholders with an interest in organizations.

If the classifications of systems and participants are now combined to yield a six-celled matrix, problem contexts can be seen to fall into the following categories: mechanical–unitary, systemic–unitary, mechanical–pluralist, systemic–pluralist, mechanical–coercive, and systemic–coercive. This is represented in Figure 2.2. Each of these problem contexts differs in a meaningful way from the others, and the characteristics of each determine the nature of the problems found within it.

The existence of these six ideal-types of problem contexts implies the need for six types of problem-solving methodologies. Important differences among problem contexts should be reflected in different types of methodologies. This provides a very convenient means of classifying available systems approaches, especially as the classification of problem contexts is far from arbitrary. It emerges naturally from a consideration of the two different ways (systems, participants) in which problems become difficult for would-be problem solvers. Support for the choice of these two key variables as the basis of classification can be found in the work of

PARTICIPANTS

	UNITARY	PLURALIST	COERCIVE
MECHANICAL	Mechanical- Unitary	Mechanical- Pluralist	Mechanical- Coercive
SYSTEMIC	Systemic- Unitary	Systemic- Pluralist	Systemic- Coercive

(row label on left: SYSTEMS)

FIGURE 2.2. Jackson's Extended Version of Jackson and Keys's Grid of Problem Contexts

Ackoff and Habermas and can be evinced from the nature of organizations as sociotechnical systems (Jackson, 1985b, 1988c). Since Habermas's work already has been discussed it might be remarked that the systems dimension corresponds to the technical interest in the prediction and control of natural and social events. The participants dimension corresponds to the practical and emancipatory interests in securing and expanding the possibilities of mutual understanding among all those involved in the reproduction of social life.

Given the grid of problem contexts, the next step in building the system of systems methodologies is to relate existing systems-based, problem-solving methodologies to it. Although this anticipates the detailed argument of Parts II and III of the book, it is worthwhile to provide some preliminary and tentative results here in order to orient the reader. It can be argued that hard systems thinking (classical OR, systems analysis, and systems engineering) assumes that problems are set in mechanical–unitary contexts. Hard methodologies take it as given that it is relatively easy to establish clear objectives for the system in which the problem resides—so the context must be unitary. They then try to represent that system in a quantitative model that simulates its performance under different operational conditions—something only possible if the system is simple and the context mechanical.

Cybernetic methodologies, such as advocated by Beer (1979) and organizations-as-systems approaches, seem suitable for tackling problems associated with systemic–unitary contexts. Mechanical–pluralist contexts respond to the kind of soft systems method proposed by Churchman (1979a), and by Mason and Mitroff (1981) in their "strategic assumption surfacing and testing" methodology. The rather different soft systems thinking proposed by Ackoff (1981a) and by Checkland (1981a) can minister to problems set in systemic–pluralist problem contexts. For example, Ackoff's "interactive planning" exhibits (through the participative principle) a method to cope with pluralism and (through the proposed design for a "responsive decision system"), an attempt to come to terms with systemicity. Coercive contexts produce their own unique difficulties, which have only recently been addressed by emancipatory systems methods such as Ulrich's (1983) critical systems heuristics. These preliminary findings are summarized in Figure 2.3.

This work, therefore, provides a "system of systems methodologies" because it demonstrates the interrelationship between different systems approaches and the relationship these have to ideal-type problem contexts. Some (Banathy, 1988; Keys, 1988) have interpreted the system of systems methodologies in a rather positivistic way, implying that it enables us to identify real-world problem situations according to the grid of problem

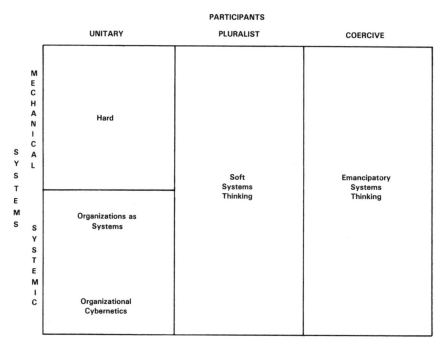

FIGURE 2.3. Preliminary Classification of Systems Approaches According to the Assumptions They Make about Problem Contexts

contexts and then to choose appropriate systems methodologies to address these problem situations. This is not, in fact, a legitimate or fruitful way to proceed, as has been argued at length elsewhere (Jackson, 1990a). The system of systems methodologies should be used, as it is in this book, to seek to provide an exact appreciation of what is being taken for granted in using each type of systems approach and to make analysts starkly aware that the choice of any systems approach is exceptionally committing in terms of the effects it brings in its wake. This should enable potential users to assess the strengths and weaknesses of different methodologies for their purposes and to be fully aware of the consequences of employing each approach. It was to this end that the dimensions of systems and participants were chosen; they seemed to bring the greatest insight to the matter of distinguishing systems approaches. The hypothesis was that systems methodologies could be usefully classified on the basis of the assumptions they made about systems and participants. And, indeed, they do seem to make up a "system of systems methodologies" in terms of these assumptions about problem contexts.

Modernism versus Postmodernism

The most important debate in the cultural arena, and in the human and social sciences, during recent times has been that centered on the attempt to establish a "postmodern" (as opposed to modern) theoretical position. This debate turns crucially on supposed changes in our culture and the way we understand knowledge and reality, but is usually linked to other developments in society as well. Thus postmodernist culture is variously associated with postindustrial society, consumer society, media society, knowledge- and information-based society, the dominance of multinational companies, a post-Fordist decentralization of enterprises, and a new stage in the development of late capitalism in which everything becomes a commodity. What is not in doubt is that postmodernism has had a significant effect on architecture, theater, literature, and art, as well as social theory. We can hardly ignore the postmodernist debate because if a new social and economic movement is being born, then systems methodologies will certainly have to respond to the "new times" that the postmodernists claim to identify.

I shall concentrate here on the debate as it has affected social theory. To begin with, some of the main points of schism between modernists and postmodernists are outlined. The key manifestations of modernism, as identified by postmodernists, are then set out. The postmodernist alternative is described, insofar as this is possible given the movement's dedication to "difference" and indeterminacy. Finally, I consider how acceptance of the postmodernist argument might affect the use and relevance of systems methodologies. For the descriptions of modernism and postmodernism, I rely heavily on Lyotard (1984) and Cooper and Burrell (1988), turning to Burrell (1989) and Jacques (1989) for the relevance of the arguments for systems thinking. The learning gained will be used in Parts II and III of the book to see if any systems methodologies show signs of being responsive to the "postmodern condition."

Modernism is committed to the achievements of the Enlightenment, upholding reason and believing that rationality can play an increasing role in helping human beings perfect themselves and their societies. The world is seen as logical and orderly so that it can be probed by science to produce objective truth. History is seen as having a meaning based upon human purpose or, if not that, upon the rationalization of social systems. There is progress toward some unitary, predictable end state, which might be the emancipation of humanity or the perfect functioning of the system. Language is "transparent" so that it is capable of conveying truth and acting as a suitable vehicle for arriving at consensus. Modernism essentially believes in the order of things and searches for unity, identity, and consensus. It offers security through rational explanations of what is happening, centering on the human subject or the increasing complexity of society. Seriousness and depth are characteristics of modernism as it plans and charts the onward march of rationality and progress.

Postmodernism seeks to puncture the certainties of modernism, particularly the belief in rationality, truth, and progress; and it delights in doing so. It denies that science has access to objective truth, and rejects the notion of history as the progressive realization and emancipation of the human subject or as an increase in the complexity and steering capacity of societies. Language is not transparent, and it certainly does not offer the possibility of universal consensus. There are many different "language games," obeying different rules, in which speakers take part in order to defeat opponents or for the sheer pleasure of playing. We have, therefore, to be tolerant to differences and to multiple interpretations of the world, and must learn to live with the incommensurable since there is no metatheory that can reconcile or decide between different positions. Postmodernism offers no security. Rather, it thrives on instability, disruption, disorder, contingency, paradox, and indeterminacy. The image is more significant than "reality," and so postmodernism emphasizes superficiality and play instead of seriousness and depth.

Lyotard (1984) recognizes two central manifestations of modernism in social theory; these can be called, following Cooper and Burrell (1988), "systemic modernism" and "critical modernism."

Systemic modernism, as its name suggests, is identified with the systems approach as a means of both understanding society and programming it for more effective performance. Parsons's work represents an early, optimistic phase of systemic modernism, reflecting the managed resurgence of capitalist economies after World War II and their stabilization using, particularly, the mechanism of the modern welfare state. The latest phase is found in Luhmann's highly technocratic, all-embracing, and despairing version of systems theory. In this, instrumental reason is completely triumphant as everything is subject to the rational requirements of the societal system. It is the system that is the vanguard of history and progress as it follows its own logic to increase "performativity" (in terms of input–output measures) and handle environmental uncertainty. Humanity is dragged in the wake of the system. Individual hopes and aspirations simply respond to the system's needs, and consensus is engineered to improve the system's functioning. Even internal dissension, strikes, and conflict represent the system readjusting to increase its viability and effectiveness.

Knowledge under systemic modernism, Lyotard argues, is completely subservient to system imperatives. First, science is privileged over other less malleable forms of learning, and then science and technology are reduced solely to programming the system. Truth gives way to performativity. Only research relevant to the functioning of complex, large-scale systems is financed, and only results that contribute to improving the input–output equation are recognized. The technocrats who subscribe to this knowledge have the power to implement the findings and so to verify their correctness. Thus a vicious circle is set up in which profit, power, and proof become indissolubly linked. Further, what is implemented also becomes associated with what is right and just. Power becomes the basis of legitimation. Questions about efficiency and salability replace those about truth or falsity and justice. Education, too, is turned to the same purpose.

The second form of modernism, critical modernism, is based upon Kant's program of enlightenment. It rests upon what Lyotard calls the power of "grand narratives" that seek to explain history in terms of progress. These grand narratives take two forms. First, there are philosophical "totalizations" that offer a unified view of all learning. Differences are overcome as previously irreconcilable sciences and knowledges are combined in one language game. A good example is Hegel's universal history of philosophy, celebrating the becoming of the "spirit." Second are those narratives that chart the emancipation of the human subject. History is seen as the progressive liberation of humanity from constraints so that it can assume mastery and take on responsibility for its own destiny. Marxism is, of course, the best example of this kind of grand narrative. The history of all societies can be explained as leading to a communist utopia in which all conflict and contradiction are overcome.

Not surprisingly, since his work combines elements from both types of grand narratives, Habermas is fingered by Lyotard as being the archetypal representative of critical modernism. Habermas proposes a unified theory of knowledge linked to different human interests, and aims his whole project at human emancipation directed by universal consensus arrived at in the "ideal speech situation," with participants presumably sticking to one language game. More surprising to the reader, perhaps, will be the idea that Luhmann and Habermas can be classified together as modernists—even if they are modernists of different varieties. For, as discussed previously, Habermas regards himself as an implacable opponent of Luhmann's systems theory and as setting out the grounds on which the imperialism of instrumental reason can be resisted. Lyotard, however, sees more similarities between their two positions than differences. Both Habermas and Luhmann believe that the world is logical and meaningful; that history has a subject—whether this is humanity or the system; that discourse can capture the order that exists "out there" in reality; and that human beings can understand and change, or at least influence, what happens in society.

Looking at the two kinds of modernism, Lyotard is convinced that systemic modernism is the most powerful. The grand narratives are no longer credible, as more "realistic" views of science and knowledge have prevailed. It is obvious, to Lyotard, that the language games people play are too numerous and complicated to be subsumed under any totalizing endeavor. Moreover, despite the commitment of critical theories to oppose the status quo, these theories are in fact easily incorporated into it. In capitalist countries the minor resistances they provoke provide a fertile source of renewal for the system. In those few places where the alternative, communist model of society has not been totally eliminated, Marxism itself has been transformed into a regulator of society. As Lyotard (1984) tellingly argues, "Everywhere, the critique of political economy (the subtitle of Marx's *Capital*) and its correlate, the critique of alienated society, are used in one way or another as aids in programming the system" (p. 13).

While recognizing systemic modernism as the strongest adversary, Lyotard is firm in his opposition to the determinacy of all forms of modernism, whether emphasizing the functionality of the system or human emancipation. He wants to construct a postmodern alternative. The certainties encouraged by modernism, the metadiscourses pretending to provide objective understanding of the whole, can exact a high price in terms of a terrorism either of the system or of the philosophical and political kind. For this reason it is necessary to "wage war" on totalizations, to emphasize dissension, instability, and unpredictability, and to activate "difference." The blind spots of modernism, those things rendered unpresentable and unspeakable in the narratives of modernism, must be brought to the fore.

This task is made easier because, although modernism is powerful, it is becoming clear that it is built upon fragile foundations. Science is seen to be only one kind of language game, with limited relevance to social affairs. Even within its sphere of relevance, the modernist account of science is prone to attack. The new physics, as in quantum theory, concerns itself with instabilities and with uncertainty and the undecidable. Put simply, science does not function as modernism would have it. Postmodern science, therefore, rejects performativity and asks questions about purposes. It sees systems not as stable but as subject to discontinuity and catastrophe. They are temporary islands of determinism within a sea of indeterminacy. The quest for precise knowledge about systems is misguided; more precision only reveals greater uncertainty. The attempt to limit individual initiative, according to systemic requirements, destroys exactly the novelty the system needs to adjust to its environment. Our new understanding of science provides no support, therefore, for modernism.

The possibility of developing a metalanguage that modernism could employ to legitimate its grand narratives is also open to attack. There is no one social subject that can be addressed using a universal metalanguage. And there are many language games, of which each of us knows only a few. Nor is it easy to sustain the modernist notion that language is oriented to achieving consensus. Language games are characterized by struggle and dissension, and this seems highly necessary in order to promote innovation and to energize and motivate human action and behavior. Communication should, therefore, be imbued with the capacity for innovation, change, and renewal, and refusal of conformity should be encouraged. Consensus can only be possible in localized circumstances and is only desirable if subject to rapid cancellation.

Cooper and Burrell (1988) reference the work of Derrida and Foucault as other prominent postmodernist writers. Derrida's "deconstructive" method seeks to reveal the deceptiveness of language, and the work that has to go into hiding contradictions so that unity and order can be privileged and rationality maintained. Foucault demonstrates how power operates to impose an order on the world so that it fits the categories of modernism. To help us recognize just how extraordinary the ordinary is, he recommends "genealogy"—the search for disparity, difference, and indeterminacy, and the granting of respect to sudden, spontaneous insight.

For modernists such as Habermas, postmodernism is a philosophy of irrationalism, leading at best to despair because it abandons the hope that humans can improve their lot through their own agency. To Lyotard and Jacques (1989), however, this is not the case; a postmodernist ethics can be constructed on the basis of the idea of justice. Giving up on performativity and the grand narratives means we can no longer hide behind "objectivity" to avoid personal responsibility. We have to live in a world of multiple partial truths. But just knowing that one does not know everything can be liberating. It opens up a new world of possibilities in which each of us has to take ethical responsibility for the truths we embrace.

Following Burrell (1989) and Jacques (1989), we can now consider some of the implications for systems methodologies if what the postmodernists say is correct. Some of these derive from the other societal changes said to accompany or give birth to postmodernism itself. Operational research, for example, is a systems methodology that is clearly associated with the postwar consensus. It flourished in the nationalized industries and other large centralized and hierarchical corporations. Classical operational research is modernist and Fordist to its core. No wonder, then, that it is having difficulty adjusting as large organizations are decentralized and even broken up into autonomous units, and in a world where consumption rather than production is dominant (and so marketing, and the superficialities of packaging and appearance, are all-important).

Other lessons stem directly from the cultural change that *is* postmodernism. If history is no longer seen as unilinear and predictable, then there is little point in promulgating forecasts of the future. If there is a decline in belief in rationality and an optimum solution to problems (increase in performativity), then the problem-solving techniques will lack legitimation. At a time when the scientific method is being challenged as the sole means of producing knowledge, other forms of learning—from the case study, from experience, from intuition—may become more acceptable. Deep analysis of systems in search of laws and regularities is unlikely to receive much support. It will be more productive to emphasize the superficial, to concentrate on image, to take note of accidents, and to respect arbitrariness and discontinuities. If there are no acceptable grand narratives to guide the idea of progress, then systems methodologies can only hope to bring about temporary and contested improvements. Indeed, in a world of multiple truths competing for prominence, systems practitioners will be impotent unless they recognize the social, political, and ethical contexts of their work. Finally, the postmodern world does not value "seriousness" very highly; we had better introduce a bit of humor, lightness, irony, sarcasm, and racy language into our systems approaches.

Which, if any, systems methodologies express the spirit of the times as portrayed in postmodernism? Part II and Part III of the book will provide the further evidence necessary for the reader to make up his or her own mind.

Conclusion

All systems methodologies make explicit or implicit assumptions about the world they seek to understand and change. Systems thinking itself does not provide the means for unearthing and discussing these theoretical assumptions. It is necessary, therefore, for systems thinkers to learn about and to consider some social scientific schemata in order that they can be more self-reflective about what they are trying to do. In this chapter I have dealt at length with assumptions systems methodologies must make, either consciously or unconsciously, about the human interests they serve; the nature of systems thinking and social systems; the appropriate way to "see" organizations; the complexity of the systems with which they deal and the relationship between participants; and such things as rationality, truth, and progress. This puts us in a position to interrogate each of the systems methodologies, set out in the next part of this volume, about all these matters. That should, in turn, equip systems thinkers with the background theory necessary so that they can reasonably choose between and use systems methodologies. It also provides the basis for questions later in the book about the possibility of reestablishing systems thinking as a unified approach to problem management at the leading edge of the management sciences.

The preparatory theoretical work done, we can now turn with enhanced capability to consider what the various systems methodologies offer to managers, organizations, and society.

II

Methodological Approaches

3

Organizations as Systems

Introduction

From the 1930s onward, three different models of management competed for precedence in organization theory—the traditional approach, human relations theory, and systems theory (Kast and Rosenzweig, 1981). The traditional approach was based upon Taylor's scientific management, Fayol's administrative management theory, and Weber's bureaucracy theory, and encouraged the view that organizations were like machines. This view was considered briefly in the last chapter; it has been subject to criticism from many commentators. Human relations theory grew out of the critique of the traditional approach, particularly its alleged failure to take account of human needs. Theorists such as Mayo, Maslow, Herzberg, and McGregor studied and drew conclusions about issues such as group behavior, individual motivation, and leadership. While it was a useful corrective to traditional theory to put humans and their needs at the center of organizational analysis, this could easily lead to the neglect of factors such as the market, technology, competition, and organizational structure; factors that, it is arguable, have far more effect on organizational performance than decisions on how to manage people. Organizations have to take account of human needs, but not at the expense of everything else (Perrow, 1972).

During the 1960s, because of the weaknesses of traditional and human relations thinking and because of its own obvious superiority, the systems approach came to dominate management theory. Systems thinkers argued that organizations should be seen as whole systems made up of interrelated parts. The trouble with other theories of management, according to the systems perspective, was that they concentrated on only one or two of the aspects of the organization necessary for high performance. The traditional approach concentrated on task and structure, and the human relations approach on people. The systems approach was said to be "holistic" because it believed in looking at organizations as wholes. The traditional

41

and human relations approaches were "reductionist" because they looked at parts of the organization in isolation. Another significant advantage claimed for the systems approach was that it saw the organization as an "open system" in constant interaction with its environment. This was opposed to the limited, "closed" perspective of the traditional and human relations models, which tended to ignore the environment.

The period when the organizations-as-systems approach could claim unchallenged hegemony in management theory came to an end in the 1970s, with the emergence of "phenomenological" (Silverman, 1970) and Marxist accounts of the nature of organizations. Nevertheless, in many ways the systems approach still remains dominant. None of the many other perspectives, described by Burrell and Morgan (1979) and Morgan (1986), have come close to toppling it from that position.

The organizations-as-systems approach has been so significant in the organizational sciences, and the variety of systems models has been so great, that it is difficult to do it justice in just one chapter. All that one can do is pick out some of the most important landmarks in its history, paying particular attention to the methodological recommendations made in the most important models for studying and changing organizations. I begin with Barnard's early systems model based on the notion of "equilibrium." I then pass on to sociological systems theory—particularly Selznick's adaptation of "structural functionalism" for the study of organizations and Parsons's "equilibrium function" model, which takes the purely sociological systems tradition to its highest level of sophistication. Katz and Kahn marry together Parsonian ideas with a rigorous working out of the nature of "open systems" derived from the biologist von Bertalanffy; this is studied in a section on general system theory. Finally, the explicitly prescriptive side of the systems model is considered with sections on the important pragmatic schools of systems thinking known as contingency theory and sociotechnical systems theory. I end with an overall assessment of the organizations-as-systems type of systems approach.

Barnard's Systems Thinking

The earliest systems models, used in management, studied organizations as mechanical systems in equilibrium. The idea of studying social systems in this way was originally derived from Pareto (1919) and was promoted in the United States by Henderson, a powerful figure at Harvard University in the 1930s. Henderson saw organizations as being complex systems made up of parts in mutual interaction. They may exhibit surface change but, at a deeper level, are in a state of unchanging equilibrium

(Lilienfeld, 1978). Henderson influenced, among others, Mayo, Roethlisberger and Dickson, Barnard, and Parsons. Roethlisberger and Dickson (1939) used this thinking to explain the findings of the famous Hawthorne experiments and to consider what factors might cause the personal disequilibrium of workers. I shall concentrate here on Barnard's use of the model to advise executives on how they should sustain organizations in equilibrium by the careful manipulation of inducements to stakeholders.

Chester Barnard was a lifelong executive himself. Between 1927 and 1948 he was president of the New Jersey Bell Telephone Company, and he also served in government agencies and charitable positions. In 1938 he produced one of the earliest systems accounts of the nature of organizations, called *The Functions of the Executive*. This has been one of the most influential books published in the entire field of management.

Barnard believed his thinking was relevant to all forms and types of organization. His aim was to discover features common to executive functions in all organizations. What was significant was that he attempted to do this by considering, first, what kind of systems organizations are. Thus he did not simply produce a list of elements of the management process, as Fayol had done. He asked himself what organizations as systems were actually like, and then derived from this analysis conclusions about what executives needed to do to manage them properly (to keep them in equilibrium). We need, therefore, to consider his work in two parts: looking first at his exposition of the nature of organizations as systems, then at his conclusions about how executives should behave to ensure that their organizations survive and are more effective.

Barnard reasoned that organizations were "cooperative systems." When an individual tries to do something, he or she is subject to strict physical and biological constraints that determine what is possible to achieve. In order to realize major tasks, therefore, individuals have to cooperate, and this gives rise to the birth of cooperative systems.

Cooperative systems will persist, Barnard argues, as long as they are effective and efficient. Barnard links effectiveness to the success of the organization in accomplishing its purpose. Efficiency relates to the need to provide, to individuals who cooperate, a surplus of satisfactions over dissatisfactions. Unless these individuals receive such a surfeit, they will not continue to remain as members of the organization (in the case of employees), or to have dealings with it (in the case of other stakeholders). Effectiveness and efficiency are achieved through the interactions among people as managed by both the formal (studied by traditional theory) and informal (studied by human relations theory) structures of the enterprise. The formal structures are the consciously coordinated activities that define a common purpose, reward organizational members, and put individuals in communication with one another. The informal structures are those that arise without a common or consciously coordinated joint purpose. They are equally significant, Barnard argues, to proper organizational functioning, and executives of necessity should pay close attention to the informal as well as formal aspects of organizations.

From this analysis of organizations as cooperative systems, Barnard derives his conclusions about what executives should do in order to manage them properly. There are essentially three functions the executive must undertake. First, organizational communication must be maintained by creating a proper structure for the enterprise, selecting suitable people for the executive role, and securing an informal organization that backs up and supports the formal. Second, essential services must be secured from appropriate individuals by making them aware of the organization, bringing them into a cooperative relationship with it, and making sure they are motivated to work for or with the organization by offering them sufficient inducements in return for their contributions. Finally, the organization's objectives should be formulated and the idea of a common purpose inculcated at all levels of the enterprise.

There is obviously too much emphasis in Barnard's work on organizations being naturally cooperative systems. The mechanical-equilibrium model that underlies it cannot deal with internal conflict nor, for that matter, with structure elaboration in response to a changing environment. Nevertheless, the idea of studying organizations as whole systems consisting of closely interrelated parts, the equal attention given to formal and informal aspects of organizational life, and the attempt to base a theory of management on the need to manage systems in equilibrium sensitively, remain lasting and important contributions.

Sociological Systems Theory

Following Barnard's pioneering work, organizations as systems gradually developed to become the dominant approach to the study of organizations in the 1960s and 1970s. Very important in this maturation process were a series of theoretical breakthroughs that further established that organizations could usefully be considered as complex systems made up of parts existing in close interrelationship, and additionally demonstrated that they could be seen as possessing "needs" and as being in constant interaction with their environments. This theoretical innovation came from two sources: first, from sociological systems theory, which is considered in this section; second, from general system theory, which is looked at in the next.

Sociological systems theory contributed the organismic analogy to organizational studies. The central figures in sociology who developed this analogy were Spencer (1969), in the nineteenth century, and Durkheim (1933). Both saw social systems as made up of mutually dependent elements functioning in ways that contributed to the maintenance of the whole. From sociology, the organismic analogy passed into anthropology and was given coherent theoretical expression, by Malinowski and Radcliffe-Brown, as "structural functionalism." In structural-functionalist analysis, recurrent activities in a society are explained by the function they perform for the maintenance of that society's structure. Social institutions function to serve the needs of a society for survival.

The organismic analogy lent itself very well, of course, to the study of organizations. Organizations could be represented as primarily geared to ensuring the survival and continuity of themselves as systems. The various parts of organizations could be understood in terms of the contributions they made to the maintenance of the whole organization. I shall consider here, as representative of this thinking, Selznick's structural-functionalist approach to organizations and Parsons's "equilibrium function" model (as Buckley, 1967, calls it).

Selznick (1948), seeking to analyze what organizations were like, found himself diverging considerably from the traditional view that they were instruments of rational action. Following Barnard, he saw that they were cooperative systems with both formal and informal aspects; rational action embodied in the formal structure was modified by the social needs of individuals. Such cooperative systems were also subject to the pressure of their environments, to which some adjustment had to be made. Organizations were, therefore, "adaptive structures" that had to adapt their goals and change themselves in response to environmental circumstances. To Selznick it appeared that many of the adjustments made by organizations, in response to both internal and external determinants, took place independently of the consciousness of the individuals involved. Organizations were acting like organisms; reacting to influences upon them in ways best designed to ensure their own survival.

If organizations behaved in this manner, then it seemed to Selznick that the best way of studying them was to use structural-functionalist analysis. Organizations were primarily oriented to their own survival. They had needs that had to be met if survival was to be ensured. For Selznick, organizations possessed the following stable needs, deriving from their nature as cooperative systems and adaptive structures:

- Security of the organization in relation to social forces in its environment

- Stability of the lines of authority and communication
- Stability of informal relations
- Continuity of policy and the sources of its determination
- A homogeneous outlook with respect to the meaning and role of the organization

Activity in an organization was best understood not in terms of conscious purpose, but by how it contributed to meeting these needs, or "functional imperatives," of the organization.

Parsons attempted to construct a sociological systems model for analyzing all elements of the social world. This consisted of a combination of the notion that social systems are made up of the interaction of individuals, the mechanical-equilibrium model (which had underpinned Barnard's work), and a form of structural functionalism, concentrating on the functional prerequisites that must be met by social systems if they are to survive. The most famous part of all this is Parsons's elaboration with Smelser (1956) of the four functional imperatives that must be adequately fulfilled for a system by its subsystems if that system is to continue to exist. The first letters of these four imperatives—adaptation, goal attainment, integration, and latency (or pattern maintenance)—make up the well-known AGIL mnemonic. Due to the recursive character of systems, this AGIL scheme can be employed to analyze and link the various levels of system right through from the individual personality system to the social system. The meaning of the terms that make up AGIL is as follows:

A = adaptation—the system has to establish relationships between itself and its external environment
G = goal attainment—goals have to be defined and resources mobilized and managed in pursuit of those goals
I = integration—the system has to have a means of coordinating its efforts
L = latency (or pattern maintenance)—the first three requisites for organizational survival have to be solved with the minimum of strain and tension by ensuring that organizational "actors" are motivated to act in the appropriate manner

We can now examine those aspects of Parsons's work specific to the study of organizations as systems.

The defining characteristic of formal organizations for Parsons (1956, 1957)—that which distinguishes them from other types of social system—is their primacy of orientation to the attainment of a specific goal. The goals of organizations could, following the functionalist logic, be directly related to the needs of the wider society, and organizations classified on that basis. So there are:

- Economic organizations, like business firms, oriented to the adaptive function
- Political organizations, like government departments, oriented to the goal-attainment function
- Integrative organizations, like those of the legal profession, oriented to the integrative function
- Latency organizations, like churches and schools, oriented to the pattern-maintenance function

Within organizations (made up of interacting individuals), order was maintained by a value system that inculcated shared norms among organizational members. To ensure harmony, this value system had to be congruent with the central value system of society, internalized by individuals during the socialization process (e.g., education). Equilibrium should be easily maintained in this manner since organizations could legitimate themselves in their participants' eyes in terms of the function performed for society. The main source of strain for organizations occurred if the central value system of society began to change. In these circumstances, organizations exhibited "dynamic equilibrium," adapting in the direction of a new type of stability.

The structure of organizations was understood by Parsons through the use of his AGIL scheme. Like all social systems, organizations have to meet four functional imperatives to survive, and so require four types of subsystems to deal with the requirements set out in AGIL.

Parsons (1960) saw the management task in organizations as differing depending upon at which of three levels it operated. At the "technical system level," it was concerned directly with the transformation process; at the "managerial level," with integrating technical-level activities and mediating between these and the institutional level; and at the "institutional level," it integrated the organization with the wider community it was supposed to serve.

Parsons's equilibrium-function model was immensely important in the development of organization theory, influencing among others Katz and Kahn (1966), Thompson (1967), and Kast and Rosenzweig (1981). In his later work, Parsons consolidated it further by incorporating cybernetic insights and certain general system theory formulations. I deal with the criticisms of his model (and Selznick's) in a later analysis and assessment of the organizations-as-systems approach as a whole.

General System Theory

Sociological systems theory contributed a profound understanding of the nature and role of organizational subsystems in meeting organizational needs. Parsons's combination of the mechanical-equilibrium and organismic analogies took this type of thinking to its apotheosis. If further progress was to be made in analyzing organizations as systems, inspiration was needed from elsewhere. In fact, it came from biology and was transmitted by way of general system theory. The inspiration came in the form of a rigorous working out of the idea that organisms—and other types of complex system—were "open systems."

Katz and Kahn's (1966) *The Social Psychology of Organizations* was the classic expression of this new development, the more so since it succeeded in integrating the open-system notion with ideas from psychology and much from Parsons's sociology. I shall treat this model at length in a minute, but first it is necessary to look at the contribution of the biologist Ludwig von Bertalanffy.

It was perhaps not surprising that the new boost to the organizations-as-systems tradition should come from biology. Biologists had been struggling with problems of organized complexity for some time. In particular, von Bertalanffy was convinced that organisms should be studied as complex wholes. His work came to fruition in 1950 with the publication of the famous article "The Theory of Open Systems in Physics and Biology." Many have argued that this essay established systems theory as a scientific movement (Emery, 1969; Lilienfeld, 1978). What von Bertalanffy did was to distinguish between two types of systems—closed and open. A system is closed if no material enters or leaves it. A closed system obeys the second law of thermodynamics, gradually running down, increasing in entropy, and reaching an equilibrium state when no energy can be obtained from it. A system is open if it imports and exports material and, in the process, changes components. An open system depends on its environment and lives off it (the environment doesn't just "impinge" on it). Open systems can temporarily defeat the second law of thermodynamics. Organisms, for example, can maintain themselves in a steady state by exchanging materials with their environments. Open systems can evolve toward states of greater complexity and differentiation, reversing the law of entropy. They are capable of self-regulation, adapting to circumstances by changing the structure and processes of their internal components. And they exhibit *equifinality*—the ability to reach the same final state from different initial conditions and in different ways.

Von Bertalanffy was important for establishing the notion of open systems on a scientific basis. He is also rightfully regarded as the founding father of general system theory. He derived his insights from biology, but he believed that they could be transferred to other disciplines as well. This was because the laws he was discovering were laws governing system behavior, not laws specific to particular disciplines. It followed that there could be a new science—general system theory—devoted to the study of complex systems of all types, whether they were of a natural, biological, or social nature (von Bertalanffy, 1968). For the rest of his life, von Bertalanffy dedicated himself to the development and promulgation of this new science. In 1954 he helped give institutional embodiment to his ambition by setting up (with scholars such as Boulding and Rapoport) the Society for General System Research. This had four aims:

- To investigate the isomorphy of concepts, laws, and models in various fields, and to help in useful transfers from one field to another
- To encourage development of adequate theoretical models in fields that lack them
- To minimize duplication of theoretical effort
- To promote the unity of science

It was not long before von Bertalanffy's original model of organisms as open systems was transferred, in the manner of general system theory, to other disciplines. By the 1960s it had become thoroughly absorbed into organization theory, with the rich armory of concepts surrounding the open system notion complementing those of structural functionalism. Katz and Kahn's (1966) account of organizations as open systems is perhaps the best known.

Katz and Kahn begin by pointing out the advantages of their approach. It is more "scientific" than the traditional view because it does not fall into the trap of identifying organizational purposes with the goals of individual members. Organizations are systems with their own goals. Further, the traditional and human relations approaches take a closed view of the organization. It is clearly advantageous to abandon this and to start looking at organizations as open systems. Organizations are best represented as entities in close interrelationship with their environments, taking in inputs and transforming them into outputs. These outputs, in the form of products, can provide the means for new inputs, so that the cycle can begin again. The main purpose is to maintain a steady state and to survive.

Reviewing and building on von Bertalanffy's findings, Katz and Kahn have it that nine characteristics define all open systems (including, of course, organizations):

- The importation of energy from the external environment
- The throughput and transformation of the input in the system

- The output, which is exported to the environment
- Systems as cycles of events—the output furnishes new sources of energy for the input so the cycle can start again
- Negative entropy—open systems "live" off their environments, acquiring more energy than they spend
- Information input and a coding process—systems selectively gather information about their environments and also about their own activities (so they can take corrective action)
- The steady state and dynamic homeostasis—despite continuous inflow and export of energy, the character of the system remains the same
- Differentiation—open systems move in the direction of differentiation and structure elaboration (e.g., greater specialization of functions)
- Equifinality

Other significant aspects of the Katz and Kahn model closely follow Parsons's thinking. Five generic types of subsystem are recognized that meet the organization's functional needs:

- The *production* or technical subsystem, concerned with the work done on the throughput
- The *supportive* subsystem, concerned with obtaining inputs and disposing of outputs
- The *maintenance* subsystem, which ensures conformance of personnel to their roles through selection, and through rewards and sanctions
- The *adaptive* subsystem, ensuring responsiveness to environmental variations
- The *managerial* subsystem, which directs, coordinates, and controls other subsystems and activities through various regulatory mechanisms

Externally, organizations seek to control their environments to reduce uncertainty or, where that is not possible, to adapt their own structures to accord with environmental demands. Organizations are seen as falling into four major types according to the functions they perform for society.

Von Bertalanffy's open system concept continued to influence theoretical work and empirical investigations (see the next two sections) in organization theory during the 1970s and 1980s. Countless books were published looking at management from a systems point of view. In at least one of its intentions, therefore, general system theory has met with success. The hope that general laws could be discovered that hold across all system types has, however, not been fulfilled. Some general system theorists have found it difficult to advance much beyond von Bertalanffy's (1968) original and preliminary assertions and formulations (e.g., Weinberg, 1975; Rapoport, 1986), some have followed mathematical avenues that are clearly not relevant to complex social systems (Klir, 1985), while others use general system theory simply to give coherence to a range of fairly traditional management science techniques (van Gigch, 1978). Partially because of the gap between its high ambitions and its actual achievements, general system theory has come in for some severe criticism (Berlinski, 1976; Lilienfeld, 1978). The Society for General Systems Research staggered on through the 1980s with a few hundred members and various name changes, and is now all but defunct. Interested readers might, however, read Miller (1978) for the most thoroughly researched attempt to integrate knowledge across biological and social systems. Miller's theory of "living systems" asserts that there are seven levels of living systems—the cell, the organ, the organism, the group, the organization, the society, and supranational systems—and that each of these has nineteen critical subsystems. Merker (1985) has suggested a methodology for applying living systems concepts to organizations in order to achieve effective management.

Contingency Theory

Introduction to Contingency Theory

I have dealt with the theoretical breakthroughs that made an organizations-as-systems approach possible. Equally significant in its emergence, however, were various empirical studies of organizations and their performance, all of which tended to throw doubt on traditional and human relations thinking about management. The organizations-as-systems approach, as a unified systems perspective, is based upon a combination of the theoretical and empirical contributions. We must now turn to the empirical work. In this section I look at the studies that contributed to the emergence of contingency theory, and in the next I consider sociotechnical systems thinking. Together, these two theories represent the more prescriptive side of the organizations-as-systems tradition, giving managers specific advice about how they should run their organizations.

The contingency approach to the study of organizations and their management came into increasing prominence during the 1970s (Kast and Rosenzweig, 1981). Based upon the theoretical innovations discussed earlier, it views organizations as consisting of a series of interdependent subsystems, each of which has a function to perform within the context of the organization as a whole. Because of their importance to the survival needs of the organization, each subsystem is conceptualized as representing a functional imperative; an imperative that has to be met if the organization is to be viable and efficient. Contingency theorists are not in complete agreement as to which subsystems should be singled out as critical. For the purposes of this account, I will identify four subsystems of significance: the goal, human, technical, and managerial subsystems. The goal subsystem is concerned with overall purpose and objectives. The human subsystem embraces the people in the organization, their leadership, and their motivation. The technical subsystem is involved with the transformation of the inputs into the organization (matter, energy, information) into useful outputs (products, services, energy, information). The managerial subsystem must coordinate the other subsystems and look to the organization's relationship with the environment. In addition, management must consider the best structure for the organization in the light of the demands of the other subsystems. Contingency theory assumes that each of the subsystems is open to a range of variation. Each should be designed so that it is congruent with the others and corresponds to the environment with which it is faced. The size of the organization will also have an important effect upon the subsystems and the organizational structure.

Contingency theory additionally rests upon the open systems view that regards the organization as dependent upon the wider environment. The organization and environment are seen as being in a state of mutual influence and interdependence. The contingency theory of organizations is concerned to understand and represent the key associations that characterize relationships between the organization and its environment. It tends to be assumed that these can be understood in terms of the organization's need to survive; the organization must be adapted in certain ways if it is to survive in its environment. The economic performance of a firm decides whether it survives or not, and this is determined in turn by the way the organization manages its relationship with the environment. The theoretical background of contingency theory is represented in Figure 3.1, showing the primary subsystems of the organization as an open system.

As was stated, contingency theory depends equally as much on the conclusions emerging from the results of various empirical investigations, and I shall discuss these in the following. For the moment, however, let me establish the main hypotheses upon which contingency theory rests. There seem to be four of these.

First is that there is no one best way to structure the activities of an organization in all circumstances. In this sense, contingency theory is a rebuff to traditional management theory and human relations theory,

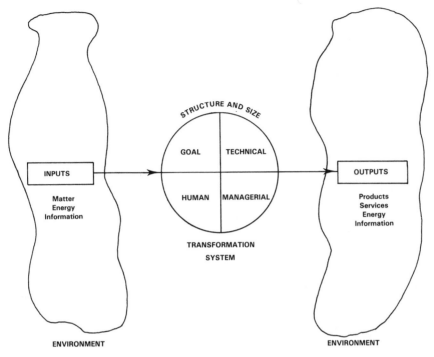

FIGURE 3.1. The Primary Subsystems of the Organization as an Open System

which pretended to produce principles of management applicable to all circumstances. According to the contingency approach, no such general principles exist.

Second, certain contextual factors determine the nature of the structure because of the constraints they impose. These constraints are assumed to have force because organizations must achieve certain levels of performance in order to survive. If organization structure is not adapted to context (technology, environment, etc.), then opportunities are lost, costs rise, and the maintenance of the organization is threatened.

Third, it follows that depending on circumstances (i.e., on the context), some form of organization structure is likely to be more effective than others. Different organizing principles are appropriate to different contextual circumstances; it all depends on certain key strategic contingencies. This offers the prospect of reconciling earlier management theories, establishing the domain to which each theory is apt. It shows the way forward by suggesting that the appropriateness of management principles depends on the nature of the situations in which they are applied. In some circum-

stances each of the earlier theories might be correct, even the much-de-
rided traditional approach.

Finally, empirical work can be conducted to establish what is the
appropriate match between the organizational structure and the nature of
the demands placed on it by humans, technology, environment, and size.

I shall now consider, in turn, the key strategic contingencies and the
effect these have upon each other and upon the most suitable organizational structure.

The Goal Subsystem

The goal subsystem obviously is closely interrelated to other internal
subsystems. Choice of goal will have an effect on the technical, human, and
managerial subsystems, and also upon the best structure to employ. Similarly, each of the other subsystems will affect the nature of the goals
pursued and the way they are pursued. Another important interrelationship will be with the environment. Goals must be chosen that ensure the
legitimacy and the viability of the organization within the context of its
wider environment. In a stable environment it may be possible to set static
goals. In a highly uncertain and turbulent environment, goals will have to
be more flexible and multiple, satisfying a variety of constraints. The
organizational structure employed will have to reflect the need for flexible
goals if the environment is uncertain. Fuller discussion of goals from the
organizations-as-systems perspective can be found in Thompson and
McEwan (1958), Etzioni (1960), and Perrow (1961).

The Human Subsystem

The role of human beings in organizations is accorded a special status
within most contemporary theories of management. Individuals are seen
to possess certain needs that must be satisfied if they are to be attracted and
encouraged to stay within the organization, and if they are to be motivated
to give their best. In other words, human needs have acquired the status
of a functional imperative. Theorists differ with regard to the nature of this
imperative according to the "model of man" to which they subscribe
(Schein, 1970). However, it is correct to see the human relations thinkers'
emphasis upon the human desire for self-realization and self-actualization
as legitimate concerns here (McGregor, 1960; Argyris, 1964). Thus human
relations theory has its place (as does traditional theory) within the contingency perspective, but now it is recognized that human needs are only
one of the various functional imperatives that have to be met. Given that

proviso, human relations thinkers have shown that attention should be given to informal groups, to the proper design of jobs, and to participation in decision making.

The Technical Subsystem

The type of structure one should choose for an organization, to get maximum efficiency, will depend also on the kind of technology employed to bring about the transformation process. The analysis of Woodward (1964) has been particularly influential here, and I shall concentrate on that. Perrow's (1967) work on the topic might also be consulted by interested readers, together with authors such as Blauner (1964) for the effect of technology on the human subsystem.

Between 1953 and 1957, Woodward led a research team in a survey of about 100 manufacturing firms in South East Essex in England. Her deliberate intention was to see if these firms were following the principles set out in traditional theory and, if so, whether this was bringing business success. In an investigation of certain specific features of the ways they were organized (division of labor, specialization, number of levels in the hierarchy, span of control, nature of communication taking place, etc.), Woodward found considerable variation among the firms. For example, regarding span of control, in some firms foremen had to supervise only a handful of personnel; in others perhaps eighty or ninety workers. Obviously, the "one best way" traditional approach was not being applied. Furthermore, there seemed to be no connection between business success and what traditional theory considered to be the best organizational structure. This was very worrying.

Eventually, Woodward found a way of explaining the variations in structure among the firms. This involved relating organization structure to the technology or production system employed. Three broad categories of technology were identified:

- Unit and small batch (production largely to customer requirement)
- Large batch and mass production (assembly line)
- Process production (continuous flow production of liquids, gases, etc.)

These differences in technology appeared to account for many of the differences in structure found. Furthermore, it seemed that firms most nearly approximating the typical structure for their technology were the most successful. There appeared to be one form of structure most appropriate to each production system, and success, therefore, was a matter of getting the technology–structure fit right. If technology changed, structure should be changed in order to bring success. In fact, in the middle range of technologies, mechanistic structures seemed to be the best; so there were *some* circumstances in which traditional theorists were correct. Their view was simply limited. Woodward demonstrated, therefore, that particular technologies need particular structures to get the best performance.

Size

Pugh and a group of other researchers, originally based at what is now the University of Aston in England (Pugh and Hickson, 1976), have carried out a considerable amount of empirical research attempting to discover the link between contextual variables and various structural aspects of organizations. They wanted to know how variables such as origin, ownership, size, charter, technology, market, location, and dependence correlated with internal factors like specialization, standardization, formalization, and centralization. Scales were developed for each contextual and internal structural element; many organizations were examined to see where they fitted on the scales, and statistical analysis was undertaken with computer assistance. Stable correlations seemed to hold between contextual and internal factors across seemingly very different types of organizations. So, for example, if one knew an organization's score on the scales of size, technology, and so forth, one could predict its specialization score. Examining their results, the researchers surprisingly found only moderate correlations between technology and structure. This was, of course, contrary to Woodward's conclusions—although it is argued that the two bits of research can be reconciled on the basis that Woodward's organizations were generally smaller than those looked at by the Aston researchers (Hickson, Pugh, Pheysey, 1969). Instead, the latter found the strongest correlation between size and structure; depending on the size of an organization, a particular structural configuration seemed to be appropriate. So, for example, increased size seemed to bring about decreased centralization but increased structuring of activities (standardization, specialization, and formalization). It follows that size is a very significant variable that managers need to take into account when designing organization structures.

Environment

The survival of organizations as open systems depends upon some degree of exchange with outside parties. Different environmental conditions and different types of relationship will, contingency theorists argue, require different types of organization structure for high performance to be achieved and sustained. The usual conclusion is that the higher the degree of environmental uncertainty and turbulence, the more the structure of an organization needs to be adaptive, with fluid role structures, coordination achieved by frequent meetings, and considerable lateral communication. Examples of such theorists are Burns and Stalker (1961) and Lawrence and Lorsch (1967).

Burns and Stalker argue that different environmental conditions require different management systems in organizations. Some circumstances favor a mechanistic structure, others an organismic structure. The mechanistic, traditional organizational form is suitable for stable environments and, indeed, made possible the large increases in scale and efficiency of undertakings characteristic of the early twentieth century. This structure is, however, unsuitable in times of rapid technological and market change. The bureaucratic firm is incapable of accommodating the demands of large-scale research and development, and the new relationships with the market, required in these conditions. Uncertain and turbulent environments require more adaptive management systems, exhibiting greater flexibility and demanding more commitment from members; what Burns and Stalker call an "organic" or organismic structure. A survey of the Scottish electronics industry, which was at the time confronted with rapidly changing environmental circumstances, allowed Burns and Stalker to specify the nature of the organismic structures suitable to an unstable environment.

Mechanistic structures exhibit specialization, independence of tasks, strict rules, vertical communication, tight job descriptions, and a hierarchy with communication coming down from an omniscient leader at the top. Organismic structures need to show less formal task definition, greater task interdependence, continual redefinition of duties, horizontal as well as vertical communication, and greater decentralization of decision making. These two types of structure represent ideal types from which actually existing organizations will, of course, diverge.

Burns and Stalker point, therefore, to the need to adjust organizational structure according to the nature of the environment faced. Unfortunately, as they also point out, this is far from easy to achieve because organizational participants develop vested interests in protecting existing organizational designs and procedures.

Lawrence and Lorsch have extended this work and conclude that different subunits within organizations (production, sales, research and development) will themselves require different structures because they each relate to different subenvironments (technical, market, and scientific, respectively). In certain kinds of environments, there will be a need for

high differentiation in an organization as each subunit necessarily de-
velops particular attributes in response to its own environmental segment.
This will demand innovative strategies on the part of managers to ensure
the overall integration of the system in the face of its total environment.
Overall organizational performance demands a degree of differentiation
among subunits consistent with the requirements of their specific environments and a degree of integration consistent with the demands of the total
environment.

The Managerial Subsystem

Management is clearly a functional imperative of efficient and effective organizations, since some function is needed to balance the pulls
exerted by the other subsystems and to fit the organization into its environment. Thompson (1967) and Kast and Rosenzweig (1981) have elaborated upon Parsons's three-level division of managerial tasks (described
earlier in this chapter). Beyond this, however, the role of management was
for some time seriously neglected by contingency theorists. The likely
explanation is that it was seen simply as the element in the system that
responded (or otherwise) to the determinations imposed on the organization by other variables. The work of Child (1972, 1984) has changed all that.
Child has argued that managers possess "strategic choice." Managers can
choose or influence some of the environmental factors that affect their
organizations (e.g., employees, customers, location); they are not simply
prey to environmental determinations. Organizations can also perform at
less than optimum performance and still survive; this gives managers slack
to exercise their judgment about what structure to employ. Finally, Child
suggests, much the same performance may be obtained with different
structures. So, again, there is room for choice. With Child's work the
deterministic version of contingency theory was shown to be flawed, and
the managerial subsystem reinstated as an important and independent
influence on the organizational structure.

Summary of Contingency Theory

An organization is viewed by contingency theory as a center of mutual influence and interaction between four subsystems (goal, human,
technical, and managerial), the variables of size and structure, and the
environment in which the organization is located. Contingency theory
postulates that the effective performance of an organization is contingent
upon the subsystems of the organization being designed in accordance

with each other and the demands of the environment with which they interact. Attention has to be paid to getting an organizational structure appropriate to the demands of the subsystems and the environment. These ideas are represented in Figure 3.2. Quite specific proposals for the design of organizations can be made on the basis of the empirical studies conducted under contingency theory—as, for example, in Lawrence and Lorsch (1969).

An interesting and more recent development in contingency theory has been to see the best way to structure an organization as contingent upon the amount of information processing it has to do, which in turn is dependent on the uncertainty and diversity surrounding its basic task. This approach, as pioneered by Galbraith (1977), was mentioned earlier as an employment of the organizations-as-brains metaphor. It certainly extends the potential of contingency theory (which was previously heavily organismic in character) and brings it closer to the sophisticated organizational-cybernetic thinking discussed in Chapter 5.

Sociotechnical Systems Theory

Introduction to Sociotechnical Systems Theory

The second set of empirical investigations that helped shape the organizations-as-systems perspective were those carried out within the sociotechnical systems tradition. Sociotechnical systems theory is associated

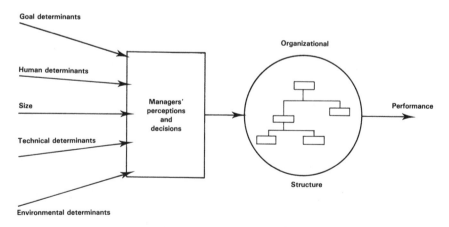

FIGURE 3.2. The Contingency-Theory Perspective

with the Tavistock Institute of Human Relations and particularly with the names of Emery, Rice, and Trist. From the 1940s onward, these theorists attempted to transfer behavioral science and systems ideas to industry through the consultancy mechanism. Particularly important in the early development of the theory were the Coal Mining Studies (Trist and Bamforth, 1951; Trist et al., 1963). In the next section I consider some of the important management concepts developed during the early stages of sociotechnical systems thinking. The Coal Mining Studies are then dealt with in some detail. Finally, later developments in the sociotechnical tradition of work are sketched out.

The Early Stages of Sociotechnical Systems Thinking

Sociotechnical systems theory sees organizations as pursuing primary tasks that can best be realized if their social, technological, and economic dimensions are jointly optimized, and if they are treated as open systems and fitted into their environments. We can consider this more fully by examining seven interrelated ideas or concepts that inspired or were developed during the early studies.

Of paramount importance is the idea that work groups or organizations should be regarded as interdependent sociotechnical systems. They have interactive technological and social aspects, and in designing the structure of the group or organization both of these should be considered. If the structure of the work organization is designed with only the technology in mind, then it may be disruptive of the social system and not achieve maximum efficiency. If it is designed with only the social and behavioral aspects in mind, it is unlikely to make very good use of the technology.

This leads onto a second idea: In designing work organizations, their social, technological, and economic elements (the subsystems recognized in sociotechnical theory) should be jointly optimized. The attainment of optimum conditions for any of the three elements may not result in optimum performance for the system as a whole. For example, the optimum structure to make use of the technology may not serve the social subsystem very well. Joint optimization means ensuring optimization of the whole, even if this requires a less than optimum state for each separate aspect.

Joint optimization is possible (and this is the third concept) because there is organizational choice. It is possible within the same technological and economic constraints to operate with different forms of work organization, with various social and psychological results. So, given the constraints, managers should exercise their choice over the type of work organization to adopt with the social system in mind.

The next concept is that of primary task. An organization's primary task is the task it has to perform in order to survive. It is for the purpose of realizing this primary task that the social, technical, and economic subsystems have to be jointly optimized.

The fifth notion is the by-now-familiar one that work organizations should be regarded as open systems. The sociotechnical thinkers were very influenced by von Bertalanffy's conclusions and employed the usual open system, input–transformation–output model to understand production systems.

The Tavistock theorists also emphasized a sixth idea, the importance of group working. They considered that workers were more satisfied if they worked in groups. Groups could tackle whole tasks, and this made work more meaningful for the individual. Sociotechnical thinking encourages, therefore, the setting up of semiautonomous work groups. These groups (which the studies showed could be forty or fifty strong) are supposed to act as self-regulating and self-developing social systems, capable of maintaining themselves in a steady state of high productivity. Control and decision making are exercised internally by the group and not externally by managers. Within the groups, great flexibility can exist with job rotation and workers who are encouraged to become multiskilled. Each group can negotiate some of the details of its own labor contract with management. Many advantages are said to follow in addition to increased job satisfaction. The system should ensure more work is done because no individual is ever short of a job—if one finishes his or her own, he or she can always help with someone else's. Problems are dealt with quickly, as they arise, and as near to the point where they occur as possible. They do not require the intervention of management.

The seventh and final concept can be seen as a directly related consequence of the setting up of semiautonomous work groups. Since the groups control themselves, they do not have to be controlled from the outside. This frees management for the much more important task of "boundary management." Instead of wasting time attempting to apply autocratic regulation, managers can invest their energies in relating the operating system (and the organization as a whole) to its environment; ensuring that the group doing the work in the operating system is supplied with the necessary input, and that its output is disposed of profitably on the market.

These concepts did not, of course, emerge all at once. Indeed, the reader studying Trist and Bamforth (1951) will find them working with a mechanical-equilibrium analogy rather than the later open system idea. And the notion of primary task itself underwent modification. Nevertheless they made up the core of sociotechnical thinking by the early 1960s.

The Coal Mining Studies

Most of the above concepts can be seen employed in the Coal Mining Studies. Trist and Bamforth (1951) and later Trist et al. (1963) used socio-technical ideas to study the mechanization of the British coal mining industry. In the traditional method of coal getting, the "hand-got method," small groups of skilled men worked in an essentially self-regulating and autonomous way on their own part of the coal face. The workers could choose who to work with, each developed multiple skills, they were responsible for their own pace of work, and supervision was internal. Each group made its own contract with management. This form of work organization seemed to provide for a social system that suited the underground situation. With the advent of mechanization, however, the traditional form of work organization was abandoned, and the "conventional long-wall" method of coal getting was set up. This was a factorylike system of work organization with forty or fifty specialists, on different pay rates, all working together on a single long face. Furthermore, a three-shift system was introduced, with each shift doing a different part of the overall task. The whole system was coordinated by constant interference from management.

The conventional long-wall system was introduced to get the most out of the new technology and, indeed, looked optimum for that technology. However, it was introduced without a thought for the social system and had extremely dysfunctional social and psychological consequences. Productivity was disappointing, absenteeism and turnover were high, and there were constant problems for management, especially in handling the changeover between shifts.

In the later study, Trist et al. (1963) found that some miners, unable to tolerate the conventional long-wall system, had originated and won acceptance by management of what was called a "composite long-wall" system. This form of work organization was able to operate the new technology efficiently, but also paid attention to the needs of the social system. Demarcation between shifts disappeared and, on each shift, self-selected groups of forty or fifty men took on responsibility for the whole task. These groups allocated work, allowed individuals to become multiskilled, and were self-regulating. They were paid on a group bonus system. Where the composite long-wall form of work organization was introduced, the miners produced more, went absent less, and were generally more satisfied with their work.

These studies consolidated the Tavistock researchers' belief in organizational choice (since different forms of work organization could operate the same technology); in the need to jointly optimize social and technical systems in pursuit of the primary task; in the usefulness of group working and the creation of semiautonomous work groups; and in the view that managers were best employed in a boundary-spanning role, controlling the inputs and outputs of an open system.

Later Developments in Sociotechnical Systems Thinking

In the 1960s, 1970s, and 1980s work based upon sociotechnical ideas continued to burgeon, and the scale of intervention became extremely ambitious. The most important studies were probably the Norwegian Industrial Democracy Project (Emery and Thorsrud, 1969, 1976; Bolweg, 1976) and the various experiments carried out in Sweden, especially Volvo's car plant at Kalmar, which was designed and built around the concept of semiautonomous group working (Gyllenhammer, 1977). In Britain there was Shell's attempt to establish a "new philosophy of management" using sociotechnical concepts (Hill, 1971; Blackler and Brown, 1980); an experiment that is described more fully as one of the case studies in Chapter 8. Alongside and in the course of these studies, at least six new ideas were added to the armory of sociotechnical thinking. These were:

- Sociotechnical theory as a means of promoting industrial democracy
- More attention given to appropriate job design
- Consideration of how technology could be redesigned to permit group working
- A greater appreciation of organization–environment relations
- Organizational goals added as an important subsystem
- The emergence of step-by-step methodologies for putting sociotechnical thinking into practice

I shall take each of these new ideas in turn and explain its significance using examples from the key studies mentioned.

In a famous project conducted for the Norwegian Employers Federation and the Norwegian Labour Organization, Emery and Thorsrud (1969) concluded that the attempt to extend industrial democracy should begin at the level of the shop floor, with control over the task itself. Allowing worker representatives on the board had, on its own, little effect on levels of commitment and perceived involvement among the mass of workers. Sociotechnical thinking, and particularly the idea of semiautonomous work groups, showed how the process of democratization could be started at the bottom of the organization, where the benefits would be immediately registered, and then proceed upward. This conclusion was accepted and an ambitious project formulated, involving employers, unions, and gradually the government, to democratize Norwegian industry. There were even hopes that the lessons learned in industry would diffuse to other sectors of Norwegian society and beyond Norway itself. Four pilot projects were set up, positioned in key industries, as demonstration models from which the ideas could be spread outward (reported in Emery and Thorsrud, 1976). The pilot projects were a moderate success, but the expected widespread diffusion did not take place (Bolweg, 1976). The main payoff was actually in Sweden where, as a direct result of studying the Norwegian experiment, literally hundreds of projects began in the early 1970s.

Around the same time as the Norwegian project, earlier Tavistock research on job design was consolidated into a list of six requirements that jobs should meet if they are to be psychologically satisfying for workers (Bolweg, 1976). A job should be demanding and challenging in terms other than endurance. It should provide for continuous learning. The individual must possess a discrete area of decision making. The individual's need for social support and recognition in the workplace should be met. The task itself and the product should be related to the worker's life outside the factory. And the job should be seen as contributing to some desirable future.

The third new development concerned the redesign of technology to facilitate group working. In the early sociotechnical studies, in spite of the notion of joint optimization, it was usually the case that the existing technology was accepted, with the real adjustments being made to the work organization and the social system. In the later work there was genuine redesign of technology in order to realize the true meaning of joint optimization. Volvo's car factory at Kalmar, for example, was especially designed to allow car manufacture by semiautonomous work groups of around twenty people (Gyllenhammer, 1977). In this factory, opened in 1974, the assembly line had disappeared. A self-propelled vehicle (the "Kalmar carrier"), following conductive tape on the floor, transported the vehicles around the different areas of the factory controlled by the thirty or so work groups. Each group could pace and organize its own work and was responsible for its own inspection. Each group made its own contract with management. Design changes made it possible for each group to be given responsibility for an identifiable part of the car. Kalmar was about ten percent more expensive to build than an equivalent ordinary factory, but Volvo regarded this as worthwhile given the better productivity and lower turnover and absenteeism that resulted.

The fourth innovation came in 1965 with the publication of Emery and Trist's article, "The Causal Texture of Organizational Environments." Emery and Trist accepted von Bertalanffy's open system formulation, but felt that it neglected to deal with processes in the environment that are, themselves, among the determining conditions of organization–environment changes. They therefore added an additional concept—the causal texture of the environment. This refers to the degree of system-connectedness that exists in the environment itself. Emery and Trist isolate four ideal types of causal texture; these form a series in which the degree of causal texturing increases.

First, there are "placid–randomized" environments in which there is no connection between the parts of the environment, and the environment is homogeneous in character. Second are "placid–clustered" environments in which there is still no connection between environmental parts, but the environment is diverse, with certain resources in certain places (so the organization must know its environment). Third are "disturbed–reactive" environments. These are dynamic environments in which a number of organizations of the same type compete. Therefore, there is connection between environmental parts, and each organization has to take account of the others. Finally, there are "turbulent fields." With increasing interaction of organizations and interconnectedness of the environment, powerful dynamic properties arise, not only from the interaction of component organizations but also from the environment itself. The environment takes on its own dynamic. For example, timber enterprises, in the cause of competing with one another, may overexploit the available timber, encouraging soil wash and erosion, and making regeneration of timber resources impossible.

Emery and Trist argue that the environments in which organizations exist increasingly resemble turbulent fields. This makes management extremely difficult since uncertainty for organizations is increased as the consequences of their actions become increasingly unpredictable. Organizations must adopt flexible structures to increase their adaptive capabilities. But even this is not enough; individual organizations cannot expect to adapt successfully simply through their own direct actions. They will have to enter into joint collaboration with other organizations to seek solutions. The development of a set of values that can be shared by organizations will be important in this.

As these last points make clear, the arguments of Emery and Trist's paper took sociotechnical thinkers beyond the mere reconsideration of organization–environment relations, and on to looking at the goals and values that organizations should adopt in turbulent field situations. This had immediate application because, as soon as the 1965 article was completed, the Tavistock researchers became involved in shaping a "new philosophy of management" for Shell UK (Hill, 1971; Blackler and Brown,

1980). Shell was certainly in a turbulent environment, faced with the beginnings of OPEC, rapid technological change, the birth of the ecological lobby, and a difficult industrial relations climate. It therefore needed to rethink its traditional values and to move toward more flexible structures. A statement of "objectives and philosophy" (issued in May, 1966) saw the primary objective of the company, maximizing its contribution to the long-term profitability of the Shell Group, as subject to certain social objectives. For example, the statement declared that the resources the company used were community resources and must be used to contribute to the satisfaction of the community's need for products and services. More specifically, employee potential had to be enhanced, the safety of employees and the public given high priority, and pollution of the environment minimized. The document then went on to spell out the usual sociotechnical requirement for joint optimization of the technical and social systems, and to detail the psychological requirements that related to the content of jobs.

The final new development was the emergence of methodologies for operationalizing sociotechnical theory. During the Norwegian project much attention was given to the need for collaborative research and to developing strategies to diffuse results. During the Shell experiment, a simplified nine-step method was produced for the actual sociotechnical analysis of production systems (Hill, 1971). Here I shall simply supply Cherns's (1976) nine-principle checklist for sociotechnical design. The nine principles are:

- Compatibility—the process of design must be compatible with its objectives (so, if the aim is a participative organization, the design process must be participative)
- Minimal critical specification—of the way in which the work is actually carried out and who should carry it out
- The sociotechnical criterion—variances from specifications are to be controlled as near to the point where they arise as possible
- The multifunction principle—to provide for flexibility and equifinality, each individual should be able to perform more than one function
- Boundary location—control of activities in a department should become the responsibility of the members, with the supervisor concentrating on boundary activities
- Information flow—information systems should be designed to provide information, in the first place, to the work teams who need it for task performance

- Support congruence—systems of social support should reinforce the organizational structure (so, if it is based on group working, payment should be by group bonus, etc.)
- Design and human values—high-quality jobs based on the six design characteristics
- Incompletion—design as an iterative process (once at the end, one must go back to the beginning again)

Sociotechnical practice has had a major impact on industry and, apparently, brings satisfactory results (Pasmore et al., 1982). This is true of the pure form of the theory and even more true if one takes into account its offshoot, the "quality of working life" movement. Some also see "quality circles" as having derived originally from sociotechnical thinking, and certainly many of the same principles are involved in quality circles, although in a less well-developed form. Those contemplating introducing quality circles could learn much from the sociotechnical literature. Among recent contributions to extending the theory, the *Journal of Applied Behavioural Science's* special issue on sociotechnical design (1986), Mumford's (1983) use of the ideas in participative information-system design, and Cherns's (1987) revisiting of his principles are worthy of note.

We are now in a position to summarize and evaluate the organizations-as-systems approach. I begin by briefly recapitulating some of the main points covered in the discussion above. The major criticisms of the approach are then set out. In a further section, I seek a deeper understanding of its nature and characteristics in terms of the theoretical considerations of Chapter 2.

Strengths and Weaknesses of Organizations as Systems

Viewing organizations as systems clearly provides a much richer picture of organizations than that supplied by the traditional and human relations models. In retrospect, it can be seen that the traditional model considered the goal subsystem and its effect upon structure, but largely ignored the human and technical subsystems and the issue of size. It was also a closed perspective, saying nothing about organization–environment relations. The human relations model considered the human subsystem, but neglected all the others. It, too, was a closed perspective. The organizations-as-systems approach looks at all the subsystems, their interrelationships, and the interactions between the subsystems (and the organization as a whole) and the environment.

According to early versions of the organizations-as-systems methodology (those governed by the mechanical-equilibrium analogy), organizations should be studied as systems of interdependent parts, and as having both formal and informal aspects. Later, as the organismic analogy began to dominate, it was seen to be appropriate, in addition, to view them as organisms striving for survival. They had needs, or functional imperatives, that had to be met by their subsystems. They had to adjust continually and adapt to internal and, especially, external forces because they were open systems dependent on their environments. Organizations had to take action in response to environmental changes if they wanted to maintain a steady state.

If we consider the organizations-as-systems approach as a methodology not for producing knowledge about organizations but for recommending action, we find that contingency theory and sociotechnical theory offer the most precise guidance. A sketchy summary of this guidance is as follows: Both recommend that if an organization is not functioning effectively, then the subsystems should be examined to ensure that they are meeting the needs of the organization, and the organization examined to see that it is well adjusted to its environment.

Although it is generally viewed as superior to the traditional and human relations approaches, the organizations-as-systems tradition has itself come in for some severe criticisms. The main charges are that it downplays purposeful action in organizations; that it reifies organizations; that it cannot properly explain change and conflict; that it exhibits a managerial bias; and that its prescriptions for improving managerial performance are ill-founded and vague. I shall consider the criticisms in turn, drawing upon various sources (Lockwood, 1956; Gouldner, 1959; Buckley, 1967; Silverman, 1970; Burrell and Morgan, 1979; Clegg and Dunkerley, 1980). It will be recognized, however, that all the criticisms are interrelated.

As we have seen, the organizations-as-systems approach sees survival rather than goal attainment as the raison d'être of organizations. It also emphasizes the nonrational aspects of organizational functioning. Both these things contribute to a neglect of the considerable amount of purposeful, goal-oriented activity that takes place in modern organizations. Rational planning activities are discounted. This also means that centers of command and control in organizations are not properly located, and the suggestion must be that little can be done to measure the performance of an enterprise in achieving goals.

There is also a tendency in the organizations-as-systems approach to reify organizations—to grant them the power of independent thought and action. Thus activity in an organization is seen as best explained by the organization's desire to meet functional imperatives and to adapt to its environment. Individuals are seen as subject to forces that are beyond their control and that they do not always understand. The conscious reasons they give for their actions are seen as no substitute for a scientific, functional explanation of what is occurring in the organization.

Although internal tensions are admitted in the organizations-as-systems model, the main explanation provided for change is as an adaptive mechanism in response to environmental disturbances and pressures. Organizations seek as far as possible to maintain the status quo by preserving their existing structures. Structures are therefore seen as semipermanent features of organizations that should form the main focus of analysis. Processes operate to support structures. Structures are not temporary manifestations of process. Why organizations should wish to protect particular structures is not explained. The notion that social systems might frequently change their structures is not entertained.

The emphasis on social order in organizations, to the exclusion of conflict and instability, is also regarded as one-sided. With the mechanical-equilibrium model, equilibrium is maintained by the inculcation of shared norms and values into organizational participants. The organismic model pictures all the parts as functioning in cooperation to serve the whole. Unity and interdependence of parts are stressed. The idea that there might be different groups in organizations pursuing their own rationalities, based on competing social and economic interests and frequently coming into conflict, is suppressed.

Many of the above points are brought together to justify the conclusion that the organizations-as-systems approach exhibits a managerial bias. The organization is seen as an integrated whole, the survival of which benefits all participants. The power of some group or groups to control the organization is hidden since the organization is regarded as pursuing its own purposes. Conflict is disguised, or seen as a dysfunctional threat to the system and, therefore, all connected with it. In contingency theory and sociotechnical theory managers act paternalistically, for the good of all, by using their expert knowledge to adjust the organization in ways that will ensure its survival. Sociotechnical theory even gets the workers to control themselves, relieving managers of one onerous chore, by convincing employees that they are getting a form of genuine control over their working lives.

Finally, since organizations as systems developed primarily as a methodology for understanding organizations, it is perhaps not surprising to find many of its remedies for changing and improving them accused of being vague and/or untested. This is probably more true of contingency theory than sociotechnical theory but, in both, adequate explanations for the statistical correlations discovered—or the improvements supposed to follow from implementing their prescriptions—are lacking. Perhaps, too, the emphasis on system maintenance might prevent necessary radical rearrangements of structure being contemplated.

Analysis and Assessment

We can now test out, for the first time, the hypothesis that the theoretical considerations of Chapter 2 will provide a deeper understanding of different systems methodologies and their assumptions, and so assist managers and management scientists to choose an appropriate methodology for whatever problem(s) they face.

Interrogating the organizations-as-systems approach using Habermas's sociological theory clearly reveals that it is oriented toward serving the technical interest in prediction and control of objectified processes (in this case, social systems). Contingency theory, for example, operates as an empirical analytic science. It aims to produce theoretical statements about the covariance of observable events from which lawlike hypotheses can be derived. These should provide the foundation for better prediction and control of organizations. The knowledge produced by the organizations-as-systems methodology seeks to guide instrumental action in developing the forces of production, and strategic action in improving the steering capacities of organizations. Further, the approach does not restrict its advocacy of instrumental reason only to those subsystems of the organization where it might be appropriate. Questions of what the organization should be doing are also defined as administrative problems to be decided by managers on the basis of their knowledge about system needs. The practical interest in maintaining and improving mutual understanding, insofar as it is considered at all, is subordinated to the technical interest. In Parsonian theory and sociotechnical thinking, social integration is wholly secondary to system integration. The emancipatory interest in freedom from unnecessary constraint is ignored.

An examination of Burrell and Morgan's (1979) account of where different theories of organization fit in terms of sociological paradigms finds the organizations-as-systems approach set squarely in the functionalist box. This is confirmed by the preceding discussion. Organizations-as-systems theorists are objectivist in terms of the assumptions they make about systems thinking. They study systems from the outside, seek causal regularities, believe that human beings can be understood scientifically and then dealt with as component parts of the system, and prefer quantitative techniques of analysis. They are also regulative in terms of their assumptions about social systems, seeking to understand how the status quo is maintained and aiming to facilitate better prediction and control. Consideration of the interpretive paradigm (which would seek knowledge of systems by trying to understand subjectively the point of view and intentions of the human beings who construct them), the radical paradigms (which emphasize conflict, contradiction, domination, and radical change), and the structuralist paradigm (which seeks explanation of regularities and not just prediction) confirms that the categorization of the organizations-as-systems approach as functionalist is correct.

Most of the shortcomings of organizations as systems can be seen as stemming from the adherence of the approach to a pair of very limited metaphors—the mechanical-equilibrium metaphor in the case of Roethlisberger and Dickson (1939) and Barnard (1938), but otherwise principally the organismic. It is this, for example, that limits the ability of the approach to explain conflict and change. As Silverman (1970, p. 22) has written, organizations may be systems but not necessarily natural systems. There remains, of course, the possibility of freeing the approach from distorting mechanical and biological analogies. Buckley (1967) advocates a "morphogenic" systems model that emphasizes dynamic processes and sees social structure as emerging from the interaction of systems elements linked together by information flows. This model has much in common with the organizational-cybernetic model that will be considered in Chapter 5. Burrell and Morgan (1979) argue that the systems model could be based on any one of a number of different analogies; mechanical, organismic, morphogenic, factional, and catastrophic analogies are suggested. Perhaps this is the way forward for those who want to retain what they see as the virtues of organizations as systems, while ridding it of the most obvious weaknesses.

Contingency theory and sociotechnical thinking seem to assume that problem contexts are systemic–unitary. These methodologies rest on the organismic rather than the mechanical analogy, and view systems as complex—made up of elements in close interrelationship, probabilistic, open to the environment, evolving over time, subject to behavioral influences, and having purposeful parts. While recognizing this complexity, they are unfortunately, given their functionalist rather than structuralist foundations, unable to deal with it. They lack the means to dig beneath the surface to find explanations for the regularities they perceive and the results they obtain. In this respect they need to be supplemented by the cybernetic explanations of Chapter 5. Contingency and sociotechnical theory also make predominantly unitary assumptions about problem contexts. This should not be overstated in relation to sociotechnical thinking, where an acknowledgement of the need for a participative and collaborative carrying through of projects demonstrates some recognition of pluralism.

The organizations-as-systems approach is an example of systemic modernism. It is modernist because it seeks objective truth by rationally probing for unity and consensus in what is perceived to be a logically ordered world. This is a case of systemic rather than critical modernism because progress is discerned in the rationalization of increasingly complex systems, rather than the emancipation of the human subject. The world has a meaning in terms of increasing the performativity of systems; improving the input–output ratio and enabling the uncertainty of the environment to be better controlled. Everything is subject to the rational requirements of systems, and individuals are dragged in the wake of systems. On minor matters, contingency theory fails to comply with the full systemic logic of Luhmann's thinking, and on these it is thoroughly taken to task by Luhmann (1976).

The full benefit of interrogating the various systems methodologies according to the schemata set out in Chapter 2 cannot, of course, be fully grasped until all the different methodologies have been studied. This is because one of the primary aims in this book is to show the diversity and range of the various systems approaches. And the practical usefulness of the theoretical investigations may not become clear until Parts III and IV, where it is demonstrated how managers and their advisors can employ an understanding of the strengths and weaknesses of alternative approaches to help them choose the right methodology for the problem at hand. Nevertheless, it is hoped that something of the enhanced knowledge and capability that can be gained by working at a higher intellectual level will be apparent.

I now pass on to give the same treatment to a set of methodologies designed much more obviously for bringing about change and improvement in systems, rather than seeking to understand them—hard systems methodologies.

4

Hard Systems Thinking

Introduction

At about the same time as Parsons and the general system theorists were perfecting their approaches to gaining understanding of social systems, other groups of systems thinkers were using systems ideas in a much more applied fashion to develop methodologies for problem solving in real-world problem situations. The work of these systems thinkers gave birth to what has come to be known, following Checkland (1978, 1981a), as hard systems thinking. Checkland originally included in this category only systems engineering and systems analysis (this incorporating additionally cost-benefit analysis and planning-programming-budgeting systems). It has become clear, however, that we can add to the list other approaches such as operational research (insofar as it embraces systems ideas at all), decision science, and management cybernetics (distinguished from organizational cybernetics in the next chapter). All these share the basic orientation, identified by Checkland (1978), as "the assumption that the problem task they tackle is to select an efficient means of achieving a known and defined end."

In this chapter, systems engineering, systems analysis, and operational research are briefly described. The nature of hard systems thinking is then firmly established and a catalogue of the criticisms that have been leveled at the approach is provided. This is followed by an attempt to put the criticisms into context. The strengths of hard systems thinking, when used appropriately, are stated; acknowledgement is made that the criticisms are not always apt in respect of the best practitioners of the hard approach; and attention is given to the development of "soft OR" in the United Kingdom, aimed at overcoming some of the weaknesses in the classic conception of operational research. Finally, the schemata of Chapter 2 are used to develop an in-depth analysis and appraisal of hard systems thinking. The chapter is kept deliberately brief. Hard systems thinking became, and remains, the orthodoxy in applied systems work, and there is naturally a huge literature associated with it. My aim is simply to equip readers with the means to examine that literature critically for themselves. The space saved can then be devoted to other less well-known and less well-developed but, perhaps, ultimately more exciting strands in the systems tradition of work.

Systems Engineering

Systems engineering has been defined by Jenkins (1972) as

> the science of designing complex systems in their totality to ensure that the component subsystems making up the system are designed, fitted together, checked and operated in the most efficient way.

It developed, as the name suggests, out of the engineering discipline as the idea took hold that the engineering approach, previously used only to engineer components, could be extended to tackle systems made up of the interaction of many components. The term *systems engineering* was, probably, first used in the Bell Telephone Laboratories in the 1940s, and they remained the leaders in the field during the 1950s as the methodology of systems engineering was gradually refined.

A. D. Hall's (1962) classic account of the methodology was based on his experience with the Bell Telephone Laboratories. Hall sees systems as existing in hierarchies. In systems engineering, plans to achieve a general objective must similarly be arranged in a hierarchy, with the systems engineer ensuring the internal consistency and integration of the plans. The methodology itself ensures the optimization of the system of concern with respect to its objectives. This requires a number of steps, the most important being problem definition, choosing objectives, systems synthesis, systems analysis, systems selection, system development, and current engineering. With Hall, the system of concern is usually a physical entity. Later accounts, however, stress the general applicability of the approach. Jenkins (1972), for example, sees the same systems engineering approach as relevant to hardware systems, parts of firms, whole firms, and local governments. In providing a more detailed description of the systems engineering methodology, I shall follow Jenkins's account.

For Jenkins, the purpose of systems engineering is to ensure the optimal use of resources, the main ones being men, money, machines, and materials. This can be achieved through a methodology incorporating four basic phases—systems analysis, systems design, implementation, and operation. In systems analysis, the real world is taken to consist of systems and is examined in systems terms. The problem is formulated and the system in which it exists is defined and analyzed in terms of important subsystems. The interactions between these subsystems are studied. Definition of the wider system and its objectives leads to specification of the objectives of the system being studied. In the second phase (systems design), the future environment of the system is forecast. The system is then represented in a quantitative model that simulates its performance under different operational conditions. The particular design that optimizes the performance of the system in pursuit of its objectives is chosen. The model therefore is an aid in the prediction of the consequences that follow from adopting alternative designs. A control system must be incorporated into the design of the optimum system at this point. The implementation and operation phases involve the construction, operation, and testing of the system in the real world. In carrying through this methodology, the systems engineer acts as a generalist inside an interdisciplinary systems team containing specialists as well as systems engineers, and focuses the team's attention on the efficient achievement of overall objectives.

An example of the various steps of Jenkins's methodology being used to design a petrochemical plant can be found in Jenkins (1969) and, reproduced, in Wilson (1984).

Systems Analysis

Systems analysis was defined by Quade (1963) as

> analysis to suggest a course of action by systematically examining the costs, effectiveness and risks of alternative policies or strategies—and designing additional ones if those examined are found wanting.

It was seen as representing an approach to, or way of looking at, complex problems of choice under uncertainty.

Systems analysis developed out of wartime military operations planning, and during the 1940s and 1950s applications were mainly military, involving work on weapons systems and strategic missile systems. At that time the approach was closely associated with the RAND (an acronym for "research and development") Corporation, a nonprofit body in the advice-giving business that was set up in 1947 and came to embrace systems analysis as its favored methodology. As set out by such as Hitch (1955) and Quade (1963), this methodology sought the broad economic appraisal of different means of meeting a defined end.

In the 1960s, systems analysis began to find broader industrial and governmental uses, the biggest breakthrough coming with the introduction of RAND-style systems analysis in the Pentagon by Secretary of Defense McNamara. In 1965 President Johnson ordered adoption of the principles of systems analysis, in the guise of planning-programming-budgeting systems, in all other departments of the federal government. Since that time, versions of systems analysis have been employed in numerous government departments and agencies, in local authorities, and in business, educational, and health institutions all over the world.

In 1972 the International Institute for Applied Systems Analysis (IIASA), a nongovernmental interdisciplinary research institution, was set up in Laxenburg, Austria, on the initiative of the academies of science (or equivalent institutions) of 12 nations. This institute has been seeking to apply RAND-style systems analysis to major world problems of, for example, energy, food supply, and the environment. In order to make its approach clear, two "handbooks" have been produced, edited by Miser and Quade (1985, 1988) and setting out the IIASA approach (a third volume of cases is to appear). It is reasonable to turn to these for a detailed modern account of systems analysis.

According to the IIASA "handbooks," systems analysis aims to help public and private decision makers to resolve problems arising in complex sociotechnical systems. It brings to bear the tools of modern science and technology, searching for regularities in system behavior and to provide evidence about the costs, benefits, and other consequences of various possible responses to the problem at hand. At the same time it tries not to neglect issues of social goals and values, matters of judgment and taste, and the need for craft knowledge to be employed alongside scientific technique. The methodology of systems analysis can be seen as consisting of seven major steps, as follows:

- Formulating the problem
- Identifying, designing, and screening alternative responses
- Building and using models for predicting the consequences of adopting particular responses
- Comparing and ranking alternative responses
- Evaluating the analysis
- Decision and implementation
- Evaluating the outcome

Miser and Quade (1985) provide, among other examples of problems to which systems analysis has been applied, the decision about how the Oosterschelde estuary in the Netherlands was to be protected from flooding. Three alternatives for this task were under review, and the consequences of adopting each of these were considered in terms of factors such as financial costs, degree of security from flooding, effects on jobs and profits in the fishing industry, changes in recreational opportunities, effects on the shipping industry and other sectors of the national economy, the ecology of the region, and social impacts. Given this wide range of factors it is not surprising that each of the alternatives had weaknesses as well as strengths, and none turned out to be uniformly better than the others. The study succeeded, however, in clarifying the issues and thus informing the political process through which the final decision was made.

Operational Research

Operational research (OR), or "operations research" as it is known in the United States, was for many years defined by the British Operational Research Society as

> the application of the methods of science to complex problems arising in the direction and management of large systems of men, machines, materials and money in industry, business, government and defence. The distinctive approach is to develop a scientific model of the system, incorporating measurements of factors such as chance and risk, with which to predict and compare the outcomes of alternative decisions, strategies or controls. The purpose is to help management determine its policy and actions scientifically.

As with systems analysis, OR was first employed in the military context. In the case of OR, its initial development was in the United Kingdom during World War II, from where it quickly spread to the United States. In both countries it soon found civilian application and played an important role in the postwar reconstruction of industrial production in the United Kingdom and in the increase in industrial efficiency in the United States.

The first textbook on OR appeared in 1957 and was written by Churchman, Ackoff, and Arnoff. It stresses the comprehensiveness of OR's aim as a systems approach responding to the overall problems of complex organizations. Interdisciplinary teams should use the most advanced scientific procedures to study all aspects of the system. The phases of an OR project are said to be:

- Formulating the problem
- Constructing a mathematical model to represent the system under study
- Deriving a solution from the model
- Testing the model and the solution derived from it
- Establishing controls over the solution
- Putting the solution to work (implementation)

Where certain classes of problems appear frequently in organizations, they are selected by OR for more intensive study. Churchman et al. (1957)

identify those associated with inventory processes, allocation processes, waiting-time processes, replacement processes, competitive processes, and combined processes as problems falling into this category.

Another well-known OR text, Ackoff and Sasieni's *Fundamentals of OR* (1968), similarly emphasizes that OR should have a systems orientation, use interdisciplinary teams, and apply the scientific method to problems of control arising in organized, man–machine systems. This book sets out the stages of the OR process in a manner similar to Churchman et al. and goes on to give in-depth treatment to those prototype, tactical problems that OR has developed some competence in tackling; problems of allocation, inventory, replacement, queuing, sequencing and coordination, routing, competition, and search. The book is clear, however, that OR must also seek to develop competence with strategic problems.

Unfortunately for OR, the problems that the pioneers of the discipline had used as examples of those that OR was currently equipped to tackle came to be identified, especially in the universities of the United States, with OR itself. OR largely abandoned any pretense of taking a systems approach or of being interdisciplinary in nature. It failed to establish itself at the strategic level in organizations and became associated with a limited range of mathematical techniques. The practical result has been, according to Ackoff (1986), a decline in the significance of the profession. As the problems that OR defined as being within its compass during the 1950s and 1960s ceased to be of first-ranking importance to corporate management, OR moved down the organization. The intellectual result has been, in Churchman's (1979b) opinion, that the original intention of a holistic, interdisciplinary experimental science addressed to problems in social systems has been betrayed, as OR has degenerated into little more than mathematical modeling. Thus two of the originators of OR as a discipline, Churchman and Ackoff, became two of the severest critics of the way the subject developed.

Hard Systems Thinking and Its Critics

Although, on occasions, protagonists of each of the strands of hard systems thinking have made claims for the superiority of their own perspective against the others, on grounds such as breadth of application and ability to engineer new as well as existing systems, the above analysis supports the contention that the similarities are more significant than the differences and that there is, indeed, a pretty unified hard systems paradigm within the systems approach. All three strands examined take *what* is required (the ends and objectives) as being easy to define at the beginning of the systems study. The job of the systems analyst is to find an optimum *how*, the most effective and efficient means to realize predefined objectives. Adapting another of Checkland's formulations (1978, 1981a), the hard systems approach presupposes that real-world problems can be addressed on the basis of the following four assumptions:

1. There is a desired state of the system, S_1, which is known
2. There is a present state of the system, S_0
3. There are alternative ways of getting from S_0 to S_1
4. It is the role of the systems person to find the best means of getting from S_0 to S_1

We are now ready to consider the criticisms that have been leveled at the hard systems way of proceeding. The catalogue of points that follow has been compiled from a wide variety of sources (Ackoff, 1977, 1979a, 1979b; Checkland, 1978, 1981a, 1983; Churchman, 1979b; Hoos, 1972, 1976; Lilienfeld, 1978; Rosenhead, 1981, 1989b). Often the same general criticisms can be found in the work of more than one commentator. I have not sought, therefore, to trace every criticism back to its source, but have broken the whole set of interrelated points down under five general headings.

First there are criticisms that suggest hard systems thinking has a very limited domain of applicability. Hard approaches demand that objectives be clearly defined at the very beginning of the methodological process. This may be fine for engineering-type problems when ends are easy to specify and attention can be concentrated on means. In the vast majority of managerial situations, however, the very definition of objectives will constitute a major part of the problem faced. Involved parties are likely to see the problem situation differently and to define objectives according to their own world views, values, and interests. This will give rise to many possible accounts of what the objectives of a particular system are, some of which might well be in conflict. In "softer" problem situations, therefore, it is not clear how hard systems methodologies can get started, since they lack the procedures for bringing about an accommodation between alternative definitions of what the objectives should be. Unfortunately, a common response to this difficulty from proponents of hard systems thinking is to distort the nature of the problem situation in order to make it fit the requirements of the preferred methodology. One objective or set of objectives will be privileged over others on the basis of the "expert" understanding of the system achieved by the systems analysts. A more appropriate response would be to admit that, outside the realm of engineering-type problems, hard methodologies are only usable in those circumstances where world views converge and unanimity is achieved about the need to maximize the performance of some relatively simple and easily separable subsystem.

A second kind of criticism relates to the failure of hard systems approaches to pay proper attention to the special characteristics of the human component in the sociotechnical systems with which they sometimes aspire to deal. People are treated as components to be engineered just like other mechanical parts of the system. The fact that human beings possess understanding, and are only motivated to support change and perform well if they attach favorable meanings to the situation in which they find themselves, is ignored. This deterministic perspective in hard systems thinking, which puts the system before people and their perceptions, extends to the ability of humans to intervene in their own destiny. Hard systems thinkers take the future to be determined by factors outside the control of organizational actors. It is the job of the systems consultant to predict the inevitable future and help managers prepare for it. Thus the opportunity to mobilize people to design their own future is missed (Ackoff, 1979a, 1979b).

The third group of criticisms concerns the demand for quantification and optimization in hard systems methodologies. When highly complex systems are involved, the building of a quantitative model is inevitably a highly selective process and will reflect the limitations of vision and biases of its creator(s). Far from recognizing this and demanding that the assumptions made in building the model be made explicit, hard systems thinking seems to acquiesce in the concealment of assumptions and to treat the model readily as synonymous with the reality. The model, which is of course far more easily manipulated than the real world, becomes the focus of attention and the generator of "optimum" solutions. It is convenient and cozy to play with the model, but the result is solutions that are out-of-date answers (since the model soon becomes an out-of-date representation) to the wrong questions.

Another consequence of the demand for quantification and optimization is the tendency to ignore those factors in the problem situation that are not amenable to quantification or, perhaps even more seriously, to distort them in the quest for quantification. Different aspirations or matters subject to differing value interpretations are forgotten or ground down on the wheel of optimization. It is this, together with the manipulation of models for its own sake, that has led to OR being characterized by Ackoff as "mathematical masturbation."

Fourthly, the degree to which hard systems thinking offers succor to the status quo, and to the already powerful, is frequently noted. As I have already shown, in order to get going in softer problem situations, hard methodologies require the privileging of one objective or set of objectives over others. It goes without saying that the best way to ensure the continuance of a consultancy project, and the implementation of the proposals, is to privilege the objectives of the most powerful stakeholders. Having inevitably been forced into making such political choices, hard approaches seek to cover their tracks by encouraging "depoliticization" and "scientization" (Rosenhead, 1981). The complicated mathematical modeling discourages ordinary people from believing that they might have anything useful to contribute to decision making. It also suggests that differences of opinion and interest can be rationally dissolved by experts using the latest tools and techniques. Thus conflict is hidden. And since conclusions emerge from a computer model programmed by white-collar scientists, they take on an air of objectivity that is, of course, entirely spurious.

The naïveté of the hard approach to complex sociotechnical problems (when it is so extended) can be accounted for, at least in part, by its roots in the engineering tradition and the "trained incapacity of engineers" (Hoos, 1976) to see systems as anything but things governed by predictable laws. The survival of such a naive orientation—the subject of the fifth type of criticism—is more difficult to explain. Lilienfield (1978) argues that systems theory of this ilk should be regarded as an "ideology." It flourishes because of the service it renders to the scientific and technocratic elites. Presenting, as it does, a view of systems as entities to be manipulated from the outside on the basis of expertise, hard systems thinking justifies the position and privileges of these elites.

Examining the points made above suggests that Keys (1987) and Jackson (1987c) are not too far wrong in summarizing the faults of hard systems thinking as arising from its inability to deal with subjectivity (criticisms one and two above), its difficulties in coming to terms with extreme complexity (criticism three), and its innate conservatism (criticisms four and five). This provides a pleasing symmetry, because it is arguable that each of the remaining methodological approaches dealt with in Part II of this book in some sense responds to one of the key weaknesses of hard systems thinking. Cybernetics (Chapter 5) aids the management of extreme complexity. Soft systems thinking (Chapter 6) is said to help with multiple perceptions of reality. Critical systems thinking (Chapter 7) is designed to free the discipline to serve interests other than the status quo. This in turn can provide grounds (see Chapter 10) for arguing in favor of a complementarist approach to systems thinking that takes advantage of the mutual strengths of different systems methodologies to promote an increased overall problem managing capability.

The Criticisms in Context

The criticisms leveled at hard systems thinking should make us wary of using hard methodologies except in a fairly narrowly prescribed set of circumstances. The "Analysis and Assessment" section that concludes this chapter offers further help in deciding the exact characteristics of such situations. For the moment, it is important to put the criticisms in context by emphasizing some of the positive achievements and features of hard systems thinking, and to stress that developments are taking place in the hard systems tradition that take account of some of the criticisms mentioned.

It cannot be denied that the systematic approach to decision making and problem solving characteristic of hard systems thinking constitutes an advance over ad hoc thinking about the management task. The careful setting of objectives, the search for alternative means of reaching those objectives, and the evaluation of the alternatives in terms of a measure of performance, made the efficient step-by-step control of projects feasible. This was perhaps particularly important in the domain of public spending, where no natural control mechanism (such as the market) exists. A further important achievement was to elaborate and popularize the use of mathematical models in order to aid decision making. Such models allowed predictions to be made about the behavior of real-world systems without the attendant risks and costs of intervening in the actual system of concern. For management scientists, constructing and working with mathematical and computer-based models stood in for the laboratory experiments of the physical scientists.

Finally, there was a recognition in hard systems thinking of the interactive nature of system parts and of the need to draw the boundaries of any investigation wide so as to include all important influences on the system. This allowed the problem of suboptimization to be identified and avoided. It was recognized that optimizing the performance of each subsystem does not always lead to optimum performance of the whole. And it led to proclamations in favor of a comprehensive approach to problem solving, even if such proclamations were then denied in the reductionist small print of the hard systems methodologies themselves.

Another feature of hard systems thinking that escapes some critics is that the practice has often been rather better than the precept. Indeed, this could hardly fail to be the case. For were OR, for example, to be simply the set of techniques described in many of the textbooks, then it could hardly have survived in modern organizations; and yet there are examples in British industry of very successful OR groups. This phenomenon of practice having stolen a march on theory, as aware practitioners deviated from the textbook representation of management science as an application of the natural scientific method, has led Tomlinson (e.g., 1984) to suggest that what is needed now is a rethinking of OR and applied systems analysis in the light of good practice. Appropriate precepts, paying much more attention to the social process of intervention, can then be constructed on the basis of successful practice. In fact, Tomlinson argues, such a rethinking is already under way, and future practitioners should have the benefit of precepts that represent much more accurately what OR and systems analysis are really about.

The position in hard systems *theory*, it must be said, has for much of the last three decades been almost as wretched as the critics have presented it. However, the contributions of Boothroyd (1978), Cook (1984), Eilon (1983, 1987), and Müller-Merbach (1984) in arguing for and keeping alive the original, broader conception of OR as an interdisciplinary, problem-centered discipline with a necessary concern for process should be acknowledged. These and others have contributed to what may be called an "enhanced OR" tradition of work (see Chapter 9). There has also been increased recognition of the legitimacy of some of the most frequent criticisms of the hard approach. Miser and Quade (1985, 1988), in compiling their "handbooks," declare their intention to restrict themselves to the known core of systems analysis but are well aware of the limitations of the methodology then described. It is a systems analysis most suited to easy-to-structure problems in which technology dominates over people. Miser and Quade's hope is that systems analysis in the future can be extended to problems set in sociotechnical systems where human behavior is much more important, and despite declared intention some of the contributors are allowed to move in this direction. A number of the papers collected in Tomlinson and Kiss (1984) are more radical still. Some authors call for a profound reorientation—and a few for the complete abandonment—of the paradigm that has hitherto dominated hard systems thinking.

One of the most interesting developments that has taken place as a consequence of the perceived failings of the hard approach has been the growth, in the United Kingdom, of what has become known as "soft OR." This is seen by its protagonists as complementary to hard OR and, indeed, exists rather on the fringes of the traditional discipline. A useful collection of papers by leading figures in soft OR has been put together and edited by Rosenhead (1989b). The methodologies discussed and illustrated in detail are "strategic options development analysis" (incorporating "cognitive mapping"), "soft systems methodology," "strategic choice," "robustness analysis," "metagame analysis," and "hypergame analysis." Rosenhead argues that these approaches have in common an emphasis on structuring decisions and problems rather than solving them. They are decision aiding and, in support of this, are transparent to users, involve participation as a key component, and are capable of incorporating conflict between different stakeholders.

The inclusion of Checkland's highly subjectivist soft systems methodology among the set of approaches examined indicates the type of shift in orientation aimed at in soft OR. Soft OR methodologies accept the need to work with a plurality of world views, to pay attention to how perceptions alter during the process of intervention, and to construct coalitions and build a consensus in favor of change through open discussion and debate. Although only Checkland's is explicitly a systems approach, the majority of soft OR writers seem to accept the conclusions of the soft systems thinkers, discussed in Chapter 6, and aspire to construct methodologies based on the same beliefs about people and organizations. At the same time, soft OR remains theoretically impoverished compared to soft systems thinking (an exception to this being Eden's "strategic options development analysis," or SODA, which draws upon the social science disciplines of psychology and social psychology). There is a vague shared commitment to respond to the individual understandings of organizational actors, but the soft OR tradition seems unable to specify exactly what new paradigm is being opened up by its endeavors.

Further, while soft OR corrects one of the major flaws in hard systems thinking by accepting subjectivity, it is less successful in addressing the others. The insights that the science of cybernetics can bring to the understanding and management of complexity are ignored, while Rosenhead (as editor of the collection) has to admit his own embarrassment at the "manipulative–reformist" stance of his contributors. Soft OR methodologies are, one imagines, designed to be of use to any client; that is, to be "neutral." But any organization represents a particular mobilization of bias in which some participants will possess more power and receive more benefits than others. There surely should be more discussion of when such approaches can be legitimately employed. In fact Rosenhead's (1989b) contributors, for the most part, avoid this kind of issue. Having embraced subjectivity in their methodologies, it becomes apparently impossible for them to decide whether the Nicaraguan *contras* should best be described as terrorists or freedom fighters (p. 81) or whether the U.S. leaders or the North Vietnamese had the right world view during the Vietnam War (p. 301). It is easy to see how the lack of guidance provided by soft OR approaches about which "side" to take, when translated down to the level of managing organizations, is likely to produce soft OR studies serving powerful managers and maintaining the existing balance of forces in organizations. The arbitrary taking of sides produces good OR for managers (in the metagame analysis) and for the English "Albatross" Sailing Association (in the hypergame analysis) but, presumably, bad OR for workers and for the Welsh "Albatross" Association.

As a last point, it should be noted that the most thorough investigation of the social context in which OR developed and is used, an issue neglected in hard OR and soft OR alike, has been carried out by OR workers (Rosenhead and Thunhurst, 1982).

This section has been necessary in order to put the criticisms of hard systems thinking into context. The hard approach has registered some significant achievements, practitioners are more sophisticated than written accounts of hard methodologies suggest, and the hard tradition is not static—changes are taking place that show an awareness of some of the concerns evinced by the critics. Finally, for it must be continually emphasized, there will be some problem situations in which hard systems methodologies yield the most satisfactory results. It is the purpose of the "Analysis and Assessment" sections in each chapter of Part II to indicate in which circumstances particular methodologies represent a sensible choice for the manager or analyst.

Analysis and Assessment

Using the categories of Habermas (explained in Chapter 2), it is clear that hard systems thinking is a manifestation of the technical interest in the prediction and control of natural and social systems. In pursuing this interest, hard methodologies seek as far as possible to follow the empirical analytic methods employed in the natural sciences. Jenkins's systems engineering methodology, for example, aims through empirical investigation to build up a systemic account of a real-world problem situation and the interactions that determine its nature. Hypotheses about how the system's performance might be improved are then incorporated into a mathematical model. The implementation and operation phases are the testing of the hypotheses. If the system performs according to plan, then the systems concepts and tools employed in the earlier phases of the methodology are validated. The purpose of Jenkins's systems engineering is very obviously to facilitate prediction and control of the system under surveillance.

So far, so good, because nobody could complain about the existence of a powerful group of methodologies seeking to assist with the prediction and control of those subsystems of organizations and society concerned with the development of the technical aspects of transformation processes. The trouble comes when the use of hard systems thinking is extended to social systems. Hard systems methodologies assume that it is possible to arrive at a clear statement of the objectives of a system from outside the system concerned. But objectives originate from within social systems, and different individuals and groups often vary considerably concerning the goals they wish to see pursued. Hard approaches have no means of engineering a consensus or accommodation between the representatives of different world views or interests. In these circumstances hard methodologies might be expected to fail because they are unable to achieve better prediction and control. This, of course, is the basis of many of the criticisms we looked at earlier. Hard systems thinking is considered to be no good in the domain of the practical interest where the issue is the creation of intersubjective understanding.

But there is a further point that is really quite sinister in its implications. In practice, hard methodologies do often seem to "work" when applied to social systems. Logically this success must depend on there being either widespread agreement over objectives among the human beings who make up the system (which is likely to be quite rare) or an autocratic decision maker who can decide on the objectives of the system. This is the dangerous authoritarian implication of hard systems thinking when it is applied to many kinds of social system. Hard systems theorists as scientists offer "objective" knowledge about how systems should be organized. Their science enables them to prescribe the "best" solution irrespective of the values of the individuals in the system. Such an approach finds ready acceptance, as Lilienfeld (1975) has argued, among those

> contemptuous of the untidiness and irrationality of the political process, [who] would prefer to replace the political process by an administrative world, a system which they as philosopher kings would manipulate from on high, from a position outside of and superior to the system they wish to control.

For Habermas (1974), the risk is that of splitting human beings into two classes, "the social engineers and the inmates of closed institutions."

It follows, as well, that the predict-and-control criterion employed by hard systems theorists as a test of their procedures may not give a fair test of hard systems methodologies when they are applied to social systems. Because of the existence of autocratic decision makers, the theory or model of social reality advocated by the analyst can be imposed upon other interests in the system—better enabling those decision makers to predict and control the workings of the system. The result is that hard systems methodologies do sometimes appear to work; they are made to work only because of the existence of compulsion. This appearance of "working" is, however, an important reason for hard systems thinking still being accepted by many.

The analysis conducted here suggests that hard methodologies can only rarely be extended to social systems. They can be legitimately employed in that context only when there is agreement over ends and means among the human beings who make up the system. In that case the purposeful character of the components of social systems becomes irrelevant, and social systems resemble hard systems. The knowledge produced by the critical sciences (tied to the emancipatory interest) is necessary in order to decide whether an encroachment of hard methodologies into the domain of the practical interest is, or is not, proper in any specific instance.

In terms of Burrell and Morgan's (1979) classification of sociological paradigms, hard systems methodologies rest upon functionalist theoretical assumptions (objective, sociology of regulation). The Jenkins methodology, for example, clearly makes objectivist assumptions about the nature of systems thinking. Systems, subsystems, and wider systems apparently are all easily identifiable in the real world. The objectives of the system to be engineered can be ascertained. Understanding of the system is gained by breaking it down into its important subsystems. The presence of human beings in the system does not require any revision of the basic systems engineering approach. Jenkins (1972) writes that

> the same systems thinking which can be applied to the design of hardware systems, such as space rockets, plants or ships, can also be applied, for example, to parts of firms, or whole firms, or to local government.

Building a quantitative model of the system plays a very important role in this systems engineering. The assumptions made about social systems in the Jenkins methodology are just as clearly regulative. The purpose of systems engineering is to understand the status quo better with a view to facilitating prediction and control of the system of concern.

Systems designers will, therefore, want to be convinced that it is valid and legitimate to view a problem situation in functionalist terms before they recommend employing a hard approach. The system should appear to have a hard, easily identifiable existence independent of observers. It should yield its most important secrets through study of the relationships among subsystems and between subsystems and the whole. The human beings in the system must accept being treated like other component parts. It has to be possible to construct a quantitative model. And the aim must be enhanced prediction and control.

The critics of hard systems thinking argue, of course, that this functionalist model badly misrepresents the nature of most of the problem situations managers face. Social systems do not have an objective existence in the real world, and it is not easy to discover what objectives they should pursue. Rather, they are ill-structured messes, and people matter quite a lot. Others would want to claim that conflict, contradiction, and power play a significant part in many social systems. Thus the dispute between hard systems thinkers and their critics can be recognized, at a more fundamental level, as being about adherence to different sociological paradigms.

Hard systems approaches unite in treating organizations as if they were machines. This metaphor presents organizations as vehicles for realizing the goals of their founders or those who currently control them. The purpose of hard methodologies is to arrange the system parts so that these goals are reached with optimum efficiency. Decision making is assumed to be rational, and strict control procedures are introduced to ensure conformance with rationally laid plans.

The sort of ideal-type problem context to which hard systems thinking corresponds is the mechanical–unitary (Jackson and Keys, 1984). The methodologies of OR, systems analysis, and systems engineering are useful as long as the problem solver can establish the objectives of the system in which the problem resides and represent that system in a quantitative model that will simulate its performance under different operational circumstances. These two conditions are only found together in mechanical–unitary contexts, to which these methodologies are therefore well suited.

Hard systems thinking, of course, exemplifies the main features of systemic modernism. Its "predict and prepare" paradigm (Ackoff 1979a, 1979b) rests upon a belief in an orderly world in which history in unilinear and the future is susceptible to forecast. Hard methodologies seek to employ systematic and rational procedures to optimize the efficient functioning of systems, thus maximizing their performance. Knowledge becomes identified with the means of programming the system. Truth is subservient to performativity. The elites that subscribe to this knowledge have the power to implement its conclusions and so validate its correctness. So the vicious circle identified by Lyotard is set up, as power becomes the basis of legitimation and vice versa. Given the power of systemic modernism, the acceptance of multiple perceptions of reality in soft OR and the recommendations for managing participation that ensue can be seen as no more than a further contribution to smoothing the functioning of the system, this time by engineering sufficient consensus around the system's purposes.

We must have respect for the contribution made by hard systems thinking to showing how systems ideas could be used by managers to intervene in real-world problem situations. This analysis and assessment demonstrates, however, that the theoretical assumptions made by the hard approach inevitably restrict its usefulness to a narrow range of problem types. It is not surprising, therefore, that in the 1970s disquiet with the dominant hard systems paradigm began to grow in the systems discipline and in management science generally. Problems that involved complex and strategic issues and had behavioral and social aspects assumed importance. These were demonstrably within the domain of management science, but they seemed to elude the methods and techniques of the discipline as it was conventionally understood and practiced. At about the same time, alternative systems approaches, challenging the traditional positivist/quantitative orientation in the discipline, began to appear. One of these was organizational cybernetics. This seemed to have a particular role to play in helping managers deal with the extreme complexity of the systems they sought to control. Organizational cybernetics is the subject of the next chapter.

Organizational Cybernetics

Introduction

Cybernetics as a recognized field of study possesses as long a history as the various methodological approaches (operational research [OR], systems analysis, systems engineering) that make up hard systems thinking. It was in 1948 that Wiener's book *Cybernetics* was published, bringing together contemporary ideas about control processes and establishing the famous definition of cybernetics as the "science of control and communication in the animal and the machine." Almost as soon as this definition was coined, however, it appeared to be too limiting. Wiener (1950) himself was soon applying the insights of cybernetics to human concerns. Ashby, in his celebrated *An Introduction to Cybernetics* (1956), noted that cybernetics should reveal numerous interesting and suggestive parallels between machine, brain, *and* society. Interest in the new science soon spread beyond engineers and physiologists to psychologists, sociologists, anthropologists, and political scientists. In 1959 Beer published *Cybernetics and Management*, and the list of those interested began to include managers and management scientists.

In this chapter I briefly trace the historical development of the cybernetic thinking that is relevant to management. I put in place the conceptual building blocks of the cybernetic approach—the notions of black box, feedback, and variety. "Organizational cybernetics" is then distinguished from "management cybernetics." Management cybernetics uses many of the same terms but interprets them according to the philosophy of hard systems thinking. Organizational cybernetics, by contrast, offers a significant break with the assumptions of the hard approach. Beer's viable system model (VSM) represents the full flowering of organizational cybernetics and is treated in some depth. Although only a model, it is possible to derive from the assumptions underlying the VSM, and from the VSM itself, a series of methodological guidelines for interrogating problem situations and improving the efficiency and effectiveness of organizations; these guidelines are spelled out in this chapter. The most commonly cited strengths and weaknesses of the VSM are then set out, and an in-depth analysis and assessment of organizational cybernetics is conducted using this book's (by now) well-rehearsed guidelines.

History

The term *cybernetics* originates from the Greek word *kybernetes*, meaning "the art of steersmanship." This word referred principally to the piloting of a vessel, a particularly hazardous occupation at the time. Plato, however, used the word to refer to steering the "ship of state." Both usages imply the identification of cybernetics with control, whether in the technical or the political spheres. From the Greek *kybernetes* came the Latin *gubernator*, and hence also the English *governor*. This last word, of course, also has technical and political meanings, both relating to control. A governor, as part of a steam engine, is a self-adjusting valve mechanism that keeps the engine working at constant speed under varying conditions of load. A governor—of a state, for example—is a public steersman or political decision maker.

By the early twentieth century, physiologists such as Claude Bernard were fully aware of analogous control processes (which they termed "homeostasis") taking place in organisms. It was not until the early 1940s, however, that the fact that there was common concern with control, originating in a number of disciplines, began to be recognized. Physicists, electrical engineers, mathematicians, and physiologists were thrown together during World War II to work on military problems. An interdisciplinary ferment was created, and one group of scientists became aware of the essential unity of a set of problems surrounding communication and control, whether in machines or living tissue. At the center of this group was Norbert Wiener.

Wiener first applied the name *cybernetics* to a specific field of study in 1947. Cybernetics was to be an interdisciplinary science. It had application to many different disciplines, Wiener argued, because it dealt with general laws that governed control processes, whatever the nature of the system under governance. The two key concepts elucidated by Wiener at this time were control and communication. In understanding control, whether in the mechanical, biological, or political realm, the idea of negative feedback was shown to be crucial. This allows a scientific explanation to be provided for behavior directed to the attainment of a goal. All such behavior depends upon the use of negative feedback. In this process, information is transmitted about any divergence of behavior from a preset goal and corrective action taken, on the basis of this information, to bring the behavior back toward the goal. Communication is equally significant, because if we wish to control the actions of a machine or another human being, then we must communicate with that machine or individual. Thus the theory of control can be seen as part of the theory of messages. Control involves the communication of information. In developing this aspect of their work, cyberneticians were able to draw on the 1949 volume *The Mathematical Theory of Communication*, by the communications engineers Shannon and Weaver.

The continuing growth of interest in cybernetics in the 1950s owed much to the work of W. Ross Ashby. Ashby published his most famous book, *An Introduction to Cybernetics*, in 1956. As well as being a popularizing text and demonstrating again how cybernetics could impact on many different areas of thought, this book introduced the important notion of variety—the number of distinct elements in a system or the number of possible states a system can exhibit. In the book, Ashby also formulated his "law of requisite variety," which is regarded by some as being as important to management as Newton's or Einstein's laws are to physics. The law of requisite variety states that only variety can destroy variety (or, put another way, the variety of a controller needs to be at least as large as the variety of the controlled system). I treat these ideas more fully in the next section.

Passing on to the 1960s and early 1970s, two names stand out in management cybernetics: those of Stafford Beer and Jay W. Forrester. Beer (1959a) was the first to apply cybernetics to management in any comprehensive fashion (in his book *Cybernetics and Management*), defining management as the science and profession of control. He also offered a new definition of cybernetics as the "science of effective organization" (Beer, 1979). Throughout the 1960s and early 1970s, Beer was a prolific writer and an influential practitioner in cybernetics. It was during this period that his model of any viable system, the VSM, was developed. This could be used to diagnose the faults in any existing organizational system or to design new systems along sound cybernetic lines.

Forrester (1961, 1969) invented system dynamics, which held out the promise that the behavior of whole systems could be represented and understood through modeling the dynamic feedback processes going on within them. Forrester's work found a great range of applications, from the study of industrial to urban to world dynamics. In D. H. Meadows et al., *The Limits to Growth* (1972), the behavior of the world system was studied as depending on interactions among demographic, industrial, and agricultural subsystems; and pessimistic conclusions were reached. Using system dynamics models, decision makers can experiment with possible changes to variables to see what effect this has on overall system behavior.

Forrester's modeling techniques have tended to be used in conjunction with essentially hard systems methodologies, and I shall not discuss them further. Beer's work on organizational cybernetics has continued, however, to develop along interesting paths during the 1980s and to become more influential. His VSM will be the focus of most of this chapter.

It is not possible to leave a historical account of the development of cybernetics without mentioning the relatively recent and significant work of Maturana and Varela (see, e.g., 1980) on autopoietic systems. Autopoietic systems are organizationally closed or "information tight." They are dedicated to maintaining themselves and respond to, and continuously seek to reproduce, the logic of their own organization. There is some dispute about whether the concept of autopoiesis, originally developed in biology, is relevant to social systems (see Mingers, 1989). Even if the idea does not transfer in any strict sense, it can still be seen as a useful corrective to the picture of organizations as open systems responding to their environments, as painted in the organizations-as-systems tradition of work.

We can now go on to put in place the building blocks of a cybernetic model of the organization.

Cybernetic Building Blocks

The starting point for a cybernetic account of the organization is the input–transformation–output model, popular throughout the systems tradition. It is an extension to the idea of the machine as a purposive system carrying out some transformation. The input–transformation–output schema is used to describe the basic operational activities of an enterprise. The cybernetic model demonstrates advantages over other models in the way it treats the command-and-control element in organizations. It supplies a basic theoretical framework that allows this element—which can be called management—to be studied as a phenomenon in its own right. The management task is determined by the nature of the system being controlled and by the nature of the environment within which the system operates. Both system and environment are likely to demonstrate the characteristics of extreme complexity, self-regulation, and probabilism that according to Beer (1959a) make a system a suitable subject of concern for cybernetics. Cybernetics provides a way of analyzing each of these characteristics and tools to enable managers to cope. Simplifying considerably (since in fact the cybernetic tools represent an interrelated response to the characteristics of cybernetic systems), extreme complexity can be dealt with using the *black box* technique, self-regulation can be appropriately managed using *negative feedback*, and probabilism yields to the method of *variety engineering* (Schoderbek, Schoderbek, and Kefalas, 1985). It is these three building blocks of cybernetic management that I seek to explain in this section.

The Black Box Technique

Let us consider first the idea of complexity and what is meant by this. According to Schoderbek et al. (1985), the complexity of a system is the combined outcome of the interaction of four main determinants:

- The number of elements comprising the system
- The interactions among these elements
- The attributes of the specified elements of the system
- The degree of organization in the system (i.e., are predetermined rules guiding the interactions or specifying the attributes)

It is extremely important to consider the last two of these factors in considering complexity. On the face of it, a car engine can look complex in terms of number of elements and interactions, but in fact is relatively simple because of the limited attributes of the specified elements and the high degree of organization in the system. A two-person interaction may appear simple, but in fact can be very complex once we add in the diverse attributes of humans and the lack of specified organization in many such systems.

Considering these four determinants of complexity, it is obvious how complexity can soon proliferate alarmingly in organizations. Exceedingly complex systems, which are so complicated that they cannot be described in any precise or detailed fashion, will be common. These systems, it follows, cannot be easily examined in order to discover what processes are responsible for system behavior. In cybernetics, systems of this type are called "black boxes." By contrast, a box within which all possible states are observable and can be understood is "transparent." Organizations and their environments are close to being black boxes. In order to cope with black boxes, managers and their advisers need to gain some knowledge of system behavior, even if they can never fully understand what causes that behavior. How can this be achieved?

According to Ashby (1956), the way *not* to proceed in approaching an exceedingly complex system—a black box—is by analysis. Reductionist analysis of each of the separate parts of the system will never enable whole interactions to be understood. If we take a complex system apart for analysis, we find that we cannot reassemble it in a way that produces the same pattern of behavior. Instead of analysis, therefore, the black box technique of input manipulation and output classification should be employed. By this procedure, an experimenter may discover some regularities that make the system more predictable. The black box technique is shown diagrammatically in Figure 5.1.

Managers of complex enterprises cannot hope to understand all the possible combinations of interactions within the systems under their con-

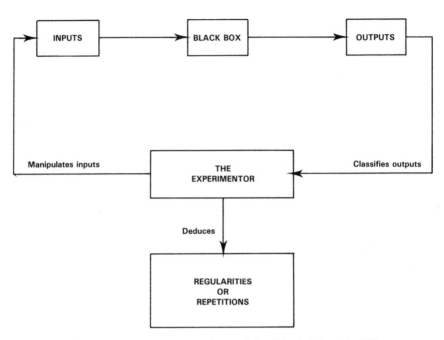

FIGURE 5.1. The Black Box Technique (after Schoderbek et al., 1985)

trol. They should not, therefore, seek to proceed by analysis, but should apply the black box technique of manipulating inputs and observing outputs. Faced with a black box, a manager does not have to enter it to learn something about it. Instead, the system is investigated by the collection of a long protocol, drawn out in time, showing the sequence of input and output states. The manager can then manipulate the input to try to find regularities in the output. Initially, if nothing is known about the box, random variations of input will be as good as any. As regularities become established, a more directed program of research can be conducted.

There are problems with the black box technique, as when a particular experiment changes a system to such an extent that it cannot be returned to its original state for further experiments (Ashby, 1956). And it is very important not to jump to conclusions about the behavior of a system without observing if for a sufficient length of time (Beer, 1979). Nevertheless, it is an important tool that managers *have* to use at all times—because only by working with black boxes can they avoid being overwhelmed by confusing detail. The more conscious they become of this, the more informed will be the way they break down their organizations into black boxes for control purposes. Once this level of sophistication is reached, the technique can be seen to have profound implications for organizational modeling and for the design of appropriate information systems.

Negative Feedback

Exceedingly complex probabilistic systems have to be controlled through self-regulation. The understanding of self-regulation that cybernetics can provide is important to managers for two reasons. First, it is the existence of mechanisms bringing about self-regulation that gives a degree of stability to the environment of organizations. It is useful to managers to know how this stability comes about and how it might be threatened, especially by an organization's own actions. Second, if managers understand the nature of self-regulation, they may be able to induce it in the organizations they manage. This is desirable because managers lack the "requisite variety" to intervene in all the decisions that will have to be made. It is also necessary because managers cannot accurately determine what types of environmental disturbance their organizations will have to face. They should therefore seek to make their organizations "ultrastable" (Beer 1981a)—capable of continuing to pursue the goal for which they were designed whatever the prevailing environmental conditions. This again requires self-regulation.

The work of Wiener (1948) has established that the way to ensure self-regulation is through the negative feedback mechanism. The feedback control system is characterized by its closed-loop structure. It operates by the continuous feedback of information about the output of the system. This output is then compared with some predetermined goal, and if the system is not achieving its goal, then the margin of error (the negative feedback) becomes the basis for adjustments to the system designed to bring it closer to realizing the goal. A simple closed-loop feedback system is represented in Figure 5.2. It seems that, for this system to work properly, four elements are required:

- A desired goal, which is conveyed to the comparator from outside the system
- A sensor (a means of sensing the current state of the system)
- A comparator, which compares the current state and the desired outcome
- An activator (a decision-making element that responds to any discrepancies discovered by the comparator in such a way as to bring the system back toward its goal)

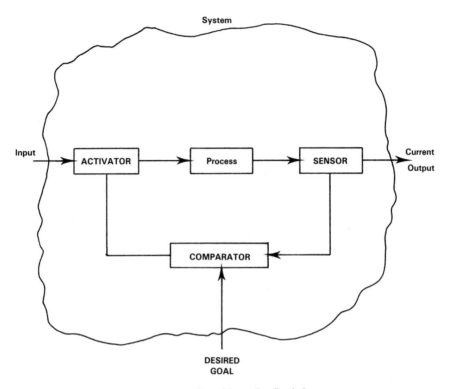

FIGURE 5.2. A Closed-Loop Feedback System

This kind of control system is extremely effective, since any movement away from the goal automatically sets in motion changes aimed at
bringing the system back onto course (Schoderbek et al., 1985). It is the
basis on which central heating and air-conditioning systems operate to
maintain a constant room temperature. Homeostasis in the body is
achieved by negative feedback; the body is able to maintain stability in
spite of extensive shifts in outside circumstances. An example is the ho-
meostatic process by which warm-blooded animals maintain their body
heat at around 37°C. Cooling of the body stimulates certain centers in the
brain, which "turn on" heat-generating mechanisms. Picking up a pen
from a desk, constantly registering the discrepancy between the position
of the hand and the pen, involves negative feedback. So, too, can managers
achieve better regulation of social organizations by ensuring that appropriate negative feedback processes are in place.

A number of additional points should be made before we leave the
concept of negative feedback. First, in designing feedback control systems,
it is important that managers ensure that there is rapid and continuous

comparison of actual performance against the desired goal, and similarly rapid and continuous taking of corrective action if necessary. If there are delays or lags in the system, then attempted adjustments may only add to instability. We are all familiar with the situation where attempts to slow down an apparently still-overheated economy only send the economy into a slump because, in fact, the economy's slowing down of its own accord has not yet been registered.

Second, it should be noted that we have been discussing only simple, first-order feedback systems (see Schoderbek et al., 1985). More sophisticated (second-order) systems are capable of considering and choosing among a variety of different responses to changes in an attempt to bring the system back toward its goal. Still more sophisticated (third-order) systems are capable of changing the goal state itself in response to feedback processes. In this case the goal is determined inside the system, and does not originate externally as in Figure 5.2.

Third, as well as negative feedback, which is deviation counteracting and therefore used as the basis for all control systems, there is also "positive feedback." This is deviation amplifying. The positive feedback process is one where the output is fed back to the input, but rather than reducing any divergence from the goal it produces a further movement in the direction in which the output is already moving. Positive feedback mechanisms are growth promoting. They may also, sometimes, be of use to managers.

Finally, it should be emphasized that feedback control alone may not be enough to achieve adequate regulation of organizations (see Strank, 1982). It is usually necessary to employ strategic control, based upon "feedforward" information that attempts to predict disturbances before they actually affect the organization. It may also be useful to try external control, attempting to intervene directly in the environment to make it more congenial to the organization.

Variety Engineering

Managers are unable to make accurate predictions either about the organizations they manage or the environments within which those organizations are situated. They are continually confronted by unexpected occurrences that they and their organizations must have the capacity to respond to if those organizations are going to be successful. They have to learn to live with probabilistic systems.

Fortunately, cyberneticians have taken an interest in probabilistic systems and, thanks to Ashby (1956), can provide some understanding of the difficulties faced by managers and ways of dealing with them. Ashby takes the credit because of his invention of the key concept of *variety*. The variety of a system is defined here as the number of possible states it is capable of exhibiting. It is, therefore, a measure of complexity. Obviously, variety is a subjective concept depending on the observer. A football team's variety will be much greater if one is assessing it as the manager of an opposing team, compared to if one is assessing it for a draw on the football pools. Just as obviously, however, organizations and their environments are systems that possess massive variety from the point of view of managers.

The problem for managers, as Ashby's "law of requisite variety" has it, is that only variety can destroy variety. In order to control a system, we need to have as much variety available to us as the system itself exhibits. So, if a machine has 20 ways of breaking down, we need to be able to respond in 20 different ways to be in control of the machine. If managers are going to control their organizations and make them responsive to environmental fluctuations, they must command as much variety as these systems themselves exhibit. Sometimes exhibiting requisite variety is easy enough. If I am engaged in a game of noughts and crosses (tic-tac-toe), and I am reasonably skilled, I can always exhibit enough variety to prevent my opponent from winning. But what if we are faced (like managers) with systems exhibiting apparently massive variety? How can we cope with this?

The answer is that we must either reduce the variety of the system we are confronting (variety reduction) or increase our own variety (variety amplification). This process of balancing varieties is known as "variety engineering" (Beer, 1979). Since the variety equation initially seems to place managers at a huge disadvantage, they will require all the skills of variety engineering if they are to balance varieties and (following the law of requisite variety) achieve control. And this must be done in ways appropriate to the organization being considered and its goals. For example, if I am manager of a relatively low-variety football team that is facing a high-variety football team, such as Liverpool, and I want to win, I have to engage in variety engineering. I must amplify the variety of my team, perhaps by improving their tactics, or by entering the transfer market. Or I must reduce the variety of Liverpool by allocating a player to take their best player out of the game, or by gaining information about their pattern of play (thereby making it more predictable).

Managers have to learn how to use variety reducers, filtering out the vast complexity of operational and environmental variety and capturing only that of relevance to themselves and the organization. And they have to learn how to use variety amplifiers, amplifying their own variety vis-à-vis the operations and the organization's variety vis-à-vis its environment. Figure 5.3 (after Espejo, 1977) represents this managerial variety engineering.

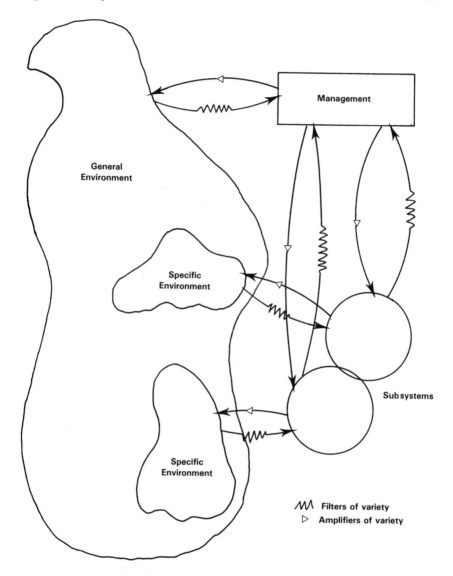

FIGURE 5.3. Managerial Variety Engineering (after Espejo, 1977)

In concluding this discussion on variety engineering, I will mention some techniques, explained by Beer (1981a, pp. 230–231), that managers can employ to reduce external variety of both kinds (operational and environmental) and amplify their own variety.

In reducing the external variety confronting them, managers can use the following methods:

- Structural (e.g., divisionalization, functionalization, massive delegation
- Planning (e.g., setting priorities)
- Operational (e.g., management by exception)

In amplifying their own variety, managers can employ the following methods:

- Structural (e.g., integrated teamwork)
- Augmentation (e.g., recruit experts, employ consultants)
- Informational (e.g., management information systems)

In putting in place the three building blocks of cybernetics—the black box technique, feedback, and variety engineering—the emphasis has been on the control part of the definition of cybernetics, the science of control and communication. The importance of the second of these concepts must not, however, be overlooked. The recognition that it is information flows and communication links that, more than anything else, bind organizations together represents significant progress over most of the organizations-as-systems models previously considered. The cybernetic model can provide the detailed understanding necessary for the effective design of information systems to aid managerial control.

Now that we have the building blocks in place, we can move forward in the next section to thinking about how they can be combined in one usable model of organization and management.

Management Cybernetics and Organizational Cybernetics

When the cybernetic ideas introduced in the previous section are combined together, they are capable of yielding two different models of the organization, which one can label *management cybernetics* and *organizational cybernetics*. Management cybernetics represents little improvement over hard systems thinking and is subject to the same criticisms. Organizational cybernetics, however, is based on a rather different philosophical orientation and is able to exploit fully the potential power inherent in the cybernetic building blocks. I shall now say a little bit more about each of these two traditions of cybernetic thinking.

Management Cybernetics

The early pioneers of cybernetics frequently employed analogies in their work to illustrate particular insights. Not surprisingly, perhaps, a tendency grew up in the secondary literature to treat organizations as if they were actually like machines or organisms. This comes through even in relatively recent books about management cybernetics (e.g., Strank, 1982). It is this kind of cybernetics—particularly that dominated by the machine analogy—that will be referred to here as management cybernetics.

The starting point for the management cybernetic model of the organization is the input–transformation–output schema. This is used to describe the basic operational activities of the enterprise. The goal or purpose of the enterprise is, in management cybernetics, invariably determined outside the system (as with a first-order feedback arrangement). Then, if the operations are to succeed in bringing about the goal, they must, because of inevitable disturbance, be regulated in some way. This regulation is effected by management. Management cybernetics attempts to equip managers with a number of tools that should enable them to regulate operations. Chief among these are the black box technique and the use of feedback to induce self-regulation into organizations. The latter is often supplemented by strategic control, based on feedforward information, and external control. Management cybernetics makes little use of the more complex, observer-dependent notion of variety.

Between this form of cybernetics and hard systems thinking there is little to choose. Conventional management scientists are able to take cognizance of its insights and to employ concepts such as feedback in their traditional analyses. Management cybernetics, therefore, offers no new direction in management science. Whether based on a machine analogy or on a biological analogy, it can be criticized for exactly the same reasons as hard systems thinking—an inability to deal with subjectivity and with the extreme complexity of organizational systems, and for an inherent conservatism (see Jackson, 1986).

Organizational Cybernetics

There is, however, another strand of cybernetic work concerned with management and organizations that breaks somewhat with the mechanistic and organismic thinking that typifies management cybernetics, and is able to make full use of the concept of variety. This type of cybernetics is not obviously subject to the criticisms mentioned above (Jackson, 1986) and does represent a genuinely new direction with respect to traditional management science. It is labeled here *organizational cybernetics*. Beer (1959b, 1966, 1972) has been pushing organizational cybernetics (though he does not use this term) for some years and has worked hard at defining its relationship with hard systems thinking. In spite of the respect that is accorded to Beer in, for example, the OR community, little serious attention has been paid to this work. This is evidence, perhaps, that Beer's thinking stems from a different paradigm. It is, however, fair to say that organizational cybernetics can only be found in fully developed form in Beer's (1979, 1983a, 1984, 1985) later works. Other sources for organizational cybernetics are the writings of two adherents of Beer's thinking, Clemson (1984) and Espejo (1977, 1979, 1987), and the collection of papers on the VSM edited by Espejo and Harnden (1989b). The "St. Gallen school" of cybernetics (see H. Ulrich and Probst, 1984) also evinces similar concerns and tackles them from a compatible theoretical position.

Beer's version of organizational cybernetics seems to have emerged from management cybernetics as a result of two intellectual breakthroughs. First, in *The Heart of Enterprise*, Beer (1979) succeeds in building his VSM in relation to the organization from cybernetic first principles. This enables cybernetic laws to be fully understood without reference to the mechanical and biological manifestations in which they were first recognized. Second, more attention is given in organizational cybernetics to the role of the observer. Clemson (1984) makes a distinction between a first-order cybernetics appropriate to organized complexity because it studies matter, energy, and information and a second-order cybernetics capable of tackling relativistic organized complexity because it studies, as well, the observing system. Organizational cybernetics is second-order cybernetics. This will become clearer in the next section, which describes Beer's VSM; this model encapsulates all the most important features of organizational cybernetics.

Beer's VSM

Introduction

The traditional company organization chart is, for Beer (1981a, pp. 77–85), totally unsatisfactory as a model of a real organization. His aim in constructing the VSM is therefore to provide a more useful and usable model.

The VSM, as its name suggests, is a model of the organizational features of any viable system. In *Brain of the Firm*, Beer (1972) builds it using as an example of any viable system the workings of the human body and nervous system. His logic is that if we want to understand the principles of viability, we had better use a known-to-be-viable system as an exemplar. The human body, controlled and organized by the nervous system, is perhaps the richest and most flexible viable system of all. The result is a neurocybernetic model containing a five-level hierarchy of systems that can be differentiated in the brain and body in line with major functional differences. From this, Beer builds up a model—consisting of five subsystems—of any viable system. In *The Heart of Enterprise* (1979), the same model is derived from cybernetic first principles, demonstrating that it is perfectly general. It can, therefore, be applied to firms and organizations of all kinds. Indeed, in a one-person enterprise, all five functions will still have to be performed by that one individual. In *Diagnosing the System for Organizations* (1985), the model is presented in the form of a "handbook" or "manager's guide," the intention being to aid application of the principles to particular enterprises. It is from these three sources (Beer, 1972, 1979, 1985) that the following account is primarily drawn. As will be seen from this detailed description, Beer makes full use of all the various concepts and tools devised by cybernetics to understand organizations and to make recommendations on how to improve their effectiveness. In the VSM, Beer encapsulates the cybernetic laws he sees as underpinning system viability and demonstrates their interrelationship.

I begin by describing the model and then pass on to the methodological recommendations for intervening in organizations that can be derived from it.

The VSM

General Overview

For Beer, a system is viable if it is capable of responding to environmental changes even if those changes could not have been foreseen at the time the system was designed. In order to become or remain viable, a system has to achieve requisite variety (at a level concordant with effective performance) with the complex environment with which it is faced. It must be able to respond appropriately to the various threats and opportunities presented by its environment. The exact level at which the balance of varieties should be achieved is determined by the purpose that the system is pursuing. Beer sets out a number of strategies that can be used by managers to balance the variety equations for organizations in a satisfactory way. These involve variety engineering, and were summarized in the earlier discussion of that topic. Essentially, these strategies are designed to fulfill two requirements. The first is that the organization should have the best possible model of the environment relevant to its purposes. The second is that the organization's structure and information flows should reflect the nature of that environment so that the organization is responsive to it. With its emphasis on engineering variety, the VSM can legitimately be seen as a sophisticated working out of the implications of Ashby's law of requisite variety in organizational terms.

With these general comments about variety engineering in mind, it is now possible to elaborate more fully on the organization of the VSM. The model is made up of five elements (Systems 1 to 5 in Figure 5.4), which may be labeled implementation, coordination, control, development, and policy. It is essential that the functions handled by these five systems be adequately performed in all organizations. Great importance is also given to the design of the information channels that link the different functions, and the system and its environment. As has already been said, this is a perfectly general model applicable to all systems. It will, however, be studied here with particular reference to organizations. I now take the five systems in turn before considering the overall structure of the model (and its recursive nature) and then the information that flows around the various communication linkages. Please refer to Figure 5.4 throughout this account.

System 1

The System 1 (S1) of an organization consists of the various parts of it directly concerned with implementation—with carrying out the task(s) that the organization is supposed to be doing. Subsidiaries A, B, C, and D in Figure 5.4 are all parts of System 1 of that viable system. It will be noted that each part has its own relations with the outside world, interacts with other subsidiaries, and has its own localized management (1A, 1B, 1C, 1D).

Each subsidiary (or part) of S1 is connected to the wider management system by the vertical command axis. Instructions for the subsidiaries arrive from higher-level Systems down this command channel. Each localized management, say 1B, therefore has a set of instructions received down the line that it interprets, instructing its operational element, B, what it should do (effector). What goes on in B is monitored (sensor) and transmitted back to 1B. 1B is then able to send this information about B's performance to higher levels along the upward communication channel. It is also, of course, able to compare actual performance with planned performance as it occurs, and to adjust the behavior of B as necessary (the negative feedback mechanism).

It should be noted at this point that each part of System 1, or subsidiary of a firm, should be autonomous in its own right so that it can absorb some of the massive environmental variety that would otherwise

FIGURE 5.4. Beer's VSM

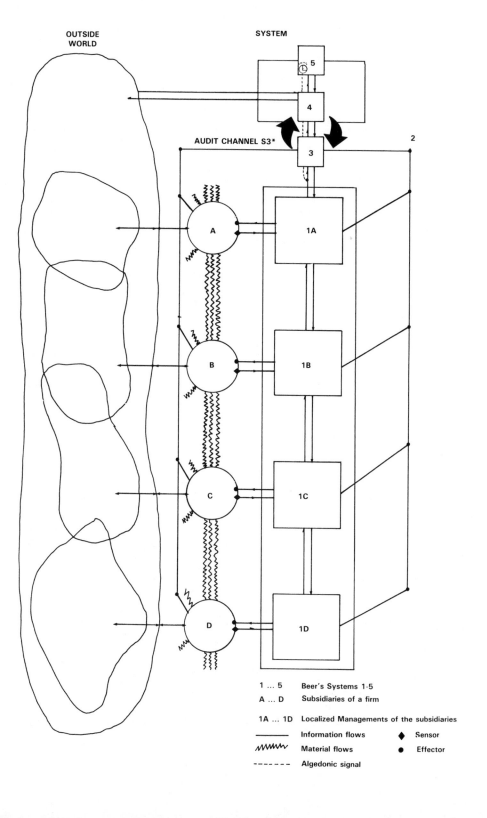

OUTSIDE
WORLD

SYSTEM

5

4

AUDIT CHANNEL S3*

3

2

A

1A

B

1B

C

1C

D

1D

1 ... 5	Beer's Systems 1-5
A ... D	Subsidiaries of a firm
1A ... 1D	Localized Managements of the subsidiaries

———	Information flows	◆	Sensor
⋀⋀⋀⋀	Material flows	●	Effector
– – – –	Algedonic signal		

flood higher management levels. If every aspect of the business had to be thought about consciously at the senior management level, then the firm would soon grind to a halt. In order to make the parts of the System 1 autonomous, they must all be viable systems designed in accordance with the VSM. Indeed, if we had a more detailed version of Figure 5.4 in which the black box representations of the subsidiaries were opened up for viewing, we should find each subsidiary also shown according to the representation of Figure 5.4. This is the basis of the model's recursion, to be discussed later. If each subsidiary is made a viable system, it will be able to make its own decisions with respect to the external world and other subsidiaries.

A subsidiary should, then, be able to do what it likes. The only restrictions on the autonomy of the parts of System 1 stem from the requirement that they continue to belong to the whole organization. Their localized managements must accept and implement instructions from higher management levels, use negative feedback to maintain performance, and report back. Additionally, each part of System 1 must accept a degree of coordination and control by Systems 2 and 3, which are designed to facilitate the effective interaction and performance of all the divisions. Local management, say 1B, has only local facts to go on, and action that local management takes in an emergency may not be best from the overall corporate point of view. It must, therefore, be subject to limitation. Here, Systems 2 and 3 are particularly significant.

System 2

System 2 is a coordination function. Under normal circumstances, compatible instructions from higher management should ensure that the various parts of System 1 of an organization act in harmony. In an emergency, however, each part of System 1 will try to act in its own best interests, but based on only local information. The interactions set off among parts of System 1 in these circumstances might then lead to unpredictable and dangerous effects for the whole enterprise and for the subsidiaries themselves. There is a need, therefore, for a coordinating function, and this System 2 provides. System 2 consists of the control centers of the parts of System 1 linked to a corporate regulatory center. The corporate regulatory center receives information about the actions of the various subsidiaries and is able to prevent dangerous oscillations arising in the system created by all the subsidiaries.

Suppose that subsidiaries A, B, C, and D in Figure 5.4 all play a part in manufacturing the firm's major product, so that output from A is passed to B, from B to C, and so on. Now what happens if something goes wrong with the production program in B, for example? Local management, 1B, will try to adjust the B plan and take corrective action, but this may not be possible locally. It may require varying supplies received from A and deliveries to C. 1B must inform 1A and 1C of what is going on, and each will try to adjust accordingly, but this is likely to send trouble reverberating throughout the system, creating violent oscillations. It is System 2's job to oversee these interactions and to stabilize the situation so as to obtain a balanced response from System 1. It sends feedback to the localized managements of System 1 to reestablish harmony, calling if necessary upon the resources of System 3.

System 3

Before passing on to System 3 itself, I must mention one other information flow, leading to System 3, which passes up the left-hand side of the model. This is the audit channel, or System 3*. It is there to give System 3 direct access to the state of affairs in the operational elements. Through this channel, System 3 can get immediate information, rather than relying on information passed to it by the localized managements of the subsidiaries. System 3 might want to check directly on quality, or on employee morale, or to see that maintenance procedures are being followed. Only System 3, with information provided to it by System 4, can know how essential any subsidiary is to the whole enterprise and therefore take action affecting its future; hence its need for direct access. System 3* is a vital function in any viable system.

We can now review the duties of System 3 itself. System 3 is a control function. It does not initiate policy but interprets it in the light of internal data from Systems 2 and 3* and external data from System 4. It is responsible for passing a coordinated plan down the line to System 1. It must oversee the effective implementation of policy and distribute resources to the parts of System 1 to achieve this. It has to monitor the performance of System 1 and take control action in accordance with information it receives up the information channel and also from System 2 and System 3*. Also, it must report upward any information needed by the policy system above it. Particularly vital information has to be rushed through on the "algedonic" (or arousal) channel shown as a hatched line in Figure 5.4.

Three kinds of information systems converge on System 3. First, System 3 is on the vertical command axis as part of corporate management. It transmits detailed interpretations of policy downward. It transmits information from the divisions upward, coalescing it into corporate information. It acts to send vital information upward extremely quickly. Second, it receives and acts upon information from System 2. It might send instructions downward on the basis of this, or consult upward. Finally, it responds to information received from System 3* advising on the fate of particular subsidiaries.

The three lower-level Systems, 1 through 3, make up what Beer calls the "autonomic management" of the organization. They are capable of optimizing the productive performance of the enterprise within an established framework and maintaining internal stability without reference to higher management levels. Autonomic management does not, however, possess an overall view of the organization's environment and is therefore incapable of reviewing corporate strategy and reacting to threats and/or opportunities in that environment. This is where Systems 4 and 5 come in.

System 4

System 4, or the development function of the organization, has two main tasks. First it acts as what Beer calls the biggest "switch" in the organization. It switches instructions down from the thinking chamber of the organization, System 5, to the lower-level systems. And it switches upward, from Systems 1 to 3, information required by System 5 to take major strategic decisions. There is a constant danger of overloading System 5 with information that is not significant enough to warrant its attention. System 4 must prevent this by carefully filtering the information it passes upward. It will further operate on aggregate information collected by System 3 to put it in a form useful to top management. With regard to information passed by System 3 for urgent attention, System 4 will act as an "algedonode"—rapidly transmitting it upward or wholly suppressing it, according to its perceived importance (Beer, 1981a).

The second major task of System 4 is to capture for the organization all relevant information about its total environment. If the organization is to be viable and effective, it has somehow to match the variety of the environment in which it finds itself. To do this it must have a model of the environment that enables predictions to be made about the likely future state of the environment and allows the organization to respond in time. System 4 provides the organization with this model. The sort of model suitable would be one constructed according to Forrester's (1969) system dynamics approach. Having recognized relevant environmental threats and opportunities, System 4 filters the information and redistributes it downward or upward according to its implications. Information with immediate implications will be communicated to System 3 for speedy action. Information with longer-term implications will require the judgment of System 5.

System 4 is the point in the organization where internal and external information can be brought together. As such, activities like corporate planning, market research, operational research, research and development, and public relations should be located there. Beer proposes that System 4 become the "operations room" of the enterprise, a real "environment of decision" in which all senior meetings are held.

System 5

System 5 is responsible for the direction of the whole enterprise. It is the thinking part of the organization, formulating policy on the basis of all the information passed to it by System 4 and communicating the policy downward to System 3 for implementation by the subsidiaries. One of its most difficult tasks is balancing the sometimes-conflicting internal and external demands placed on the organization. The internal demands are represented by the commitment of autonomic management to optimizing ongoing operations. Whereas the external demands are represented by System 4, which with its links to the environment tends to be outward and future oriented. System 5 must ensure that the organization adapts to the external environment while maintaining an appropriate degree of internal stability.

System 5 must also represent the essential qualities of the whole system to any wider system of which it is part, acting in this capacity simply as the localized management of a particular part of System 1 of the wider system.

Beer recommends that System 5 be arranged as an elaborate, interactive assemblage of managers—a "multinode." Decision making needs to be formalized and the effects of decisions monitored without threatening the freedom and flexibility of interaction allowed in the multinode.

The basic structures and processes of the VSM have now been described. What is further required is some discussion of two of the most important features of the model: its approach to corporate structure and to measures of performance.

Corporate Structure

It is worth discussing the idea of recursion on which the model depends. Recursion refers to the fact that the structure of the whole model is replicated in each of its parts. As was seen, the subsidiaries of an organization should be treated as viable systems in their own right and must, therefore, possess their own Systems 1 to 5. The organization, which is itself a viable system, might well at a higher level of recursion simply be an implementation subsystem or System 1 part of another viable system. The generality of the model and its applicability to different system levels allows elegant diagrammatic representations of management situations to be constructed and acts as a great variety reducer for managers and management scientists. Lower-level systems that will inevitably appear as black boxes at high levels of recursion can become the focus of interest in their own right with only a slight adjustment of attention.

Measures of Performance

Next, it is worth considering the nature of the information that flows around the various connections linking Systems 1, 2, 3, 4, and 5. This will often, given the importance of negative feedback for control, be information about how the different divisions of the organization and the organization as a whole are doing in relation to their respective goals. Achievement in most organizations is measured in terms of money, the criterion of success being the extent to which profits are maximized and costs minimized. This is not, however, regarded as satisfactory by Beer. It ignores how well the organization is doing in terms of preparing for the future by investing in research and development or in terms of more abstract resources like employee morale. It fails to reveal the cost-cutting manager who, in search of immediate profits, is damaging the organization's long-term future. Instead, Beer (1981a, pp. 162–166) advises adopting three levels of achievement (actuality, capability, and potentiality) that can be combined to give three indices (productivity, latency, and performance) expressed in ordinary numbers. These can be used as comprehensive measures of performance in relation to all types of resources throughout the organization. These measures are able to detect the irresponsible cost-cutting manager.

Using the VSM for Diagnosis and Design

Now that the VSM has been described, it is time to say how it can actually be used by managers and their advisers as part of a methodology for understanding and improving the performance of organizations. Obviously the VSM itself is a model and not a methodology, but it is based on such firm cybernetic principles that it is not difficult to extrapolate from those principles, and the model itself, exactly how to proceed in uncovering the faults of organizations. In essence the methodology must center on looking at enterprises, or potential enterprises, to discover whether they obey cybernetic laws (in which case they will be viable and effective) or flout them (in which case they are likely to fail).

I will consider this in a little more detail. One use of the VSM, obviously, is to ensure that new organizational systems are designed according to the cybernetic principles elucidated in the model. The most ambitious attempt to use the model in this way—Project CYBERSYN, involving the regulation of the Chilean social economy under the Allende government—is described by Beer (1981a) in *Brain of the Firm* (second edition) and elsewhere (Beer, 1975, 1981b; Espejo, 1980). Other examples are given by Beer (1979) in *The Heart of Enterprise*. The model can also be employed as a diagnostic tool; the organization being analyzed can be compared to the VSM to check that its structures and processes are such as to ensure viability and effectiveness. Advice on how to proceed with diagnosis and examples can be found in various sources (Beer, 1984, 1985; Clemson, 1984; Espejo, 1979; Espejo and Harnden, 1989b; Keys and Jackson, 1985). To complete this account of the VSM, I set out a summarized procedure for using the model and then outline some common threats to viability that are always worth looking for while carrying out intervention using the VSM.

Detailed Procedure

The procedure for using the model to diagnose the faults of a proposed or existing system design is quite complicated. However, it can roughly be divided into two parts:

- System identification (arriving at an identity for the system and working out appropriate levels of recursion)
- System diagnosis (reflecting on the cybernetic principles that should be obeyed at each level of recursion)

Various tasks have to be undertaken in each part as described below. This procedure was first set out in Jackson and Alabi (1986) and refined in Flood and Jackson (1991a). In Flood and Jackson, a fully worked example is provided using the steps outlined. More detail on each of the tasks can be found in Beer's (1985) *Diagnosing the System for Organizations*, from which the procedure was originally derived. Espejo (1989) has done useful work on how the VSM can be used to help stakeholders with different viewpoints arrive at some sort of agreement about organizational identity (for example, by considering the structural implications of alternative viewpoints). This considerably enlarges our understanding of the first phase of system identification and should be consulted by interested readers. I will now set out the procedure step-by-step.

A. System Identification
- Identify or determine the purpose(s) to be pursued
- Taking the purpose as given, determine the relevant system for achieving the purpose—this is called the "system in focus" and is said to be at recursion level 1
- Specify the viable parts of the System 1 of the system in focus—these are the parts that "produce" the system in focus and are at recursion level 2
- Specify the viable system of which the system in focus is part (wider systems, environments, etc.); this is at recursion level 0

B. System Diagnosis

In general, draws upon cybernetic principles to:
- Study the System 1 of the system in focus
  - For each part of System 1, detail its environment, operations, and localized management
  - Study what constraints are imposed upon each part of System 1 by higher management
  - Examine how accountability is exercised for each part and what indicators of performance are taken
  - Model System 1 according to the VSM diagram
- Study the System 2 of the system in focus
  - List possible sources of oscillation or conflict between the various parts of System 1 and between their environments
  - Identify the elements of the system (various System 2 elements) that have a harmonizing or damping effect
  - Ask how System 2 is perceived in the organization (as threatening or as facilitating)
- Study the System 3 of the system in focus
  - List the System 3 components of the system in focus
  - Ask how System 3 exercises authority
  - How is the resource bargaining with the parts of System 1 carried out?
  - Ask who is responsible for the performance of the parts of System 1
  - What audit (or System 3*) inquiries into aspects of the parts of System 1 does System 3 conduct?
  - What is the relationship between System 3 and the System 1 elements? Is it perceived to be autocratic or democratic? How much freedom do System 1 elements possess?
- Study the System 4 of the system in focus
  - List all the System 4 activities of the system in focus

- ○ How far ahead do these activities consider?
- ○ Do these activities guarantee adaptation to the future?
- ○ Is System 4 monitoring what is happening to the environment and assessing trends?
- ○ Is System 4 open to novelty?
- ○ Does System 4 provide a management center/operations room, bringing together external and internal information and providing an environment for decision?
- ○ Does System 4 have facilities for alerting System 5 to urgent developments?
- • Study the System 5 of the system in focus
  - ○ Who is on the board, and how does it act?
  - ○ Does System 5 provide a suitable identity for the system in focus?
  - ○ How does the ethos set by System 5 affect the perception of System 4?
  - ○ How does the ethos set by System 5 affect the relationship between System 3 and System 4—is stability or change emphasized?
  - ○ Does System 5 share an identity with System 1 or claim to be something different?
- • Check that all information channels, transducers, and control loops are properly designed

Common Threats to Viability

When one examines an existing or proposed social system design using the procedures outlined above, it is likely that a number of faults in its organization will be revealed. The following are some of the most common faults discovered by cybernetics. Discovery of any of these would be regarded by Beer as a threat to the organization's continued existence.

1. Mistakes in articulating the different levels of recursion, so that a system is not properly managed at each of its levels of operation. Often the importance of certain System 1 parts is not recognized. They are not treated as viable systems in their own right and therefore lack a localized System 1 management to attend to their affairs. In Beer's work in Chile (1981a), problems were encountered in regulating the social economy because the "allocation system" and the "people system" were not initially seen as independent viable systems at the same level of recursion as the production

system. Another example is provided by Espejo (1979) in the context of a small firm.

2. The existence of organizational features that, according to the VSM, are additional and irrelevant to those required for viability. These are likely to hamper the organization in striving for effectiveness and may eventually threaten its ability to survive. These irrelevant features should therefore be dispensed with.

3. System 2, 3, 4, or 5 of an organization showing a tendency toward becoming autopoietic. An autopoietic system is one that has the ability to "make itself"—to continue to produce those aspects of its organization that are essential to its identity. This is what makes systems viable and autonomous (Maturana and Varela, 1980). However, following the VSM, viability is a property that should be embodied only in the system's totality and in the parts of its System 1. A system developing autopoiesis in any of its Systems 2, 3, 4, or 5 is pathologically autopoietic, and this threatens its viability. In an organization, Systems 2, 3, 4, and 5 should serve the whole system by promoting the implementation function (System 1) and should not be allowed to become viable systems in their own right. If they do develop as autopoietic systems, it will inevitably be at the expense of the system as a whole. The faults typical of bureaucracies can be traced to these organizations becoming pathologically autopoietic (Beer, 1979, pp. 408–412).

4. Certain key elements as revealed by the VSM being absent or not working properly in the actual organization. Corrective action should be taken to ensure that the functions concerned receive due attention. Beer (1984) particularly picks out Systems 2 and 4 as elements that are often weak in organizations. System 2 is frequently not fully established because the localized managements of the parts of System 1 resent interference from this relatively junior control echelon. Unless System 2 is able to assert itself, however, coordination between the various activities of the parts of System 1 will be put in jeopardy. System 4 is often weak in relation to System 3 because it is regarded in many organizations as being a "staff" function. For this reason, it may lack good communications with other parts of the organization, and its recommendations may frequently be ignored. If System 4 is weak, however, System 5 will lack the knowledge of the enterprise's environment necessary for it to give proper attention to development activities. It will forget its higher-level duties and will instead tend to get too involved with the work of System 3 or even try to intervene at System 1 level. Beer insists that System 4 must be a "line" function

for its importance to be recognized, and it is represented as such in diagrams of the VSM. It will then prevent System 5 from collapsing into System 3, and System 5 will be able to perform its proper function, balancing the internal and external demands on the organization.

5. System 5 not representing what Beer (1984) calls "the essential qualities of the whole system" to the wider systems of which it is a part. Failure to do this will entail problems for the system's viability and effectiveness.

6. If the communication channels in the organization and between the organization and the environment do not correspond to the information flows shown to be necessary in any viable system. These channels must be carefully designed for the rapid transmission of information about how the system is doing in terms of the three indices of performance.

I have set out Beer's VSM as the most developed and usable expression of organizational cybernetics. The model has been described, a detailed procedure for applying it outlined, and six of the diagnostic points noted that often emerge when the VSM is employed to make a detailed check on the operational effectiveness of an organization. A critique of organizational cybernetics, with the VSM as its representative, can now be put in place.

Strengths and Weaknesses of Organizational Cybernetics

A useful starting point in considering the strengths of the organizational cybernetic model is to stress its generality. This stems from its very nature. The recommendations endorsed in the model do not tightly prescribe a particular *structure*; they relate more to a system's essential *organization*, to use a distinction drawn by Varela (1984). They are concerned with what defines a system and enables it to maintain its identity, rather than with the variable relations that can develop between components integrating particular systems. As a result, the VSM has been found to be applicable to small organizations (Espejo, 1979; Jackson and Alabi, 1986), large firms (Beer, 1979), training programs (Britton and McCallion, 1985), industries (Baker, Elias, and Griggs, 1977), local government (Beer, 1974), and national government (Beer, 1981a). I can testify that it was the only management model capable of integrating in one volume six diverse contributions to a seminar series about the management of transport systems (Keys and Jackson, 1985). A number of other, very varied applications are set out in Espejo and Harnden (1989b). From an analysis of all these cases, it is possible to pick out those features of the VSM that serve it most advantageously when it is used to assist management practice.

First, the model is capable of dealing with organizations whose parts are both vertically and horizontally interdependent. The notion of recursion enables the VSM to cope with the vertical interdependence displayed in, say, a multinational company that itself consists of divisions embracing companies, which embrace departments, and so on. The applicability of the VSM at different system levels acts as a great variety reducer for managers and management scientists. The idea of recursion is not unique to Beer's writings—Parsons's AGIL schema (see Chapter 3) is applied at different system levels—but only in the VSM is it incorporated into a usable management tool. Horizontally interdependent subsystems, the parts of System 1, are integrated and guided by the organizational meta-system, Systems 2 through 5. The hoary old problem of centralization versus decentralization is dealt with in the VSM by arrangements to allow to the subsystems as much autonomy as is consistent with overall systemic cohesiveness. There are some close parallels between Beer's account of this issue and the contingency-theory approach to differentiation and integration offered by Lawrence and Lorsch (see Chapter 3).

Second, the model demands that attention be paid to the sources of command and control in the system. The relative autonomy granted to the parts within the VSM should again be noted. In the VSM, the source of control is spread throughout the architecture of the system. This allows the self-organizing tendencies present in all complex systems to be employed productively. Problems are corrected as closely as possible to the point where they occur. Motivation should be increased at lower levels in the organization. Higher management should be freed to concentrate on meta-systemic functions. The importance of encouraging self-organization and freeing management for boundary-management activities has been well documented in the literature of sociotechnical systems theory (see Chapter 3). It is also one of the main planks of the "St. Gallen school" of organizational cybernetics. H. Ulrich, Malik, and Probst all offer reasons why it should promote greater efficiency (H. Ulrich and Probst, 1984). Some restrictions on autonomy are of course essential, and these are imposed by Systems 2 and 3 (so as to ensure overall systemic cohesiveness) and by System 4 in its role as a development function collecting together relevant environmental information and, in the light of threats and opportunities, suggesting necessary changes to systemic purpose and consequent altera-tions of organizational structure. System 5 has overall responsibility for policy, and this will often involve balancing internal and external demands as represented in the organization by the desire of System 3 for stability

and the bias of System 4 for adaptation. The System 3–4–5 interrelationship, as described by Beer, shows interesting similarities with Thompson's
(1967) well-known discussion of the administrative process.

Third, the model offers a particularly suitable starting point for the
design of information systems in organizations, as indeed has been con-
vincingly argued by Espejo (1979), Espejo and Watt (1978), and Schumann
(1990). Most designs for information systems are premised upon some
taken-for-granted model of organization—usually the outdated classical,
hierarchical model. It takes a revolutionary mind to reverse this, to put
information processing first and to make recommendations for organizational design on the basis of information requirements, as revealed by the
law of requisite variety; yet this is what Beer succeeds in doing with the
VSM (see particularly Salah, 1989). As was mentioned in Chapter 3, Galbraith achieves a similar reversal with his model of the organization as an
information-processing system.

Fourth, the organization is represented as being in close interrelationship with its environment, both influencing it and being influenced by it.
The organization does not simply react to its environment but can proac-
tively attempt to change the environment in ways that will benefit the
organization. Morgan (1983a) sees dangers in this proactive aspect of
cybernetics because it might lead organizations to damage the field of
relationships on which they depend. He need not worry about the role of
the VSM. There is as much emphasis in the Beer model upon surviving
within and developing a set of relationships as upon goal seeking.

Fifth, the VSM can be used very effectively as a diagnostic tool to
make specific recommendations for improving the performance of organizations. A system of concern can be compared to the model to check that
its structures and processes support an underlying organization capable of
ensuring survival and effectiveness. Advice on how to proceed with diagnosis was given in the earlier subsections on using the VSM.

Finally, having dealt with the role of the VSM in promoting organizational efficiency, I should also acknowledge the contribution it can make
to helping the realization of human potentiality in enterprises. The model
provides powerful cybernetic arguments for granting maximum autonomy to the parts of an organization and for the democratic definition of
purposes. Beer advocates decentralization of control because of the implications of the law of requisite variety. The parts must be granted autonomy
so that they can absorb some of the massive environmental variety that
would otherwise overwhelm higher management levels. The only degree
of constraint permitted is that necessary for overall systemic cohesion and
viability, and this constraint facilitates the exercise of liberty rather than
limits it. If less control were exercised the result would not be greater

freedom for the parts, but anarchy (Beer, 1979, chapter 6). The constraints imposed on the parts of System 1 by the metasystem should be regarded as being like the laws enacted in a democratic society. We do not regard laws against assault and theft as infringements of our liberty because they increase our freedom to go about our normal business unhindered. The degree of autonomy granted to the parts by the VSM is the maximum possible if the system as a whole is to continue to exist.

The cybernetic argument for the democratic derivation of purposes effectively follows from this. For only with democratic involvement can the parts be convinced that the system is serving their purposes, and that they stand to gain from its continuance. And only then can they be expected to accept metasystemic constraints as legitimate and use the autonomy granted to promote efficiency rather than disruption. Just because System 5 is labeled "policy," therefore, does not imply that it is solely responsible for deciding the purposes of the enterprise. In Beer's (1985) view the board, as well as looking after the shareholders,

> also embodies the power of its workforce and its managers, of its customers, and of the society that sustains it. The board metabolizes the power of all such participants in the enterprise in order to survive. (p. 12)

If, then, the stakeholders in a system have agreed about the purposes to be pursued, and those purposes are embodied in System 5, the VSM offers a means of pursuing the purposes efficiently and effectively with only those constraints on individual autonomy necessary for successful operation.

Because of the link between efficiency and democracy established cybernetically by Beer, it is clear that the model depends for its full and satisfactory operation on a democratic milieu—ideally perhaps on a president who, when System 5 is presented during an explanation of the workings of the VSM, can exclaim "At last, el pueblo" (Beer, 1981a, p. 258). This, of course, is why Beer (1985, p. 91) counsels us in *Diagnosing* on the unfortunate effects the exercise of power can have in viable systems.

I have now, I hope, constructed a forceful argument to the effect that Beer's model supplies principles of great value to managers seeking to design and operate organizational systems. The VSM is often criticized (Checkland, 1980; Rivett, 1977) for offering a simplistic picture of the organization based upon mechanical or organismic analogy. In fact, it provides a highly sophisticated organizational model. I have argued elsewhere (Jackson, 1985c) that it is superior to the traditional, human relations, and systems models—the others commonly offered in organization theory. In the course of the analysis above, I have often had reason to mention the work of well-known organizations-as-systems theorists—Parsons, Lawrence and Lorsch, Thompson, sociotechnical thinkers, and Galbraith. The principles encapsulated in the VSM fit well with the most advanced findings of modern organizational science (Flood and Jackson, 1988). Moreover, the model integrates these findings into an applicable management tool that can be used to recommend specific improvements in the functioning of organizations. Perhaps even more significant, the VSM is underpinned by the science of cybernetics. This ensures that its use generates enormous explanatory power compared with the usual analyses carried out in organization theory. But justification for that assertion must wait until the "Analysis and Assessment" section of this chapter. And before that we need to look at some of the criticisms that have been leveled at the VSM.

Considerable effort has been made elsewhere in clarifying, classifying, and debating the most frequent criticisms raised against Beer's model (Jackson, 1985c, 1986, 1988a, 1989a; Flood and Carson, 1988; Flood and Jackson, 1988). Of the eight criticisms in general circulation, two (misplaced mechanical or biological analogy, and encouraging organizations to damage their field of relationships) have been touched on above and dismissed. Two other arguments, that variety is a "poor measure" (Rivett, 1977) or "unexceptional" in its implications (Checkland, 1980), and that cybernetics emphasizes stability at the expense of change (Ulrich, 1983), are also obviously misplaced in relation to the VSM, as the previous description of that model shows. A fifth criticism, that cybernetics is difficult to apply in practice (Rivett, 1977; Thomas, 1980), is gradually being addressed in the literature (Beer, 1985; Clemson, 1984; Espejo, 1989, 1990). For the record, the conclusion reached in the debates about these five criticisms was that they held against management cybernetics, but they could not be sustained against organizational cybernetics.

That still leaves three, in fact interrelated, criticisms that are troubling in relation to organizational cybernetics, and these we need to review more fully. It has already been argued that the idea that cybernetics offers a simplistic picture of the organization is impossible to sustain against Beer's model. The VSM more than stands comparison with the most advanced theories produced by orthodox organization theory. Yet that word "orthodox" reveals a nagging doubt. Our standard of comparison for the VSM so far has been the functionalist organizations-as-systems tradition. Consider the VSM from the point of view of another sociological paradigm—the interpretive, for example—and it does seem to capture only a subset of what is generally accepted as significant about organizations. For Checkland (1980), working within the interpretive paradigm, the VSM is at best only a partial representation of what an organization is. It is a representation, moreover, that misses the essential character of organizations: the fact that their component parts are human beings, who can attribute meaning to their situation and can therefore see in organizations whatever purposes they wish and make of organizations whatever they will. Because of this, it is as legitimate to regard an organization as a social grouping, an appreciative system, or a power struggle as it is to see it through the eyes of the VSM.

This links in to perhaps the most frequent criticism of the model: that it underplays the purposeful role of individuals in organizations. Morris (1983), while not agreeing with this criticism, captures its flavor nicely with his phrase "the big toe also thinks!" For Adams (1973), the VSM implies that man, the basic unit in organizational systems, is free only in the same way that the knee is free to jerk—as a reflex action. In Ulrich's (1981a) view, cybernetic models leave out perhaps the most important feature of sociocultural systems, human purposefulness and self-reflectiveness. This charge has very practical consequences, for it suggests that the VSM could mislead managers into placing too much emphasis on organizational design and too little on the role of individuals in organizations. If the criticism is correct, managers seeking to promote the efficiency and effectiveness of their enterprises by concentrating effort on their logical design as adaptive goal-seeking entities (as recommended by the VSM) may be misplacing their energies. Social organizations can, perhaps, exist and perform well while employing a host of apparently illogical structures. The emphasis placed on organization design may preclude proper attention being given to the generation of shared perceptions and values (to "organizational culture"). The point can, of course, be overdone. In Beer's work, the tendency has been to pay increased attention to the perceptions and roles of individuals. In principle, the VSM does cater for the purposeful role of individuals in organizations. The model suggests that it is to the advantage of organizations to grant maximum autonomy to individuals. Nevertheless, the emphasis remains overwhelmingly on systemic/structural design to the neglect of the requirement to manage processes of negotiation between different viewpoints and value positions.

Following very much from this point, a further criticism is made that underplaying the role of individuals carries autocratic implications when cybernetic models are used in practice. This is an old criticism. Lilienfeld (1978) comments on a 1948 review of Wiener's *Cybernetics* in which a Dominican friar, Pére Dubarle, expresses his fear that cybernetic techniques might help some humans to increase their power over others. Against management cybernetics the criticism is fair enough. Models that treat organizations as simple input–transformation–output systems, with an externally defined goal, clearly lend themselves to autocratic usage by those who possess power. The criticism is also, however, leveled against the VSM (Adams, 1973; Rivett, 1977; Checkland, 1980). It is believed that, when applied, the VSM inevitably serves the purposes of narrow elite groups. Much of this criticism has to be misplaced; for Beer (1985), an organization's goal is not externally defined but emerges as a compromise from among the various internal and external influences on the organization. Further, despite the terminology of Systems 1 through 5, he insists that the VSM should not be seen as hierarchical—all five functions are dependent upon each other. What the VSM arguably achieves, when it is used in organizations, is an increase in efficiency and effectiveness. There is nothing to prevent the application of the VSM to democratic organizations in which all participate fully in the process of goal setting. The model might improve the efficiency and effectiveness of these organizations as well. Indeed, I have already rehearsed the argument that it requires only that degree of control over individual freedom necessary in order to maintain cohesiveness in a viable system—law and order for the benefit of all. It cannot therefore be argued that the VSM *inevitably* serves autocratic purposes.

Of course, the problem still arises of the model being misused by a powerful group. Ulrich (1981a) argues that Beer's VSM does in fact lend itself to this kind of usage. He insists that design tools should be so constructed that they are impossible to subvert for authoritarian use. Beer replies (1983b) that the risk of subversion does exist but that safeguards can be built into the system to minimize the danger.

This final argument can only be further elucidated if we move to a metalevel of analysis. I shall therefore pick it up again in the following "Analysis and Assessment" section when I bring back into play the theoretical schemata introduced in Chapter 2. The aim will be, as usual, to put into context the debates that have gone on about the strengths and weaknesses of organizational cybernetics, so that a more balanced appraisal of its potential usefulness as a systems approach is acquired.

Analysis and Assessment

The reader will recall Habermas's argument that, stemming from their sociocultural form of existence, human beings necessarily possess technical, practical, and emancipatory cognitive interests. It should be instructive to begin an assessment of Beer's VSM, therefore, by considering how successful it is in serving these different human species imperatives.

The discussion in previous sections of this chapter strongly suggests that it is in terms of the technical interest in prediction and control that the VSM makes its most substantial contribution. More particularly, it contributes powerfully to that type of knowledge related to the technical interest that supports strategic action oriented to regulation in the social domain. It can potentially deliver a massive increase in the steering capacities of organizations and societies. The VSM is a sophisticated systems model of great generality, pinpointing various systemic/structural constraints that must be observed if an enterprise is to succeed as an adaptive goal-seeking entity. It is geared to tackling problems of differentiation and integration, providing insight into the proper arrangement of command-and-control systems and into the design of appropriate management-information and decision-support systems, treating organization–environment relations sensitively, and yielding specific recommendations for improving the performance of organizations. All in all, it seems to embody great explanatory power and to lend itself to ready application by managers and management scientists.

The practical interest receives support rather than substantive assistance from the VSM. Cybernetic justification is provided for the need to extend understanding and consensus, and communication systems and procedures for decentralizing control (which could under certain circumstances assist this process) are outlined. However, little attention is paid to methods that might help, at the level of conscious meaning, to achieve and establish shared understanding about purposes. Ulrich's (1981a) distinction between "syntactic" and "semantic–pragmatic" levels of communication helps to further establish this argument. The syntactic level is solely concerned with whether a message is well formed or not in the sense of whether it can be "read." This matter can be dealt with by information-processing machines. The semantic and pragmatic levels are concerned, respectively, with the meaning and the significance of messages for the receiver—they inevitably involve people. Ulrich argues that the concept of variety, which underpins the VSM, operates only at the syntactic level. It is an information-theoretic measure of complexity referring "to the number of distinguishable states that a system or its output (the 'message' it sends out) can assume at the syntactic level" (Ulrich, 1981a).

We can see that this is severely restricting as soon as we consider what criterion of "good" management must be entailed in the VSM. For Beer, apparently, good management can be no more than management that establishes requisite variety between itself and the operations managed, and between the organization as a whole and its environment. The lesson from the practical interest is that good management must also concern itself with the meaning and significance of purposes for participants in an enterprise and the creation of intersubjective agreement to pursue a set of purposes.

The need for an emancipatory interest is implicitly accepted by Beer. Indeed, I have argued elsewhere (Jackson, 1990c) that the VSM contains a "critical kernel." Beer seeks to demonstrate on cybernetic grounds that decentralized control and democracy are necessary for viability and effectiveness. He also suggests some of the problems existing social arrangements present to the proper operation of the VSM. At the top of the list are the existence of power relationships and our acquiescence in the concept of hierarchy (Beer, 1985, pp. 91–92). The implication is that we should redress power imbalances and abandon the hierarchical concept of organization. Acknowledgment of the unfortunate effects the exercise of power can have in viable systems is scarcely enough, however, in relation to such a pervasive aspect of organizational life. In an organization disfigured by the operation of power, many of the features of the VSM that Beer sees as promoting decentralization and autonomy instead offer to the powerful means for increasing control and consolidating their own positions. Even the granting of maximum autonomy to the parts can be interpreted, not as a step on the road to industrial democracy, but rather as the imposition of a more sophisticated (but equally compelling) management control technique. Workers are encouraged to believe they possess freedom, but this is only the limited freedom to control themselves in the service of someone else's interest.

Beer, as was mentioned earlier, accepts that there is a risk of subversion and that realistically, even if "immunological systems" are incorporated, the model can be used for good or ill. He goes on to suggest that, in this, "cybernetic approaches mirror advances in all other branches of science" (Beer, 1983b). The important question to ask, perhaps, is whether scientific advances that are to be applied in the management context to the design of social systems should mirror advances in other branches of science. According to Ulrich (1981a, 1983), it is exactly Beer's belief that this is the case that leads to problems. Beer conceives of his task as tool design rather than social system design, and this directly determines that he will create a model that lends itself to autocratic usage. Certainly, at the present stage of development of the emancipatory dimension of the VSM, it does require the theoretical support of other critical sciences in order to ensure that its use is as liberating as its creator intends it to be.

Further insights into the most appropriate role for the VSM, and its potential, can be gained by considering the sociological paradigm to which it most closely relates. I have argued that Beer's model can be seen as an excellent device for integrating the findings of the organizations-as-systems tradition into an applicable management tool. From this, it might be supposed that the VSM shares the functionalist assumptions of that body of work. In fact the sociological paradigm underpinning organizational cybernetics is structuralism rather than functionalism, and this has some very important consequences.

Structuralism, as the term is employed in this book (the reader is referred back to the discussion of this issue in Chapter 2), refers to a particular theoretical orientation based upon what Keat and Urry (1975) call a "realist" epistemology. This is the most fundamental difference from functionalism, which embraces a positivist epistemology. Positivism encourages empirical observation, analysis, and classification of surface elements—the sort of approach we have witnessed being used by organizations-as-systems theorists and hard systems thinkers. Structuralists, by contrast, believe that these surface phenomena are generated by underlying structures or systems of relationships that should be uncovered and understood. It is therefore incumbent upon scientists to provide explanations of the phenomena available to our senses in terms of the underlying, unobservable mechanisms that produce them. Structuralists seek to model the causal processes at work at the deep structural level that generate the surface phenomena and the relationship between them.

As was noted in Chapter 2, the convergence in approach between cybernetics and structuralism has long been apparent to structuralist writers. Cyberneticians have been much slower to recognize the similarity in concern. This is surprising given the number of concepts that are the common currency of both cybernetics and structuralism—concepts such as organized complexity, regulation, transformation, equilibrium, information exchange, and feedback and control. It is even more surprising given some of Beer's (1966) comments in the relatively early text *Decision and Control*, in which he clearly demonstrates a structuralist orientation. He argues, for example, that scientific management should not be content simply with discovering the facts but should also seek to know what the facts mean, how they fit together, and should seek to uncover mechanisms that underlie them. Ever since, of course, he has been shouting loud enough that the VSM is an attempt to set out, in terms of cybernetic laws, the necessary and sufficient conditions of viability for any autonomous system (e.g., Beer, 1979, 1990).

The link between cybernetics and structuralism is confirmed in other sources. N. V. Jackson and Carter (1984) demonstrate a correspondence between the function of myth in Levi-Strauss's structural anthropology and the way variety attenuation works in Beer's cybernetics. Molloy and Best (1980) argue that Beer's VSM can be used as an "iconic model" to reveal underlying mechanisms supporting surface system behavior and to provide explanations of observable phenomena. In general, there is little reason to doubt that cybernetics is based upon structuralist assumptions. It serves to develop explanations of observable occurrences in social systems based upon principles and laws governing the behavior of all systems under control. Even the emphasis placed in organizational cybernetics on the role of the observer has its corollary in structuralism. At least in Levi-Strauss's (1968) and Piaget's (1973) versions of the doctrine, the fundamental structures uncovered relate back to the basic characteristics of the human mind.

If Beer's VSM integrates the findings of the organizations-as-systems school, we can now understand that it goes beyond them as well. Underpinned by the science of cybernetics, and thus realizing a structuralist project, its use generates enormous explanatory power compared with the usual analyses carried out in organization theory. Organization theorists (at least those driven by positivism) cling to perceived relationships between surface phenomena as the source of their insights. Cybernetics allows an explanation of such perceived relationships to be extracted from consideration of processes at work at a deeper, structural level. For example, sociotechnical thinkers find that delegating control to autonomous work groups improves the effectiveness and efficiency of organizations by improving performance in the groups themselves and by freeing managers for boundary management. The VSM can provide a scientific explanation of this in terms of requisite variety. It is not farfetched to see the whole history of functionalist organization theory as an empirical commentary upon the cybernetic principles underlying the viability of systems as unearthed deductively by Beer.

The link between organizational cybernetics and structuralism also helps to explain why hard systems thinkers have had such difficulty absorbing Beer's work. Organizational cybernetics is based on alternative sociological foundations and represents a genuinely new direction in management science. Further, we can begin to grasp more fully the basis of the criticisms aimed at the VSM. Once we step outside the structuralist paradigm and view the VSM using the assumptions of the interpretive and radical paradigms, as defined by Burrell and Morgan (1979), then doubts inevitably begin to appear. Perhaps too much emphasis is placed upon organizations as logically designed structures of communication and control, and not enough on organizations "as *processes* in which different perceptions of reality are continuously negotiated and renegotiated" (Checkland, 1980). Perhaps, if the social world consists of antagonistic class formations with some groups exploiting others, then the VSM does provide too convenient a vehicle for increasing the power of dominant groups.

The ascription of structuralist underpinnings to organizational cybernetics, and the setting out of a particular procedure for using the VSM, have been based upon what it is hoped the reader will regard as logical and coherent extrapolation from the model. It must be acknowledged, however, that some of the conclusions reached are implicit rather than explicit in Beer's writings, and other readings are possible. Even if the reading provided is seen as true to the spirit of Beer's books, it is still possible to argue that the VSM *should* be interpreted and employed differently. Harnden (1989, 1990), for example, would probably class the interpretation given as "representational" in that it pictures the VSM as trying to express certain fundamental laws governing the organization of complex systems—laws that we ignore at our peril (although Harnden's analysis is aimed at positivist rather than structuralist readings). Harnden wants to align the VSM with interpretive theory; to him it is best regarded as an "hermeneutic enabler." Organizational models should be seen not as seeking to capture objective reality, but as aids to orienting ongoing conversations about complex social issues. The VSM is a particularly good model, Espejo and Harnden (1989) argue, because it permits an extremely rich discourse to unfold about the emergence and evolution of appropriate organizational forms. It provides an "umbrella of intersection" for different perspectives, and this should help us to coordinate our interactions in a consensual domain.

Harnden has been convinced by the work of Maturana and Varela of the need to "bracket" objectivity. As part of their studies on autopoiesis, Maturana and Varela have concluded that cognition is an organizationally closed system and that, therefore, we must give up any claim to have direct access to the phenomena around us. Not a particularly original conclusion, one might think, given the history of philosophical debate on this issue and the fact that this point is taken for granted in soft systems thinking—but enough to give life, apparently, to the version of second-order cybernetics to which Harnden associates himself and to which he would like to attach the VSM.

Ultimately, Harnden (1989) believes that it is a matter of choice whether we adopt a representational view of the VSM or see it as an hermeneutic vehicle for orchestrating diverse viewpoints. But this in itself is an interpretive conclusion. For those who see the VSM as expressing in a coherent and usable form cybernetic principles of effective organization (and all the evidence of his writings suggests Beer is one of these), there is no choice about the cybernetic laws expressed in the VSM. If an enterprise does not respect the law of requisite variety, for example, it will not work as well as one that does and, indeed, its viability will be threatened. If their conversations lead participants to ignore the lessons of the law of requisite variety with that result, then I suppose they have made a choice. But such a choice hardly respects the history of cybernetics or Beer's endeavors.

The tension between the structuralist and interpretive readings of the VSM reaches a crescendo in Espejo's proposed methodology for using the model (Espejo, 1989, 1990). Although theoretically Espejo seems willing to go all the way with Harnden in embracing the interpretive view (Espejo and Harnden, 1989b) and seeks to embed the VSM in an interpretive methodology based on learning, the more logical structuralist use of the model keeps thrusting through, offering a contradictory direction for analysis. Thus the VSM is employed to reveal the cybernetics of the situation, and "diagnosing communication problems leads to a discovery of the causes of operational problems, thus making it possible to improve the situation" (Espejo, 1990). Forced to choose between what his cybernetic diagnosis tells him and what the participants in the situation believe, what would Espejo decide to do?

Cybernetic laws governing the viability of complex systems either exist or they don't. If they don't, the game is up for cybernetics in the social realm and the prize can be handed to the soft systems thinkers. The VSM might find some use at stage 4 of Checkland's methodology (see Chapter 6). But this is a depressing and unnecessary conclusion. The structuralist reading of organizational cybernetics provides it with its own domain for exploration and its own field of application, dealing with problems of communication, control, and organizing in complex systems. It would also be a damaging conclusion to reach for the overall strength of the systems movement, because soft systems thinking is certainly not equipped—in the way that organizational cybernetics is—to enhance the steering capacities of organizations and societies, and this is central to their successful evolution.

Inevitably the procedure for interrogating systems methodologies using the range of schema set down in Chapter 2 creates some redundancy. We have now dealt with most of the major issues surrounding the VSM, and so we can proceed swiftly with the rest of the analysis.

In terms of metaphor, the VSM successfully combines the strengths implicit in viewing organizations as machines with what is to be gained by conceiving of them as organisms and brains. The arrangements at the operational level (Systems 1 through 3) ensure the optimum use of resources in carrying out transformation processes, while Systems 4 and 5 ensure adaptation to the environment and the institutionalization of learning. System 5 is charged with maintaining a balance between the "inside and now" and the "outside and then." The model pays less attention to the culture and coercive-system images of organization. Beer, of course, is aware of the need for a shared culture in an enterprise. However, ways of engineering values and beliefs are neglected in the VSM. Again, there is recognition of the importance of power in organizations, but relatively little on how it is distributed or how its worst effects can be redressed.

The system of systems methodologies would have organizational cybernetics making systemic–unitary assumptions about problem contexts.

The tools provided by organizational cybernetics give the problem solver the best chance of dealing with difficulties in this type of problem context. The VSM is about the design of goal-seeking, adaptive systems. It is claimed that organizations designed according to cybernetic principles will be self-regulating and even self-organizing in the face of environmental perturbations. This is the best that can be achieved in systemic contexts when the systems of concern are exceedingly complex and probabilistic. In such situations mathematical modeling and optimization are impossible, so hard systems thinking is inappropriate. On the other hand, the VSM is weak on mechanisms for resolving conflict and differences of value and opinion in organizations and so depends on a preexisting (unitary) agreement among participants about the goals to be pursued. Espejo (1989) is working on the extension of the VSM to more pluralistic contexts, and it is true that the construction of different VSMs of the same problem situation, showing how different purposes would work out in terms of organizational structure, could assist with the alleviation of pluralism.

Finally, I should comment on the VSM in relation to the modernism-versus-postmodernism debate. Briefly, it seems obvious that the VSM is an expression of modernism. The world is perceived as logical and orderly to the extent that it can be probed with a view to discovering the laws of viability of systems. The chief contribution of organizational cybernetics, as we have seen, is to the technical interest in prediction and control in the social domain. This, and a lack of self-reflectiveness about the social use to which it is put, demonstrates a systemic rather than a critical modernist orientation. As Ulrich (1981a, 1983) says, Beer conceives of his task as tool design, rather than social system design. Thus the model lends itself to the increased rationalization of social systems; its use can assist their "perfect" functioning. There is, however, in Beer's writings a happy assumption that there is a correspondence between the demands of viability and the requirements of democracy, and Beer would certainly want to see his efforts as assisting human emancipation. Further, since I have not stressed it already let it be said here that the VSM is only one part of Beer's contribution to human knowledge. His work as a whole can be seen as a grand cybernetic narrative geared to curing the ills of humankind and putting men and women more in control of their own destinies (e.g., Beer, 1983a, 1990). So critical modernism is also reflected on Beer's agenda.

The fact that Cooper and Burrell (1988) seemingly regard the cybernetician Varela as a postmodernist should not make us pause for long. Varela's work on autopoiesis has an as-yet-undetermined relationship to organizational cybernetics. Further, the attribution of the label *postmodernism* to Varela's thinking seems at best dubious. True, he forgoes the idea of objective truth, but Luhmann (1986) seems to have little difficulty relating Varela's notion of organizationally closed systems, following their own logic, to his version of systemic modernism. And the idea of structural coupling, such an integral part of Maturana and Varela's thinking (see Mingers, 1989), is supportive of the possibility of creating consensual domains. But we cannot follow all the interesting avenues thrown up by all of our theoretical schemata.

To conclude this chapter let me remind the reader that cybernetics as a recognized field of study has been around approximately as long as hard systems thinking. It has not yet, however, made the same impact on management science. It is hoped that this review will help put matters right, and the role that organizational cybernetics in particular can play as an important stream of thought—and means of action—in management science will be more widely recognized.

Soft Systems Thinking

Introduction

Soft systems thinking opens up a completely new perspective on the way systems ideas can and should be used to help with decision making and problem resolving. It arguably brings within the scope of proper treatment all those wicked, messy, and ill-structured problems that either escape or are distorted by the systems methodologies so far considered because of the strict prerequisites that need to be met before those methodologies can be employed. The result has been a massive extension of the area within which systems thinking can be used to help with real-world problem management.

In terms of the crude approximations I am using initially to orient readers' thoughts in these chapters, if organizational cybernetics offers progress over hard systems thinking along a dimension concerned with the nonhuman aspects of complexity (the systems dimension of the system of systems methodologies), soft systems thinking is an advance along the dimension dealing with people and their perceptions, values, and interests (the participants dimension). Hard systems thinking ignores issues of subjectivity. Soft systems thinking, by contrast, admits that there are multiple perceptions of reality and is able to help analysts deal with this. Anticipating part of a later argument, soft systems thinking avoids the functionalism of organizations as systems and of systems engineering, systems analysis, and operational research, and it is not structuralist as organizational cybernetics is. Instead, it is interpretive in character. Interpretive theorists, as we know from Burrell and Morgan (1979), will adopt a more subjectivist approach to systems thinking and practice. They do not seek to study objective "social facts" or to search for regularities and causal relations in social reality. The social world is seen as being the creative construction of human beings. It is necessary, therefore, to proceed by trying to understand subjectively the point of view and the intentions of the human beings who construct social systems. Hence the importance in soft systems thinking of probing the worldviews or *Weltanschauungen* (Churchman, 1979a;

Checkland, 1981a), or the "appreciative systems" (Vickers, 1970; Checkland, 1981a), that individuals employ in understanding and constructing the social world.

In this book I am taking the word *methodology* to embrace both procedures for gaining knowledge about systems and structured processes involved in intervening in and changing systems. In introducing soft systems thinking, therefore, it might be useful to consider in what sphere of methodological development interpretive systems ideas have had the most impact. We shall find that they have had very little impact by way of helping to produce an interpretive systems theory, but considerable influence (implicitly, at least) on the development of methodologies to resolve problems in systems. I will attend to this in a little more detail.

The interpretive sociological paradigm is resourced by two great human science traditions, the hermeneutic tradition associated with the name of W. Dilthey and the phenomenological tradition associated with the names of E. Husserl and A. Schutz. Systems ideas have played virtually no part in the construction of the paradigm. Certainly there is, as yet, no fully elaborated systems methodology that serves the paradigm by providing knowledge about the social world, in systems terms, from a phenomenological or hermeneutic perspective. This is in marked contrast, of course, to the many variants of the functionalist systems approach described in Chapter 3. In these circumstances it is not surprising that there is a widespread belief (e.g., Silverman, 1970) that systems thinking is inevitably functionalist in nature. The absence of an interpretive systems methodology for gaining knowledge does not, however, mean that one could not be developed. There seems to be no good reason why a methodology could not be constructed that would probe the systemic nature of the interpretations individuals employ in creating the social world. In fact two particular theoretical notions, mentioned above and well-known in the soft systems tradition, seem to presage the development of just such a methodology.

The first is the notion of *Weltanschauung* (W). This carries the implication that an individual's interpretations will be far from random; they will be consistent in terms of a number of underlying assumptions that constitute the core of that individual's worldview or W. Ws can therefore be studied systemically. The W idea has been used by Churchman (1979a) and Checkland (1981a) in the development of methodologies to solve problems in systems. Checkland has suggested that his methodology can be applied to reveal any recurrent Ws and that it therefore opens up the prospect of discovering "the universal structures of subjective orientation in the world" (Luckmann, quoted in Checkland, 1981a, p. 279). Apparently, then, it can be employed to gain knowledge about the social world from the hermeneutic standpoint; but this idea remains undeveloped.

Then there is Vickers's notion of an "appreciative system." This is the most important concept employed by him in developing his study of the "peculiarities of human systems" (Vickers, 1983). Vickers argues that the components of human systems—active individuals attributing meaning to their situation—make it impossible to study such systems using the methods of the natural sciences. The only way to understand decision making in human systems is to understand the different appreciative systems that the decision makers bring to bear on a problem (Vickers, 1965, 1970). Appreciative systems are "the interconnected set of largely tacit standards of judgement by which we both order and value our experience" (Vickers, 1973, p. 122, note 2). An individual's appreciative system will determine the way he or she sees and values various situations and hence how he or she makes "instrumental judgments" and takes "executive action"—in short, how he or she contributes to the construction of the social world. It follows, according to Vickers, that if human systems are to achieve stability and effectiveness, then the appreciative systems of their participants need to be sufficiently shared to allow mutual expectations to be met. Human systems depend upon shared understandings and shared cultures.

It should be pointed out that Vickers's social theory (as far as it can be pieced together from hints in his various writings) is not itself interpretive. For Vickers, developments in human society do not depend solely upon changes in appreciative systems. Nevertheless, an interpretive element in his thinking does offer a fruitful starting point for anyone interested in developing a systems methodology for producing interpretive systems theory. It was Checkland who first recognized Vickers's significance in this respect, and he has since used Vickers's work as an important theoretical support for his own interpretive systems-based methodology for problem solving (Checkland, 1981a, 1989; Checkland and Casar, 1986).

There is in the established literature, therefore, no more than a fore-shadowing of a systems methodology to produce a genuinely interpretive systems theory. However, a full-scale research program designed to provide just this kind of theory, and to reflect upon the process of doing so, is currently under way. This is being conducted at the University of Los Andes, Merida, Venezuela, by Fuenmayor and his colleagues (Fuenmayor, 1985, 1989). It is too early yet to judge the results of this important work.

If there is a current lack of interpretive systems theory, the same cannot be said of methodologies for problem management based upon interpretive assumptions, for (as I shall be arguing later) an interpretive orientation to intervention is one of the most important characteristics that marks the soft systems tradition of work.

The soft systems approach emerged as a result of dissatisfaction with the development and limitations of hard systems thinking. C. W. Churchman and R. L. Ackoff were, as noted already, among the most influential pioneers of operations research in the postwar period in the United States. During the 1960s and 1970s, however, they became increasingly disillusioned with OR. The original intention of a holistic, interdisciplinary, experimental science addressed to problems in social systems was, in their view, being betrayed (Ackoff, 1979a; Churchman, 1979b). Churchman's educational program in "social systems design" at Berkeley was an attempt to keep the original dream alive. His work influenced (among others) Mason and Mitroff, whose soft methodology is considered in this chapter, and Ulrich, whose emancipatory systems approach is featured in the next. Ackoff continued to develop OR according to its original prescription as an approach that could deal with ill-structured and strategic issues. He too, however, felt the need to give an alternative name—"social systems sciences" (S^3)—to the educational and consultancy activities he initiated at the University of Pennsylvania. In the United Kingdom in 1969, P. B. Checkland and his colleagues at Lancaster University began an action-research program designed to extend the usefulness of systems ideas to ill-structured management problems. Initially they used the systems engineering methodology of Jenkins; as this methodology was found wanting, it was gradually modified. Eventually an entirely different kind of approach—Checkland's soft systems methodology—emerged (Checkland, 1976, 1981a).

The work of Churchman, Mason and Mitroff, Ackoff, and Checkland can be considered representative of soft systems thinking and is dealt with in more detail below. Similarities between the soft systems trend and soft OR have already been noted. The reader interested in following up other related work would do well to consider Argyris and Schon (1974, 1978) on organizational learning and Warfield and Christakis et al. (Warfield, 1976; Christakis, Keever, and Warfield, 1987; Janes, 1988) on "interactive management."

Churchman's Social Systems Design

Churchman's perspective on systems thinking, social systems design, is the result of careful and profound philosophical speculation and is difficult to summarize. Perhaps a sensible approach is to take the four aphorisms that close his book *The Systems Approach* (Churchman, 1979a) and to expand on these.

> "*The systems approach begins when first you see the world through the eyes of another.*"

One implication for Churchman is that the systems approach begins with philosophy that allows the world to be viewed from the radically different perceptions of opposed philosophical positions. *The Design of Inquiring Systems* (Churchman, 1971), in many respects his most important book, considers the different ways in which five important philosophers might design systems for finding things out. This first aphorism contains lessons from Kant and Hegel. We are reminded that whatever view of the world we hold is inevitably based on certain taken-for-granted, a priori assumptions (Kant). It is wise for systems designers to recognize, following Hegel, that there are many possible worldviews, constructed upon alternative sets of taken-for-granted assumptions. Once we appreciate this, it becomes clear that subjectivity should be embraced by the systems approach. Systems designers must accept that completely different evaluations of social systems, their purposes, and their performance can and do exist. The only way we can get near to a view of the whole system is to look at it from as many perspectives as possible (Churchman, 1970).

> *"The systems approach goes on to discovering that every world-view is terribly restricted."*

In *The Design of Inquiring Systems*, Churchman shows that each of the five designs for finding things out is incomplete in itself, resting upon assumptions that cannot be proved using its own logic. Increased sophistication in inquiry comes with recognition of the limitations of whatever inquiring system is employed. This opens the way, for Churchman, to a different understanding of objectivity. Subjectivity is not to be rigorously excluded (in practice it can't be, anyway), but must be included in any definition of objectivity—so that by bringing together different subjectivities the restricted nature of any one worldview can be overcome. A further point is that although individual worldviews are terribly restricted, they are also usually highly resistant to change. Worldviews cannot be seriously challenged just by exposing them to apparently contrary "facts," which they will simply interpret according to their fixed presuppositions. "No data can ever fatally destroy a W" (Churchman, 1970).

The conclusion of these ruminations is that we need a dialectical approach to objectivity such as suggested by the philosopher Hegel. In practice, Churchman charges systems designers with the task of making those responsible for social systems (decision makers) aware of the restricted nature of their own worldviews. This can best be done through a process of "dialectical debate" (Churchman, 1970). The worldview that makes the decision makers' proposals meaningful should be unearthed. This prevailing worldview (thesis) should then be challenged by another "deadly enemy" worldview based on entirely different assumptions and giving rise to alternative proposals (antithesis). Whatever facts are available can then be considered in the light of both worldviews. This should help to bring about a richer (i.e., more objective) appreciation of the situation, expressing elements of both positions but going beyond them as well (synthesis). The dialectical process advocated by Churchman can, therefore, be represented as consisting of the following steps:

Thesis

- Understand decision makers' proposals
- Understand the *Weltanschauung* (W) that makes these proposals meaningful

Antithesis

- Develop an alternative W (a "deadly enemy")
- Make proposals on the basis of this W

Synthesis

- Evaluate data on the basis of both Ws and
- Arrive at a richer appreciation of the situation

"There are no experts in the systems approach."

This admonition should be taken to heart most strongly by systems designers themselves. When it comes to matters of aims and objectives (and appropriate means), which inevitably involve ethical considerations and moral judgments, there can be no experts. Systems designers, because they seek to take on the whole system, may become arrogant in the face of opposition from apparently sectional interests. It is incumbent on them to listen to all "enemies" of the systems approach (such as religion, politics, ethics, and aesthetics) since these enemies reflect the very failure of the systems approach to be comprehensive (Churchman, 1979c).

"The systems approach is not a bad idea."

The attempt to take on the whole system remains a worthwhile ideal, even if its realization is unattainable in practice. From this arises the need for the system designer to pursue his or her profession in the "heroic mood." This is the spirit advocated by Churchman's mentor, the pragmatist philosopher E. A. Singer. Increasing purposefulness and participation in systems design, through the process of dialectically developing world views, is a never-ending process. "Hence," Churchman (1971) writes, "the Singerian inquirer pushes teleology to the ultimate, by a theory of increasing or developing purpose in human society; man becomes more and more deeply involved in seeking goals" (p. 254). There is a need to help bring about a (Lockean) consensus around a particular worldview so that decisions can be taken and action occur. Before this worldview can congeal into the status quo, however, it should itself be subject to attack from forceful alternative perspectives (Churchman, 1971).

A number of points that emerge from the discussion so far are worthy of further attention because they help establish the significance of Churchman's contribution to soft systems thinking. First, there is the shift proposed by Churchman in our understanding of objectivity in the systems approach. In the organizations-as-systems, hard, and cybernetic traditions, objectivity is perceived to rest on the accuracy and efficacy of some model of the system of concern. Either the model is taken to represent the system of concern (as in organizations-as-systems and hard approaches) or it is held to suggest, because of the scientific laws it encapsulates, faults in the system of concern (as with the VSM). In both cases the objectivity of the model is demonstrated, and the results of the systems study "guaranteed," if the implemented solutions derived from the model work in practice. For Churchman, systems and whether they work or not are as much in the mind of the observer as they are in the real world. A model can only capture one possible perception of the nature of a system. Objectivity, therefore, can only rest upon open debate among holders of many different perspectives. And the results of a systems study can only receive their guarantee from the maximum participation of different stakeholders, holding various worldviews, in the design process.

This is a fundamental shift indeed, and it is one that is necessarily adhered to (in theory at least) in all the softer systems methodologies that will be considered here. Once the claim to be modeling some real world "out there" is abandoned, the only possible reason why anyone should want to follow the prescriptions of systems methodologists is that they can provide the means of better organizing open and free debate about the value or otherwise of existing and proposed systems designs.

A further point derives from Churchman's desire to strive for "whole system" improvement. Because decision makers inevitably have a restricted worldview (as does everybody else), following their worldview could lead to suboptimization in terms of the whole system. The system designer's first obligation in carrying out a systems study therefore is not to the decision makers, even if they are paying the bills; rather, it is to the "clients," customers, or beneficiaries of the system (Churchman uses various words to describe this group). This is a very broadly defined set of people, all of whom have an interest in the system and whose objectives should, in view of this, be served by the system. In the case of an industrial firm it will include employees, stockholders, customers, and interested sections of the public. The purpose of social systems design must be to help social systems serve their clients. Its role, therefore, is to identify the interests of the clients and to influence the decision makers in the system to realize those changes that benefit the clients of the system. If a systems designer becomes convinced that the decision makers are serving the wrong clients, then he or she has a professional obligation to change the decision-making process (Churchman, 1970). The decision makers must be persuaded to confront their most cherished assumptions with plausible counterassumptions.

The final point also stems from Churchman's insistence that social systems design (originally OR) has to take on the whole system. To some (e.g., Bryer, 1979) this makes Churchman's work appear hopelessly idealistic and impractical. All that Churchman is doing, however, is pointing out the fate of all applied sciences, which have no option but to live with the prospect that localized actions based on limited information can have disastrous consequences in terms of whole-system improvement. As Ulrich (1981b) argues, all such critics are doing is "blaming the messenger for the bad news." What Churchman does, following Ulrich's (1985) reading, is to use the theoretical indispensibility of comprehensive systems design as an ideal standard to force us to recognize the need to reflect critically on the inevitable lack of comprehensiveness in our actual designs.

So Churchman is not asking for the impossible, but is suggesting a way of proceeding given that what is necessary if we are to be sure our designs are justifiable—that we should understand the whole system—is, in fact, impossible. We need to make the lack of comprehensiveness of our designs transparent so that we can easily reflect on their limitations. A good way of doing this is to expose our designs to the "enemies" of the systems approach and learn from what they have to say about them. It is this reading of Churchman that Ulrich has seized upon and developed in creating his own "critical systems heuristics" (Ulrich, 1983). Accepting this reading allows us to see Churchman as anticipating the emergence of at least one school of critical systems thinking. The question with which he ends *The Design of Inquiring Systems* (1971) suggests that he should have much sympathy with the endeavors of another. The question is: "What kind of a world must it be in which inquiry becomes possible?" (p. 277).

The extent to which Churchman's methodology comes as a shock to those reared on hard systems thinking is well illustrated by a story he tells in *The Systems Approach and Its Enemies* (Churchman, 1979c). During the 1960s, NASA was in the middle of the Apollo space program to put a man on the moon. It was thought a good idea to have various scholars come to study the innovative methods NASA was using to manage this complex project. Churchman's was one such group; they, however, went far beyond NASA's intentions and began asking challenging questions and debating about the purpose of the Apollo program, which from a systems point of view did not obviously contribute to the betterment of the human species. A NASA group was monitoring the groups monitoring them, and graded the approaches used in terms of both relevance to NASA's mission and interdisciplinarity. Churchman's group received an F for the first category and an A for the second.

Mason and Mitroff's Strategic Assumption Surfacing and Testing (SAST)

There are a number of versions of the SAST methodology that differ in their precise details. The substance, however, is the same. SAST is undoubtedly a soft methodology, and finds its proper home here because it focuses managers' attention on the relationship between the participants involved in a problem situation, and not on the supposed characteristics of the system(s) that constitute the context. In the language of the system-of-systems-methodologies matrix, it is the participants dimension rather than the systems dimension that receives attention. The human and political aspects of organizations are brought to the fore, while the issue of organizational structure slides into the background. The account of SAST given here is drawn from the main sources with which either R. O. Mason or I. I. Mitroff, or both, have been associated (Mason and Mitroff, 1981; Mitroff and Emshoff, 1979; Mitroff, Emshoff, and Kilmann, 1979). It is an attempt to present the substance of the methodology in the clearest possible way and may not correspond to the detail of any one account. The methodology itself is approached through the underlying philosophy and principles on which it is based. The reader will recognize in SAST a profound debt to Churchman's work. It is because it neatly operationalizes many of Churchman's ideas, and not because it ranks alongside the intellectual contributions made by Churchman, Ackoff, and Checkland to soft systems thinking, that I give such prominence to SAST in this chapter.

SAST is designed for use with complex systems of highly interdependent problems, where problem formulation and structuring assume greater importance than problem solving using conventional techniques. It is argued that most organizations fail to deal properly with such "wicked" problems because they find it difficult to challenge seriously accepted ways of doing things; policy options that diverge considerably from current practice are not given systematic consideration. SAST aims to ensure that alternative policies and procedures are considered. This necessitates the generation of radically different policies or themes since data alone, which can after all be interpreted in terms of existing theory, will not lead an organization to change its preferred way of doing things. An organization really begins to learn only when its most cherished assumptions are challenged by counterassumptions. Assumptions underpinning existing policies and procedures should therefore be unearthed, and alternative policies and procedures put forward based upon counterassumptions. A variety of policy perspectives can be produced, each supportable by the data available in an organization.

It is recognized that tensions may well ensue, since the success of the process depends upon different groups being strongly committed (initially at least) to particular policy options. However, to believe that ill-structured problems can be adequately tackled in the absence of such tensions is thought to be naive. Organizations are arenas of conflict between groups expressing alternative worldviews. This offers great potential for developing alternative strategies and policies, but it must also be managed. SAST attempts to surface conflicts and to manage them as the only way, eventually, of achieving a genuine synthesis.

This philosophy is incorporated in a number of clearly articulated principles (Mason and Mitroff, 1981). SAST is adversarial, based on the belief that judgments about ill-structured problems are best made after consideration of opposing perspectives. It is participative, seeking to involve different groupings and levels in the organization, because the knowledge needed to solve a complex problem and implement a solution will be widely distributed. It is integrative, on the assumption that a synthesis of different viewpoints must eventually be sought so that an action plan can be produced. And it is "managerial mind supporting," believing that managers exposed to different assumptions will possess a deeper understanding of an organization, its policies, and its problems. These principles are employed throughout the phases of SAST.

The idea that an approach can be both adversarial and integrative may appear perverse to some. That it is not was strongly brought home to me by one particular intervention in a firm that was in the process of introducing a quality-management program (see Ho and Jackson, 1987). In that firm there was an apparent consensus around the need for the kind of quality program proposed. However, this apparent consensus was founded upon very varied interpretations of the key concepts in the program. Only through a process of adversarial debate could these very significant differences be highlighted and the ground prepared for a more soundly based consensus built upon common understanding.

The SAST methodology itself can be regarded as having four major stages: group formation, assumption surfacing, dialectical debate, and synthesis. The aim of group formation is to structure groups so that the productive operation of the later stages of the methodology is facilitated. As wide a cross-section of individuals as possible who have an interest in the relevant policy question should be involved. It is important that as many possible perceptions of the problem as can be found are included.

The participants are divided into groups, care being taken to maximize convergence of viewpoints within groups and to maximize divergence of perspectives between groups. A number of techniques, such as personality-type technology and vested-interests technology, are suggested as means to accomplish this. Each group's viewpoint should be clearly challenged by at least one other group.

During the assumption-surfacing stage, the different groups separately unearth the most significant assumptions that underpin their preferred policies and strategies. Two techniques assume particular importance in assisting this process. The first, "stakeholder analysis," asks each group to identify the key individuals or groups on whom the success or failure of their preferred strategy would depend. This involves asking questions such as: Who is affected by the strategy? Who has an interest in it? Who can affect its adoption, execution, or implementation? And who cares about it? For the stakeholders identified, each group then lists what assumptions it is making about each of them in believing that its preferred strategy will succeed. Each group should list all the assumptions derived from asking this question of all the stakeholders. These are the assumptions upon which the success of the group's preferred strategy or solution depends. The second technique is "assumption rating;" for each of the listed assumptions, each group asks itself:

- How important is the assumption in terms of its influence on the success or failure of the strategy?
- How certain are we that the assumption is justified?

The results are recorded on a chart such as that shown in Figure 6.1. Each group should now be able to identify a number of key assumptions—usually in the most important/least certain quadrant of the chart—upon which the success of its strategy rests.

The groups are brought back together to begin a dialectical debate. Each group makes the best possible case for its preferred strategy while clearly identifying the most significant assumptions it is making. Points of information only are allowed from other groups at this time. There is then an open debate focusing on which assumptions are different between groups, which are rated differently, and which of the other groups' assumptions each group finds most troubling. Each group should develop a full understanding of the preferred strategies of the others and their key assumptions. After the debate has proceeded for so long, each group should consider adjusting its assumptions. This process of "assumption modification" should continue for as long as progress is being made.

The aim of the synthesis stage is to achieve a compromise on assumptions from which a new, higher level of strategy or solution can be derived. Assumptions continue to be negotiated and modifications to assumptions

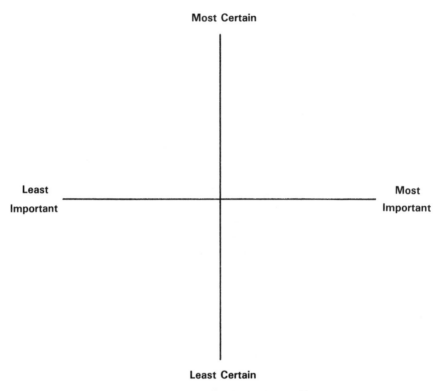

FIGURE 6.1. An Assumption Rating Chart

made. A list of agreed assumptions should be drawn up. If this list is sufficiently long, then the implied strategy can be worked out. This new strategy should bridge the gap between the old strategies and go beyond them as well. The assumptions on which it is based can be evaluated as it is put into effect. If no synthesis can be achieved, points of disagreement are noted and the question of what research might be done to resolve those differences is discussed. Meanwhile, any strategy put into effect can be more fully evaluated.

Mason (1969) has detailed what he sees as the advantages of a dialectical approach to strategic planning over the alternative expert and devil's-advocate methods. In the expert approach, some planner or planning department simply produces an "objective" plan, based upon the "best" evidence, for managerial consumption. The planners' assumptions remain hidden, and the opportunity is lost to produce plans premised upon other points of view. In the devil's-advocate approach, managers and planners produce a planning document that is then subject to criticism by top management. The criticism may uncover some assumptions. However, this approach often encourages top management to be hypercritical, with the added problem that if they are too destructive, the suggested plan disintegrates with no alternative to replace it. In these circumstances planners may be tempted to produce "safe" plans to protect themselves from severe criticism. Again, with the devil's-advocate approach, the chance is lost to develop alternative plans constructed on different world views. A dialectical approach, such as SAST, is seen as overcoming all the weaknesses of the other two methods.

Examples of SAST in action can be found in Jackson (1989b), Mason (1969), Mason and Mitroff (1981), and Mitroff, Barabba, and Kilmann (1977).

Ackoff's Social Systems Sciences (S³)

Like his friend and sometime colleague Churchman, Ackoff has been much influenced by the pragmatist philosophy of E. A. Singer. I described in an earlier section how Churchman's interpretation of that philosophy produced a new understanding of objectivity in the systems approach; Ackoff has endorsed and contributed to that new understanding. For him, the conventional view that objectivity results from constructing value-free models that are then verified or falsified against some real world "out there" is a myth. Purposeful behavior cannot be value free. Objectivity in social systems science must therefore be rethought as resulting from the open interaction of individual subjectivities. It is "value full," not value free. "Objectivity," Ackoff (1974b) writes, "is the social product of the open interaction of a wide variety of individual subjectivities." From this the need for wide participation and involvement in planning and design follows.

Ackoff's general philosophical orientation takes on precise form when it is related to the profound changes he believes advanced industrial societies are undergoing. About the time of World War II, he argues (Ackoff, 1974a, 1974c, 1981a), the "machine age"—associated with the industrial revolution—began to give way to the "systems age." The systems age is characterized by increasingly rapid change, interdependence, and complex purposeful systems. It demands that much greater emphasis be put upon learning and adaptation if any kind of stability is to be achieved. This, in turn, requires a radical reorientation of worldview. Machine-age thinking—based upon analysis, reductionism, a search for cause–effect relations, and determinism—must be complemented by systems-age thinking, which proceeds by synthesis and expansionism, tries to grasp producer–product relations, and admits the possibility of free will and choice.

Those who manage corporations in the systems age need to alter the way they think about their enterprises. In the past it has been usual to regard corporations either as machines serving the purposes of their creators or owners, or as organisms serving their own purposes. Today, organizations must be considered as serving three sets of purposes. They are themselves purposeful systems and have their own goals, objectives, and ideals that should be taken into account. But they also contain, as parts, other purposeful systems: individuals, whose aspirations need to be met. And they exist, themselves, as parts of wider purposeful systems whose interests also should be served. Hence corporations have responsibilities to themselves (control problem), to their parts (humanization problem), and to the wider systems of which they themselves are parts (environmentalization problem). Managers, and the social systems scientists who support them, should seek to serve all three sets of purposes, developing all the organization's stakeholders and removing any apparent conflict between them. If this is done, internal and external stakeholders will continue to pursue their interests through the organization and ensure that it remains viable and effective.

Drawing upon his philosophy, and reflecting upon these changing conceptions of the world and of the corporation, Ackoff sets out a new approach to planning that, he believes, is more appropriate to our current predicaments. This "interactive planning" is the main operating tool of Ackoff's S^3. Its aim is to confront "messes"—systems of interdependent problems (Ackoff, 1981b). Interactivist planners do not want to return to the past (like reactivist planners), keep things as they are (like inactivists), or accept some inevitable future (the "predict and prepare" approach of preactivists). They take into account the past, the present, and predictions about the future, but use these only as partial inputs into a process of planning aimed at "designing a desirable future and inventing ways of bringing it about" (Ackoff, 1979b, 1981a). Interactivists believe that the future can be affected by what organizations and their stakeholders do now, and that what they should do is reach out for ideals. If inactivists "satisfice" in seeking to resolve problems and preactivists aim to optimize through solving problems, then interactivists idealize and thus hope to dissolve problems. They change the system and/or the environment in which the problem is embedded so that the problem simply disappears. A good example of the dissolving approach at work in a large machine-tool manufacturing company is provided in Ackoff (1981b).

Three principles underpin interactive planning. These are the participative principle, the principle of continuity, and the holistic principle. The participative principle rests upon two related ideas in Ackoff's thought. The first is that the process of planning is more important than the actual plan produced. It is through involvement in the planning that stakeholders come to understand the organization and the role they can play in it. It follows, of course, that no one can plan for anyone else—because this would take away the main benefit of planning (Ackoff, 1970). The second idea is that all those who are affected by planning should be involved in it. This is a moral necessity for Ackoff, but it also stems directly from the philosophical argument that objectivity in social systems science is "value full."

The participative principle states, therefore, that all stakeholders should participate in the various stages of the planning process. If top management is reluctant to permit full participation, stakeholders can usually gain admittance as "consultants." It is usually then possible to increase their involvement over time. To help in institutionalizing participation, Ackoff (1981a) has produced an organizational design for participative planning. It should be noted here that professional planners are by no means excluded from the interactive planning process; it is simply that their role has changed. They now use their expertise not to plan for others, but to help others plan for themselves. Thus the benefits of the solving approach (and the resolving, supplied by managers, as well) can be included in an essentially dissolving orientation. Perhaps the major paradox of the professional planner's existence—how to quantify quality of life so that it is possible to plan well for others—is also removed, once it is recognized that people should plan for themselves. All that is needed is a planning methodology that people can use, with the aid of professional planners, but ensuring that it is their own ideals and values that are paramount.

The second principle is that of continuity. The values of an organization's stakeholders will change over time, and this will necessitate corresponding changes in plans. Also, unexpected events will occur. The plan may not work as expected, or changes in the organization's environment may change the situation in which it finds itself. No plan can predict everything in advance, so plans, under the principle of continuity, should be constantly revised.

The final principle is the holistic; we should plan simultaneously and interdependently for as many parts and levels of the system as is possible. This can be split into a principle of coordination, which states that units at the same level should plan together and at the same time (because it is the interactions between units that give rise to most problems), and a principle

of integration, which insists that units at different levels plan simultaneously and together (because decisions taken at one level will usually
have effects at other levels as well).

With these principles in mind, we now consider the interactive planning methodology itself. This has five phases. These phases should, however, be regarded as constituting a systemic process and so may be started
in any order; none of the phases, let alone the whole process, should ever
be regarded as completed. The five phases are (Ackoff, 1981a):

- Formulating the mess
- Ends planning
- Means planning
- Resource planning
- Design of implementation and control

Formulating the mess involves analyzing the problems and prospects,
threats, and opportunities facing the organization at present. This requires
three types of study. A "systems analysis" is needed, giving a detailed
picture of the organization, its stakeholders and relationships with its
environment. An "obstruction analysis" sets out any obstacles to corporate
development. "Reference projections" are prepared, which extrapolate on
the organization's present performance in order to predict the future the
organization would be faced with if it did nothing about things, and if
developments in its environment continued in an entirely predictable way.
Synthesizing the results of these three types of study yields a "reference
scenario," which is a formulation of the mess in which the organization
currently finds itself.

Ends planning concerns specifying the ends to be pursued in terms of
ideals, objectives, and goals. The process begins with "idealized design,"
which is both the most unique and most essential feature of Ackoff's
approach. An idealized design is a design for the organization that the
relevant stakeholders would replace the existing system with today if they
were free to do so. It is prepared by going through three steps: selecting a
mission, which outlines general purposes and responsibilities, and aims to
generate commitment; specifying the desired properties stakeholders
agree should be incorporated in the design; and designing the system,
showing how all the desired properties can be obtained.

Idealized design is meant to generate maximum creativity from all
those involved. To ensure this, only two types of constraint upon the
design are admissible. First, it must be technologically feasible and not a
work of science fiction. In other words, it must be possible with known
technology or likely technological developments. Second, it must be oper-
ationally viable. It should be capable of working and surviving if it were

implemented. Constraints of a financial, political, or similar kind are not allowed to restrict the creativity of the design.

Ackoff is equally clear that the aim of idealized design is not to produce a fixed, utopian design that seeks to specify what the system should be like for all time. This would not be sensible since the values and ideals of stakeholders are bound to change. Nor would it be possible, because the designers cannot have at their disposal all the information and knowledge necessary to settle all important design issues or to predict the state of the organization's environment far into the future. For all these reasons it is essential that the designed system be capable of modification and of rapid learning and adaptation. It must be flexible and constantly seeking to improve its own performance. In short, what is intended is the design of the best "ideal-seeking" system that the stakeholders can imagine. This will not be static, like a utopia, but will be in constant flux as it responds to changing values, new knowledge and information, and buffeting from external forces.

An ideal-seeking system obviously requires a very particular kind of organizational design—one that encourages rapid and effective learning and adaptation. Ackoff (1983), in fact, supplies an outline for such a design, which he calls a "responsive, decision system." This contains five essential functions:

- Identification and formulation of threats, opportunities, and problems
- Decision making—determining what to do about these
- Implementation
- Control—monitoring performance and modifying actions
- Acquisition or generation, and distribution of the information necessary to perform the other functions

There are further recommendations in Ackoff's work about the design of appropriate management information systems, issues of organizational structure (e.g., centralization versus decentralization), and, as we mentioned, how to achieve a participative organization.

The remaining three stages of interactive planning are directed at realizing the idealized design as closely as possible. During means planning, policies and procedures are generated and examined to decide whether they are capable of helping to close the gap between the desired future, the idealized design, and the future the organization is currently locked into according to the reference scenario. Creativity is needed to discover appropriate ways of bringing the organization toward the desirable future invented by its stakeholders. Alternative means must be carefully evaluated and a selection made.

Resource planning sees four types of resources being considered: inputs, facilities and equipment, personnel, and money. For each of the chosen means, suitable resources have to be acquired. It must be determined how much of each resource is wanted, when it is wanted, and how it can be obtained if not already held.

Design of implementation and control looks at procedures for ensuring that all the decisions made hitherto are carried out. Who is to do what, when, where, and how is decided. Implementation is achieved and the results monitored to ensure that plans are being realized. The outcome is fed back into the planning process so that learning is possible and improvements can be devised.

The advantages said to follow from pursuing interactive planning are many. In particular, Ackoff claims (1979b, 1981a) that the methodology:

- Facilitates the participation of all stakeholders
- Allows incorporation of aesthetic values into planning
- Generates consensus
- Generates commitment and mobilizes participants
- Releases suppressed creativity and harnesses it to individual and organizational development
- Expands the participants' concept of feasibility
- Eases implementation

Ackoff's development of S^3, with its commitment to the notion that problems should be dissolved by "designing a desirable future and inventing ways of bringing it about," has taken him a long way from some of his erstwhile colleagues stuck in the predict-and-prepare paradigm of hard OR. In Ackoff's (1977) view, those who continue to work in the vein of hard systems thinking, with its emphasis on optimization and objectivity, inevitably opt out of tackling the important social issues of the age. To cling to optimization in a world of multiple values and rapid change is to lose one's grip on reality. The emphasis has to be upon learning and adapting. Objectivity in the conventional sense is also a myth. It has to be rethought as resulting from the open interaction of multifarious individual subjectivities; hence the need for wide participation and involvement in interactive planning.

Checkland's Soft Systems Methodology (SSM)

The aim of Checkland and his colleagues when they began their action-research program was to produce a systems methodology capable of intervening in "soft" problem situations and of sharpening up, under special circumstances, to tackle more structured problems. The systems engineering methodology that was initially employed demanded well-structured problems and clearly defined objectives and measures of performance. Obviously, these demands had to be loosened and the methodology radically adapted to make it appropriate for dealing with the complexity and ambiguity of the softer contexts in which it was now to be applied. What eventually emerged after considerable project work, and reflection upon the experience gained, was Checkland's soft systems methodology.

In the first full account of the methodology, published in 1972 (Checkland, 1976), Checkland describes three of the most significant early project experiences that led to the formulation of SSM. In all three it was clear that serious problems existed, but the clients simply could not say what these were in precise terms. Each of the problem situations was, therefore, vague and unstructured. One of the projects, in a textile firm, gave rise to at least a dozen candidates for the role of "the problem." Generalizing from the three projects, Checkland was able to specify what the key features of SSM had to be, and how these differentiated SSM from hard approaches.

First, in confronting softer problems, the analysis phase of a methodology should not be pursued in systems terms. In the absence of agreed goals and objectives, and an obvious hierarchy of systems to be engineered, using systems ideas too early can only lead to distorting the problem situation and to jumping to premature conclusions. Analysis, in soft systems approaches, should consist of building up the richest possible picture of the problem situation and not of trying to represent it in a systems account. Second, given that it is not obvious which system needs to be engineered, it is more appropriate to draw out of the analysis a range of systems relevant to improving the problem situation, each expressing a particular viewpoint of it. These notional systems can be named in "root definitions" and developed more fully in "conceptual models." The use of SSM will therefore lead to the construction of a number of models to be compared with the real world, rather than just one as in hard methodologies. Finally, while the models produced by hard approaches are blueprints for design, conceptual models are contributions to a debate about change. Hard methodologies, therefore, lead to the design of systems, SSM to the implementation of agreed changes.

Although the three characteristics just discussed may be regarded as distinguishing features of SSM, this does not mean that the job of describing the methodology is particularly easy. Difficulties arise in trying to capture the way in which the methodology is actually used in practice. During the early period of development and promotion of SSM, it was necessary to present it as a stage-by-stage process with definite outcomes at the end of each stage and to emphasize the procedures necessary for properly carrying out each stage. Later, such a presentation was seen to be counterproductive since it encourages users into thinking that the methodology is a kind of technique, and runs counter to the spirit of SSM as a "learning system." I shall follow the convention of going through the methodology stage by stage (since it is virtually impossible to introduce it any other way), but readers should be warned that it is meant to be used much more flexibly in practice, with constant iteration between different stages and quickly around the whole methodological cycle. Indeed, in recent avant-garde uses, the methodology has been employed more to orientate projects by providing a basis for reflection on what has been and is being done than to give strict guidelines for action (Checkland and Scholes, 1990).

Other problems arise because even those who might be regarded as familiar with the methodology and practiced with it seem to use it in rather different ways (Atkinson, 1986). Checkland would want to retain considerable flexibility for practitioners but needs to be able to say that some examples are simply not proper uses of SSM. This is a significant point because many declared uses of the methodology turn out, on closer examination, to be following "hard" reasoning, although dressed in soft language. In order to judge whether SSM is being employed correctly or not requires reference to the philosophy on which it is based. That is why it is even more important for those learning how to use SSM to become completely familiar with its underlying philosophy than it is for them to be adept at the techniques that support its various stages. Checkland has spent considerable time and effort explicating this philosophy, and I shall deal with the main conclusions later in the section. Indeed, despite the achievement of the methodology itself, the early highly innovative ideas, and the later patient building of the superstructural support for these ideas, any claim for the preeminence of Checkland among soft systems thinkers would have to rest upon his more rigorous working out of the different theoretical assumptions underlying the hard and soft systems traditions. Suffice it to say, for the moment, that the methodology cannot be fully grasped or properly used without a thorough understanding of the philosophy on which it is based.

Bearing these provisos firmly in mind, the methodology can now be summarized in terms of the seven stages or activities recognized by Checkland (1981a, 1989). Reference should be made throughout this discussion to the representation of SSM in Figure 6.2. In the first and second stages, a problem situation is entered and analyzed, and a "rich picture" of the situation is built up. As was mentioned, it is important not to impose a definition on the problem by viewing it in systems terms. The aim is not to delimit particular problems "out there" in the real world, but to gain an understanding of a situation with which various actors feel a degree of unease. The way of gathering information for display in the rich picture has changed as SSM has evolved. The early guidelines, which emphasized finding out about structure and process and thinking about the relationship between them (the "climate"), have given way to an analysis in three stages.

Analysis 1 considers the intervention itself and the roles of client(s), problem solvers(s), and problem owners. Analysis 2 takes a cultural view of the social system, looking at social roles, norms of behavior, and what values are used in judging role performance. The work of Davies (e.g., 1988), who has argued that the practice of SSM would benefit from the more explicit analysis of culture, has contributed here. Early recognition of cultural aspects of the situation can assist the process of arriving at recommendations that are "culturally feasible." Analysis 3 examines the

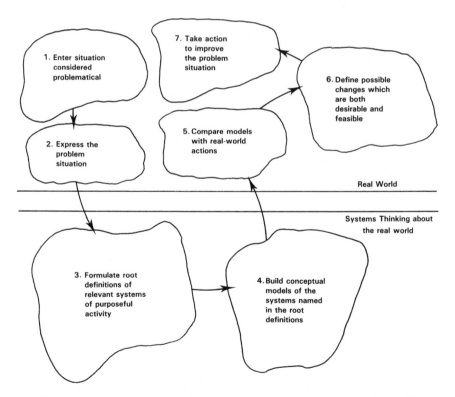

FIGURE 6.2. The Learning Cycle of Soft Systems Methodology (after Checkland, 1989)

politics of the problem situation and how power is obtained and used. Stowell's (e.g., 1989) thoughts on power as manifest in various "commodities" (e.g., command of resources, personality, talent) that are exchanged or otherwise used in organizations have had some impact on this. Understanding of how power is disposed might make it possible to assuage some of its more baneful effects. The rich picture, which is the outcome of Stage 2, is a pictorial, cartoonlike representation of the problem situation that (it is hoped) expresses it in a way that will assist with the insightful choice of relevant systems.

The third stage or activity involves the preparation of "root definitions" from the systems that appear relevant to the problem situation. A root definition should be a condensed representation of a system in its most fundamental form. To ensure that root definitions are well formulated, they should be constructed giving consideration to all the elements brought to mind by the mnemonic CATWOE (customers, actors, transformation process, *Weltanschauung,* owners, environmental constraints). As an example of a well-formulated root definition, Checkland (1989) provides the following: "A professionally-manned system in a manufacturing company which, in the light of market forecasts and raw material availability, makes detailed production plans for a defined period." This is, in fact, a primary-task root definition setting out an official, explicit task to be performed. Issue-based definitions should also be put forward at Stage 3, designed to address particular issues of consequence in the problem situation (e.g., conflict between two departments). As the W in CATWOE indicates, each root definition reflects a different way of looking at the problem situation. For example, in considering a prison, it might be helpful to consider it as a punishment system, a rehabilitation system, a system for taking revenge, a system to protect society, and as a system that constitutes a "university of crime" (Checkland, 1987). It follows that there are not correct or incorrect root definitions, only more or less insightful ones.

Stage 4 involves the construction of conceptual models of the systems defined in the root definitions. Conceptual models consist initially of seven or so verbs, structured in logical sequence and representing those minimum activities that are necessary to produce the systems enshrined in the root definitions. They can be developed to further levels of resolution by taking any of the activities as the source of a new root definition, which can then itself be modeled in more detail. Conceptual models do not seek to describe the real world or some ideal system to be engineered, but are merely accentuated, one-sided views of possible, relevant human activity systems. For this reason it is important that they are derived solely from their root definitions so that a complementary pair of artifacts is produced; the root definition expressing what the system *is,* the conceptual model what it *does*. Once constructed, conceptual models can be checked against Checkland's (1981a) "formal system model" to ensure that they are not fundamentally deficient. This is also the point in SSM where other systems thinking can be introduced as appropriate. For example, an analyst modeling a whole institution might review a conceptual model in the light of the logic of Beer's VSM. The general structure of conceptual models is shown in Figure 6.3.

Conceptual models constructed in the approved manner can now (Stage 5) be formally compared with what was perceived to exist in the real world according to the rich picture produced at Stage 2. Four different

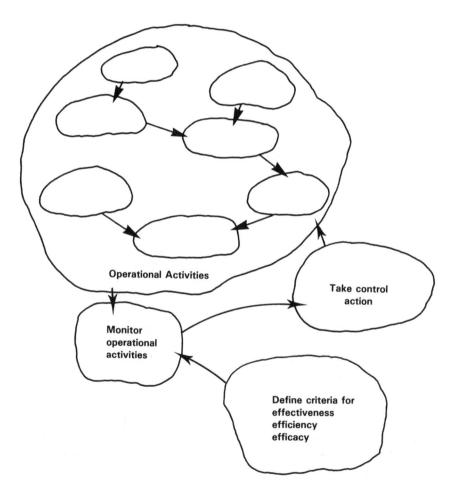

Operational Activities

Take control action

Monitor operational activities

Define criteria for effectiveness efficiency efficacy

FIGURE 6.3. The General Structure of a Model of a Purposeful Activity System (after Checkland, 1989)

ways of doing such a comparison have been developed (Checkland 1981a, 1989). Whichever method is used, the comparison should help to structure a debate about possible change among the actors concerned with the problem situation. Thus the methodology facilitates a social process in which Ws are held up for examination and their implications are discussed. Stage 6 should see the analyst(s) and the various actors agreeing on changes that are both desirable and feasible. Changes that appear desirable on the basis of systems models may still not be feasible given the history of the situation, the power structure, or prevailing attitudes. For example, it may seem desirable to implement a quality control system, but only feasible to set up procedures for dealing with customer complaints. Once agreement has been reached, the analyst (Stage 7) helps with action to implement the changes. The conclusion of the methodological cycle does not see a "solution" to the original problem but merely the emergence of another, different problem situation. Problem resolving in social systems is, for Checkland, a never-ending process of learning.

It will be useful to outline some of the important features of this methodology before becoming involved in discussion of the philosophy and theory upon which Checkland argues SSM is premised. Most of the points I shall make at this stage can be linked to Checkland's (1985a) assertion that the methodology is doubly systemic; combining a cyclic learning process with the use of systems models within that process.

The cyclic learning process that SSM seeks to articulate builds naturally upon the complex social processes, including processes of management, that normally occur in organizations. Organizations, for Checkland, are made up of different individuals and groups possessing different evaluations of the situation they are in. Their evaluations will overlap to some extent (otherwise, the organization could hardly exist), but there will usually be sufficient difference among world views to give rise constantly to issues that have to be managed. SSM takes as its task the management of the "myths and meanings" (Checkland, 1989) that are so central to the functioning of organizations, because they are the means by which individuals make sense of their situations. The aim therefore is to structure a debate, among different individuals and groups, in which different assumptions about the world are held up for examination and discussed. This debate does not lose touch with the facts and logic of the situation, since the models used to help structure it are systems models relevant to the real-world problem situation. But it is made clear that the "facts and logic" can be interpreted differently from different perspectives. If successful the debate will lead, if not to the creation of shared perceptions, at least to an accommodation between conflicting viewpoints and interests so that desirable change can be implemented.

The participants in a soft systems study learn their way to a new conception of feasibility as attitudes and perceptions are tested and changed. Changes that could not have been conceived of because of the culture of the situation before the study began can seem obvious by the time it has finished. In order for this to occur, of course, the process of using SSM must be as participative as possible, including all interested parties. It is also essential that participants come to "own" the study by being involved in using the methodology. The soft systems practitioner is as concerned to give away this approach to making decisions as to provide a set of recommendations for action.

The notion that the methodology is a cyclic learning process draws upon Vickers's account of the process of appreciation and the way appreciative systems originate, develop, and change in organizations. SSM is said by Checkland (1985a) to articulate in a formal way the process Vickers calls appreciation. Also explicit (Checkland, 1981b) is the connection with Churchman's work on inquiring systems. The methodology searches for a possible Lockean consensus through a Kantian and Hegelian route in which different assumptions about reality are counterposed. SSM is Singerian in that it accepts that learning is never ending and should be sought in the heroic mood.

The methodology is doubly systemic in that it uses systems models as part of the systemic learning process just described. Checkland (1981b) is prepared to make an "epistemological commitment" to systems models as a means of seeking to understand the world outside ourselves, because that world does appear to be densely interconnected and to reveal a degree of coherence, interconnectedness, and interrelatedness. Systems models are constructed during the formal systems thinking stages (4 and 5) of SSM and input into the real world to help structure a debate in which different perceptions of the facts and logic of the situation and different value positions are revealed and discussed. Appropriate models for this had to be invented; thus the "human activity system" concept was born. The idea was that pure models of purposeful activity (human activity system models) could be built, each expressing explicitly a particular viewpoint on the problem situation. These would contain sets of logically linked activities that when combined together produced, as an emergent property, a purposeful whole. As we know, SSM seeks to assist learning by making a comparison between these models and what is perceived to be taking place in the real world.

In reflecting upon the shift of perspective achieved by SSM, Checkland (1983) suggests—and here we move into somewhat deeper theoretical waters—that whereas hard systems methodologies are based upon a paradigm of optimization, his own methodology embraces a paradigm of learning. Hard methodologies are concerned with achieving objectives. They are modeled on the natural scientific method and so aim to provide generalizable knowledge about structured occurrences. They seek this knowledge in management science by concentrating on the "logic of the situation" in organizations seen as driven by the official goals. Thus the world is taken to contain systems whose performance can be optimized by following systematic procedures. Unfortunately for the hard approach, in social systems the logic of the situation is usually much less significant in terms of what happens than the cultural interconnections forged from the meanings attributed to the situation by individuals and groups. SSM, recognizing this, seeks to work with the different perceptions of the situation, setting in motion a systemic process of learning in which different viewpoints are discussed and examined in a manner that should lead to purposeful action in pursuit of improvement.

Checkland's methodology takes reality to be problematical and ceases to worry about knowing it ontologically, instead concentrating on using a systemic methodology to investigate problems arising from the existence of different accounts of that reality. Put concisely (Checkland, 1989), it shifts "systemicity from the world to the process of enquiry into the world." Because hard systems thinking depends on objectives and purposes already being agreed (or imposed)—the very thing SSM concentrates on engineering—hard methodologies are a special case of the soft. They become relevant when learning reduces to optimizing because, given agreement over goals, only one system appears relevant, and problem resolving turns on the best way to design that.

Using slightly different terminology, Checkland (1985a) argues that hard systems methodologies are predicated on the goal-seeking model of human behavior as exemplified in Herbert Simon's work, while SSM reflects a model of human behavior oriented to "relationship–maintaining" as set down in the writings of Vickers. This is demonstrated by the concern of hard systems thinkers with *how* we should achieve known goals, with prediction and control and with optimization. In soft systems thinking, the emphasis is rather on *what* we ought to do and on participation and learning.

Checkland (1981a) judges other systems thinking according to how far it has managed to rid itself of the goal-seeking and optimizing orientation. Hard approaches, as we have seen, stand irredeemably condemned, suitable for only a small subset of the difficulties that confront managers. The work of the sociotechnical thinkers and of Beer is seen to rest firmly in the hard tradition. These authors each offer only one model of the whole system, which they take to encapsulate the optimum organizational arrangements for an enterprise intent on goal seeking. SSM prefers to generalize the methodology rather than the content of models. Ackoff's interactive planning is taken to resemble soft systems methodology in some respects, but too much use of the goal-seeking model is made, as with the emphasis put on the idealized design of the future. For Checkland, attempting to define an ideal future and get consensus on it presents immense difficulties. There is also evidence that Ackoff continues to believe in systems "in the world." Even Churchman does not escape completely from the hard paradigm. His work is wedded to the notion of design, which Checkland takes to be essentially a hard concept. Further—and this is extremely controversial, as this book's account of Churchman's work shows—Checkland believes Churchman's main concern to be with the design of goal-seeking systems in a systemic world (1981a, 1988).

What Checkland (1981a, 1981b) knows he has achieved at a still deeper theoretical level, and what all the above arguments announce, is a complete break with the functionalism/positivism that has traditionally dominated the systems approach. SSM is closer to the interpretive sociology of Weber than the functionalism of Durkheim, and to the phenomenology of Husserl and Schutz—and the hermeneutics of Dilthey—than to the positivism of Comte and Durkheim. It has more in common with the action theory Silverman (1970) constructed in opposition to the dominant "systems" approach to organizations than to the functionalist organizations-as-systems approach he attacks. Checkland rightly argues, therefore, that the social theory implicit in his methodology is interpretive rather than functionalist, and that its underlying philosophical base is in phenomenology rather than positivism. In soft systems methodology, systems are seen as the mental constructs of observers in the world. Different descriptions of reality, based on different worldviews, are embodied in root definitions. These root definitions are turned into conceptual models that are explicitly one-sided representations expressing one *Weltanschauung*—in other words, they are Weberian ideal types. A debate is then structured around the implications of these different perceptions of what reality could be like. Systemicity is transferred "from the world to the process of enquiry into the world."

Referring to Burrell and Morgan's (1979) grid of sociological paradigms, Checkland argues that the implied social theory of hard systems approaches is functionalism. They are clearly regulative and objectivist in orientation. SSM, however, is more subjectivist in character and extends somewhat toward the radical change axis (refer to Figure 2.1), so

> the social theory implicit in soft systems methodology ... would lie in the left-hand quadrants with hermeneutics and phenomenology, although the position would be not too far left of the center line because the methodology will over a period of time yield a picture of the common structurings which char-

acterize the social collectivities within which it works. Also, given the analyst's complete freedom to select relevant systems which, when compared with the expression of the problem situation, embody either incremental or radical change, the area occupied must include some of the "subjective/radical" quadrant. (Checkland, 1981a, pp. 280–281)

In support of his claim that the implied social theory of SSM embraces aspects of radical humanism (the subjective/radical quadrant), Checkland refers to a paper by Mingers (1980) that reveals some apparent similarities between the social theory of Habermas and SSM. This matter will require further attention in the upcoming "Analysis and Assessment" section.

As a further argument, Checkland suggests that the failure experienced by himself and his colleagues when trying to use systems engineering, in their action research program, to solve problems in social systems discredits the functionalist account of social reality. In contrast, the success of SSM suggests that the phenomenological version of what the social world is like is correct. Examples of the success of SSM can be found in Checkland (1981a, 1985b), Checkland and Scholes (1990), and Wilson (1984).

Checkland likes to insist that SSM has been derived experientially on the basis of his action-research program. If this is meant to downplay the role of theory then it is misleading, for it is clear that the development of the methodology has benefited all along from being theoretically informed: early on by the work of Churchman and Vickers, later by the interpretive philosophical and sociological theories of Dilthey, Husserl, Schutz, and Weber and the social theory classification of Burrell and Morgan. Certainly it is because he has been able to theorize so thoroughly his break with hard systems thinking that his writings do not betray the "tensions" between hard and soft positions he identifies in Ackoff and Churchman. Checkland is the purest of the soft systems thinkers because he recognized the theoretical direction in which soft systems thinking was heading, made this explicit, and consciously constructed SSM on the basis of new, interpretive theoretical foundations. It is because of this, more even than because of the methodology itself, that he has made such a great contribution to systems thinking and practice.

Soft Systems Thinking and Its Critics

Some general conclusions about the nature of soft systems thinking will now be proffered as a way of leading into the most common criticisms leveled at the approach. The writers taken to be representative of soft systems thinking do have their differences—to which the reader has seen Checkland alluding—but it is the similarities in the four methodologies that are most significant. All are concerned to cope with ill-structured problems, or messes, at the strategic level. All are opposed to tackling messes by the method of reductionism. Rather than attempting to identify and analyze systems in the real world, all four approaches prefer to work with the different perceptions of systems that exist in peoples' minds. Multiple perceptions of reality are admitted and explored. Values are included explicitly rather than being excluded (in theory) from the methodological process. The privileged role of experts in the systems approach is questioned. The aim in each case is to encourage learning so that an accommodation can be reached among participants involved with a problem situation.

Taking all this into consideration, it is clear that the positivism/functionalism that underpins the organizations-as-systems approach and hard systems thinking has been abandoned in soft systems thinking. An epistemological break (in the sense of a shift between paradigms) has occurred, and a new direction in management science has been opened up based upon other philosophical/sociological foundations. If this epistemological break has only been fully theorized in Checkland, it is implicit as well in all the other methodologies considered. Despite occasional functionalist language, it is perverse to read Churchman, Mason and Mitroff, and Ackoff in other than an interpretive way—an argument for which I shall provide still further evidence in the next section.

Another argument that can be advanced in favor of the unity of the soft systems tradition is the consistency found in the criticisms made of the work of its chief proponents. Churchman, Ackoff, and Checkland are criticized for remarkably similar things. In reviewing these criticisms I shall adopt the policy employed with hard systems thinking and summarize the points made under some general headings, not always attributing them to their sources. The reader should therefore refer to the original papers for more detailed expression of the criticisms and to understand the evolution of the critical stance. These are Chesterton et al. (1975), Rosenhead (1976, 1984), Bryer (1979), Thomas and Lockett (1979), Bevan (1980), Jackson (1982, 1983), Burrell (1983), and Mingers (1984). What is remarkable about this assault is that it has come not by way of counterattack from the hard systems thinkers and cyberneticians bludgeoned in soft systems writings, but from advocates of other, more radical theoretical positions anticipating what would now be called the critical systems perspective. In Dando and Bennett's (1981) terms, proponents of the "official" position in OR and systems have been unable to defend themselves against "reformist" soft systems thinkers and have been intellectually routed. It is a group of "revolutionary"-minded workers in systems and OR who have taken up the reformist challenge and sought to advance the debate further.

There are perhaps four main thrusts to the critical attack on soft systems thinking. I shall consider these in turn, taking appropriate examples to show how each tells against the work of Churchman, Ackoff, and Checkland.

First, it is argued that soft systems thinking is set squarely on a consensus worldview. The alternative position, that deep-seated conflict is endemic in organizations and society, is not given serious attention. This means that soft methodologies are constructed on a very one-sided appreciation of social reality. Ackoff, for example, is accused of believing that there is a basic community of interests among stakeholders that makes it likely that they will enter into interactive planning and participate freely and openly in idealized design. If any conflict of interest does arise between system, supersystem, and subsystems, it can be dissolved by appealing to this basic community of interests at a higher level of desirability (Ackoff, 1975).

Ackoff, then, apparently denies the existence of fundamental conflict and has to deny its existence. If irreconcilable conflict between stakeholders is frequent (as some assert it is), then his methodology is impotent because no agreement can be reached in such cases concerning the idealized future. Ackoff (1975) rather fixes the argument in his favor by defining irreconcilable conflicts as those that involve logically incompatible ends. Since his methodology is oriented to the world of ideas, to expanding individual conceptions of the feasible, it is always going to be open to him to claim that a conflict is resolvable at a higher level of desirability. As Bryer (1979) argues, "It is an axiom of Ackoff's systems view that a 'higher' system can always be found as the only limits to systems boundaries are the subjective conceptualisations of the analyst." In the real world, however, it is easy to see that a social structure can operate such that it is impossible for all different groups to achieve their ends. Rosenhead (1976) argues that "only by abolishing the sweat-shop owner as a social category can his interest and those of his labourers be made compatible." From this perspective we need to talk about the social incompatibility of ends, not their logical incompatibility.

Checkland's SSM has similarly been accused of being consensual (Thomas and Lockett, 1979), playing down conflicts of real interest and believing that any conflicts that do exist can be resolved, temporarily at least, through a debate structured around root definitions and conceptual models. The same argument could be made against Churchman's belief in the possibility of achieving synthesis. Soft systems thinkers assert that the social world is basically consensual, the critics that it is (sometimes at least) characterized by asymmetry of power, structural conflict, and contradiction.

Second, it is argued by the critics that it is only because soft systems thinkers believe in a basically consensual social world that they are able to take the possibility of participation for granted and see it as the remedy for so many organizational problems. Participation is essential to soft systems thinking, philosophically because it provides the justification for the objectivity of the results and practically because it generates creativity and ensures implementation. Perhaps because of its significance, soft systems thinkers play down the obstacles to full and effective participation. To get started, Ackoff's interactive planning depends on all the stakeholders being prepared to enter into participative planning about the future. But will the powerful be willing to forgo their dominant position and submit their privileges to the vagaries of idealized design?

Even if interactive planning can be gotten under way, another problem will be encountered. The methodology depends for the objectivity of its results on free and open discussion between stakeholders, but planning is complex and time-consuming. We cannot realistically expect that less privileged stakeholders will be able to participate equally in the planning process. Despite whatever help the analyst can give to less fortunate groups, the various stakeholders will enter the interactive planning process with widely divergent informational, political, and economic resources. The less privileged may additionally feel threatened by the massive resources that can be mobilized by the powerful, and limit their demands to what is "realistic" (Rosenhead, 1984). The organization will already represent a "mobilization of bias" against them in a way that requires no representation or advocacy (Bevan, 1980). The less privileged may even find themselves under the sway of a dominant ideology, through the mists of which they fail altogether to recognize their own true interests. Any discussion or debate among stakeholders can only, therefore, be exceptionally constrained.

Thomas and Lockett (1979) have suggested that power can shape which world views come to the fore and influence change in Checkland's SSM. Jackson (1982) has argued at length that the debate about feasible and desirable change at Stages 5 and 6 of SSM will be crucially inhibited by power imbalances deriving from the structure of organizations and society. In general, therefore, it seems that the results obtained by soft systems methodologies will favor the powerful. It is impossible for them, in many circumstances, to bring about the objectivity that their originators seek.

Third, it is said that the belief of soft systems thinkers in a consensual social world, and in the efficacy of participation, is only sustained because they artificially limit the scope of their projects so as not to challenge their clients' or sponsors' fundamental interests. Burrell (1983) is convinced that the reason why Checkland is never faced with incommensurable worldviews is that he works with a community sharing similar interests (i.e., managers). This is a community, moreover, that usually has the power to impose agreement on any other groups involved in its proceedings. Thomas and Lockett (1979) can quite easily see how working for powerful clients will restrict the emergence of alternative, radical world views in SSM and lead only to reformist recommendations for change. The client can restrict the information fed into the project at the analysis stage. If the soft systems practitioner wants to continue working for the client, he or she will quickly abandon any radical root definitions as not being "culturally feasible" given the realities of the problem situation. The choice of which changes to implement will be subject to existing decision-making processes in which the client is dominant.

If the position of powerful stakeholders is not threatened by soft systems studies because significant issues can be kept off the agenda for debate, then the powerful might be willing to let other groups participate. And it might seem that all stakeholders share common interests. If, however, soft systems practitioners were to challenge the hierarchical nature of organizations, the ultimate decision-making rights of powerful stakeholders, or the unequal distribution of organizational resources to different stakeholders, then they would soon provoke conflicts that revealed deep status, economic, and other inequalities in organizations that could not be spirited away by soft approaches. In his researches Ackoff goes only so far as "circumstances permit." No matter, as Rosenhead (1976) states:

> These "circumstances" are not facts of nature, but are the consequences of particular social institutions (especially the projects sponsors) and their purposes. The circumstances "permit" acts of social engineering which appear to resolve social conflicts; they do not "permit" analyses or acts which challenge the sponsors' interests.

Finally, related to the other points (at the root of the other points according to Mingers, 1984), soft systems thinking is criticized for its "subjectivism" or its "idealism," and for its consequent failure to come to terms with structural features of social reality such as conflict and power. The social world may very well be created by people, the criticism runs, but it is not necessarily created by them in the full awareness of what they are doing. Further, it is created by people who have conflicting aims and intentions and who bring different resources to bear when the social construction is taking place. It follows that the social world escapes the understanding and control of any one person or group of people. It takes on the form of a highly complex and structured external reality that exercises constraint on the individuals who make it up.

Churchman, like other soft systems thinkers, neglects objective features of social reality. The highly structured, resistant social world studied by functionalist and structuralist social scientists is foreign to him. His book *The Systems Approach and Its Enemies* surprises one reviewer (Sica, 1981), because in a book supposedly about social systems we are told remarkably little about what they are actually like. Because for Churchman there are no objective aspects of social systems to worry about, bringing about change means simply changing the way people think about the world—changing their *Weltanschauungen.* But there are problems here. From the point of view of objectivist social science, Ws are not so easily changed. They are closely linked to other social facts (political and economic) in the social totality. Changing Ws may depend crucially on first of all changing these other social facts. If we really wish to bring about change, we need some understanding of the laws that govern the transformation of the social totality. Only then can the real blockages to change (which may not be in the world of ideas) be located and pressure applied. While he confines himself to the world of ideas of a society, all that Churchman can guarantee by the process of dialectical inquiry is a continual readjustment of the ideological consensus.

Burrell (1983) argues that Checkland always sees conflict as related to a clash of values and not to a difference in material interest. For Ackoff, too, it can be argued, conflict is always at the ideological level and is essentially dealt with by ideological manipulation. Perhaps it is possible to alleviate conflict temporarily at the ideological level by getting people to believe they have interests in common. But the subjective beliefs of groups about their interests do not necessarily coincide with their objective interests. Permanent reconciliation of conflicts between stakeholders might need to be in terms of objective and not merely subjective interests. All soft systems thinkers are criticized for paying too little attention to power. To Rosenhead (1984), the fact that Ackoff and Churchman ignore conflict and power is attributable to their "idealism"—the fact that "they ascribe prime motive power to the force of ideas." Another consequence of this idealism is that it limits their ability to understand how change comes about and, hence, their ability to promote change.

Unlike hard systems thinkers under attack, Ackoff (1975, 1982) and Checkland (1982) have responded vigorously to the charges leveled against their methodologies. They do not think much of any of the critics' arguments.

If his work appears consensual to the critics, Ackoff believes it is because they are obsessed with the notion of irresolvable conflicts. Ackoff (1982) has never encountered one of these in more than 300 projects on which he has worked. All the conflicts he has met he has been able to address with the interactive-planning approach. He suspects that the critics merely assert that such conflicts exist; if they went out and tried to use interactive planning on conflicts they see as irresolvable, they might find out differently.

With regard to participation, Ackoff (1975) accepts that it might meet with some resistance from powerful stakeholders. But there are ways around this, such as by introducing stakeholders first as consultants and then gradually increasing their role. The ability of low-level stakeholders to participate can, of course, be aided by professional planners. The idea that such stakeholders might not recognize their own true interests is elitist. In any case, just because full and equal participation cannot be immediately realized is a poor reason for not making whatever progress can be made. A similar point to this last one is made by Checkland (1982) in criticizing the "utopian" demands Jackson insists on for the legitimate use of SSM. Since SSM is a learning system it might, given the chance, assist in changing things in a manner that can contribute to realizing those demands. Better incremental change, Ackoff and Checkland are arguing, than waiting for some judgment day when all wrongs will be corrected.

Checkland (1982) accepts that SSM has tended to be used in a rather managerialist and conservative way. But he argues that because it is impossible to know in advance what learning will be generated by the methodology, it must in principle be capable of bringing about emancipatory/radical changes as well as regulatory/conservative results. Ackoff (1982) does not apologize for spending much of his time working with managers. They are often the most enlightened social group, he finds, and can see that benefiting other stakeholders will also benefit themselves.

Finally, Ackoff (1975, 1982) simply does not accept the existence of the structural aspects of social reality that the critics discuss. The chief obstruction between people and the future they most desire is the people themselves and their limited ability to think creatively and imaginatively. Provide people with a mission, with a mobilizing idea, and the constraints on their development will largely disappear. Checkland (1982) similarly argues that the critics assert rather than demonstrate the existence of objective and constraining features of social reality. Checkland's experience (unlike that of Rosenhead, 1984) is that *Weltanschauungen* are amenable to change and do alter—sometimes incrementally, sometimes radically. Critics, therefore, should use SSM to try to bring about the changes they deem desirable.

What the critics of soft systems thinking are essentially arguing is that just as hard systems thinking has a limited domain of effective and legitimate application, so too does soft systems thinking. If it is impossible to achieve genuine consensus through open and free participation, if there is fundamental conflict, if *Weltanschauungen* refuse to shift, if power determines the outcome of debate, then soft systems methodologies cannot be properly employed in many situations. It is obviously of importance to soft systems thinkers to resist this conclusion. The following "Analysis and Assessment" section should provide us with the necessary overview to be able to decide the issue between soft systems thinking and its critics.

Analysis and Assessment

Soft systems methodologies do not give a great deal of useful support to the technical interest in predicting and controlling natural and social systems. In social systems design and SAST, there is no intention to do so. Mitroff and Mason (1981) dismiss a critique of their work because it assesses SAST as an approach to well-structured problems rather than what it is intended to be—an approach to ill-structured problems. There would be no difficulty with this if the value of other systems approaches that did support the technical interest were fully recognized by Churchman and by Mason and Mitroff. Unfortunately, this is not altogether the case. While they would accept the usefulness of hard systems thinking once ill-structured problems had been tamed, there is no similar recognition of cybernetics as a guide to strategic action and the improvement of steering capacities. There seems to be an unwarranted assumption that once problems arising from the existence of different worldviews have been dissolved, then the difficulties stemming from nonhuman complexity of communication, control, and organization will disappear as well. Thus Mason and Mitroff (1981, p. 10) support Rittle's conclusion that "every formulation of a wicked problem corresponds to a statement of solution and vice-versa. Understanding the problem is synonymous with solving it." This is to miss altogether the daunting problems concerned with organizing large-scale complex systems that are identified and worked upon in organizational cybernetics.

Ackoff does recognize the value of systems approaches that support the technical interest, and incorporates aspects of the hard, organizations-as-systems, and cybernetic traditions in his own work. His "responsive, decision system" is a cybernetic model that, in intent and in some of its features, resembles Beer's VSM. However, apart of course from in OR, Ackoff could not claim to be an innovative thinker in this area.

Checkland's is a difficult case. We have seen him using systems models as an input into a systemic learning process. These are rigorously constructed, with root definitions being based on CATWOE and the formal system model available to check that conceptual models are not fundamentally deficient. The formal system model incorporates cybernetic principles and is "a compilation of 'management' components which arguably have to be present if a set of activities is to comprise a system capable of purposeful activity" (Checkland, 1981a, p. 173). However, as we know, conceptual models are used only to help structure debate and not to suggest what ought to exist in the world. Hence Checkland is prepared to lose most of the value of his cybernetic thinking. The feasible and desirable changes that are eventually implemented may derive from a number of different models, and there is no check that the set of changes made are such as to support a viable system. To Checkland it is the creation of shared appreciative systems that contributes most to the survival and effectiveness of organizations, and not the design of logical communication and control systems. One is left wondering why so much emphasis is put in SSM on building elegant conceptual models accurately derived from well-formulated root definitions.

The main value of soft systems thinking, in terms of Habermas's schema, lies in the support it offers to the practical interest in promoting intersubjective understanding. All the methodologies considered offer effective means of securing and expanding the possibility of mutual understanding among individuals in social systems—whether through dialectical debate, focusing attention on an idealized design, or engaging in a cyclic learning process. It is indeed an incredible achievement that the systems approach associated in the minds of many, including Habermas, with the functionalism of Parsons and the "advanced technocratic consciousness" displayed in Luhmann's systems theory should be the source of methodologies providing the most effective assistance yet developed for the practical interest. It is a tribute to the systems idea and to the work of Churchman, Ackoff, and Checkland. However, before we get carried away by that achievement, we need to remind ourselves that appropriate rationalization in the sphere of social interaction demands not just any kind of understanding, but genuine understanding based on communication free from distortion. Methodologies purporting to support the practical interest must pay attention to the possibility that systematically distorted communication might jeopardize the emergence of *genuine* shared purposes. To what extent do soft systems methodologies give consideration to this matter?

The answer is not very much. We have seen the critics arguing that Churchman fails to take account of any of the objective features of the social world that might lead to distorted communication, and that Ackoff's interactive planning can only lead to exceptionally constrained discussion or debate among stakeholders. I offer detailed argument now in relation to Checkland's methodology. The argument centers around two of the key stages in SSM—Stages 5 and 6, the discussion stages. It is here that the various relevant systems, expressed in root definitions and conceptual models, are examined and compared to what is perceived to exist in the real world, and that agreed changes emerge. If these changes are to reflect a true consensus among the actors, the discussion stages must conform as far as possible to the model of communicative competence proposed by Habermas. All actors must be willing to enter into discourse, and this must be conducted in conditions that approximate the ideal speech situation. All participants must have equal chances to select and employ speech acts and to assume dialogue roles. There must be unlimited discussion that is free from constraints of domination, whether the source of these is the behavior of other parties or communication barriers secured through ideology or neurosis. The ability of some participants to impose sanctions on others (because they are more powerful) must not affect the outcome of the discussion.

Only if such conditions are met will the consensus at the end of the debate reflect the strength of the better argument and not simply various constraints on discussion. Of course, in organizations and societies characterized by great inequalities, the kind of unconstrained debate envisaged here cannot possibly take place. The actors bring to the discussion unequal intellectual resources and are more or less powerful. The result of the unequal intellectual resources is that the ideologies of the powerful are imposed upon other actors who lack the means of recognizing their own true interests. The result of the inequalities in power is that the existing social order from which power is drawn is reproduced. As Giddens (1976) writes:

> The use of power in interaction involves the application of facilities whereby participants are able to generate outcomes through affecting the conduct of others; the facilities are both drawn from an order of domination and at the same time as they are applied, reproduce that order of domination. (p. 122)

SSM therefore merely facilitates a social process in which the essential elements of the status quo are reproduced—perhaps on a firmer footing, since differences of opinion will have been temporarily smoothed over. In doing so it supports the interests of the dominant group or groups in the social system. Checkland (1981a) does seem to take the point that the debate at Stages 5 and 6 can be crucially inhibited by society's structure, but he concludes rather weakly from this that "it is the nature of society that this will be so" (p. 283). This is not at all helpful. It tells us nothing about the degree of constraint on discussion imposed by particular social arrangements and institutions or about the possibility of changing such institutions and arrangements in order to facilitate communicative competence. The social environment in which the methodology has to operate nullifies, therefore, its attempts to bring about changes based on a true consensus. The methodology is culpable in that it is prepared to accept for implementation changes emerging from a false consensus, or accommodation, produced by distorted communication.

This takes us naturally on to consider whether soft systems thinking has anything to contribute to the emancipatory interest—the analysis of power and the way it can operate to prevent free and open discussion, and so proper rationalization in the sphere of the practical interest. In fact there is a critical kernel in soft methodologies, though this is much underdeveloped (Jackson, 1990c). As I have argued previously, the only possible justification for implementing the results of a soft systems study must be that the results and implementation have been agreed upon after a process of full and genuine participatory debate among all the stakeholders involved or affected. Soft systems thinkers should therefore be critical of all social arrangements that prevent the kind of open, participative debate that is essential for the success of their approach and is the only justification for the results obtained. However, despite Checkland's (1981a) assertion that SSM could be used in an emancipatory way that Habermas would approve, this critical opportunity has not been pursued by soft systems thinkers. When Fairtlough (1989) has tried to pursue it in practical applications in Celltech, he has found himself driven to conclusions and making proposals more consistent with critical systems thinking than soft systems thinking.

The reasons are not hard to see. In order to make more of the critical kernel, soft methodologies would have to use Habermas's conceptualization of the ideal speech situation to unmask situations of systematically distorted communication and would then have to challenge those social arrangements that produce distorted communication. Unfortunately, there is a major deficiency in soft approaches that prevents them doing this. For, as Willmott (1989) argues in relation to SSM:

> Its major shortcoming lies in its unnecessarily limited capacity to promote reflection upon the possibility that the content and negotiation of Weltanschauungen are expressive of asymmetrical relations of power through which they are constructed and debated. . . . Phenomenology, and SSM in particular, simply lacks a social theory capable of accounting for why particular sets of perceptions of reality emerge, and why some perceptions are found to be more plausible than others.

So soft methodologies lack any social theory that might allow them to understand, let alone challenge, the social arrangements that produce distorted communication. That this is so is starkly revealed by Checkland's (1981a) attempts to get to grips with what he calls the "common structurings" found in social reality—what a more positivist thinker would take as the objective aspects of the social world. This acceptance of common structurings is rather surprising given the overall subjectivist orientation of the methodology. The notion that social systems are not completely malleable has, however, been a theme running through Checkland's work. At one time it found expression in the special position accorded social systems on the "systems map of the universe" (Checkland, 1971). As well as being the context for human activity systems, they also had to be seen as natural systems. They reflected the human need for community life. This created difficulties for those who were concerned to "engineer" social systems. In the fully worked-out version of the methodology, the word *feasible* (as we have seen) draws our attention to the need to arrive at changes that take into account the realities of the problem situation. The kind of change that can be considered will be limited by the historically determined attitudes and behavior patterns of the actors in the particular social situation.

A more recent development is based upon Dilthey's concern to discover the common types of *Weltanschauungen* that occur. It is, of course, the nature of such Ws that sets the limits to change in SSM. They operate at every important stage—embodied in root definitions, structured into conceptual models, and brought to bear again at the discussion stages. The methodology can be used, according to Checkland, to reveal any recurrent Ws, and it opens up the prospect of discovering "the universal structures of subjective orientation in the world" (Luckmann, quoted in Checkland, 1981a, p. 279). This search for common structurings is an admirable aim and one that the methodology is well suited to pursuing. It echoes the concern of interpretive sociologists to understand the social world as it is—to understand how order and cohesion are achieved. But to go beyond regulation and to challenge the status quo, one would have to possess some theory of the origins of such common structurings. For example, which of the common structurings are historically contingent (and therefore amenable to change), and which are physiologically determined attributes of the human race (and therefore not amenable to change)? And one would have to put such a theory to the test of challenging the social institutions that carry what are regarded as the historically contingent structurings.

The Checkland methodology, tied as it is to subjectivism, has no such theory. There are odd references to "historically determined behavior patterns," "genetic inheritance," and "previous experiences" as placing limitations on the capacity of human beings to change. But nothing much is made of this, and as mentioned earlier, rather than challenge those structures that are historically based, the methodology prefers to deal in changes that are feasible given the existing social situation.

In summary, soft systems thinking offers little to the technical interest but has massive potential in relation to the practical interest. Its weakness, as far as the practical interest is concerned, lies in a failure to take account of the possibility of systematically distorted communication. This weakness is not easily remedied because of soft systems thinking's inability to develop in terms of the emancipatory interest. (I leave aside Churchman's anticipations of critical systems thinking, mentioned earlier in this chapter.) It could seize upon and use Habermas's theory of communicative competence as a critical standard, but would require in addition an appropriate social theory. The development of such a social theory is currently precluded by soft system thinking's attachment to subjectivism.

There is one final issue stemming from Habermas's schema that should be discussed. Other systems approaches (organizations-as-systems, hard, cybernetic) have been criticized for encouraging the dominance of the technical interest at the expense of the practical, with the result that questions about what ought to be done become defined as administrative problems. How does soft systems thinking define the relationship between these two fundamental cognitive interests? The answer is that it somewhat overcorrects the balance. Churchman and Mason and Mitroff, as was mentioned, rather downplay the significance of systems methodologies serving the technical interest. The worst offender, though, is Checkland. To Checkland, hard methodologies (and he includes organizations-as-systems and cybernetic approaches under that label) are a special case of the soft, usable when worldviews have coalesced to such an extent that there is consensus about what system to design. But this is to privilege the practical over the technical interest. The proper use of methodologies serving the technical interest is a matter of their allocation to appropriate domains of application, not of achieving a consensus. And within those domains (extensive enough in the case of organizational cybernetics) it is their own rationality, as witnessed by their ability to increase prediction and control, that must hold sway. What the best queuing system is for a particular supermarket or what would be an effective information-systems design for a particular organization are not simply matters of intersubjective agreement. Ackoff has it about right, for Habermas, when he sees machine-age thinking and systems-age thinking as complementary, and allocates space for the solving and resolving approaches within his basically dissolving orientation to social systems sciences.

The preceding discussion of soft systems thinking tended to take for granted that the soft approach has made a significant break from other forms of systems thinking and established its own theoretical home in the interpretive paradigm as defined by Burrell and Morgan. It is now time to justify that assumption. One defining feature of the interpretive paradigm, according to Burrell and Morgan, is its subjectivist approach to social science. Let us therefore look for evidence of a nominalist ontology, anti-positivist epistemology, voluntarist approach to human nature, and ideographic methodology in the writings of the soft systems thinkers.

Systems are perceived by adherents of the soft systems approach as having a subjective existence, as the product of individual consciousness. Checkland (1981a) argues that the emphasis of SSM "is not on any external 'reality' but on people's perceptions of reality, on their mental processes rather than on the objects of those processes" (p. 279). Ackoff does countenance an analysis of the systemic characteristics of messes ("formulating the mess") as a way of probing the future we are in. However, the way messes are interpreted depends very much on the point of view of the analyst: "Problems are products of thought acting on environments; they are elements of problematic situations that are abstracted from these situations by analysis" (Ackoff, 1974c, pp. 20–21). Thereafter, interactive planning concentrates on people's perceptions of a desirable future. Churchman (1979c) sees the social world as the product of individual consciousness acting on what is "given" in experience. It is not external to the individual, imposing its structure on the consciousness of the individual. Rather, the structure is imposed by the concepts and labels used by individuals.

Theorists of a subjective orientation seek knowledge by attempting to understand the point of view of the people involved in creating social reality. Checkland's methodology explores the different Ws relevant to a system of concern by encapsulating them in root definitions and then elaborating them in conceptual models. Ackoff hopes to involve all the stakeholders of a system in the design of a desirable future for that system. For Churchman (1979a), "the systems approach begins when first you see the world through the eyes of another" (p. 231). Even the points of view of the enemies of the systems approach—politics, morality, religion, aesthetics—should be "swept in" in order to make the approach as comprehensive as possible (Churchman, 1979c).

Theorists with a subjective orientation see human beings as possessing free will rather than as being determined in their behavior by external circumstances. In Checkland's methodology, the various actors are presumed capable of learning and of making whatever changes to the system they deem to be both desirable and feasible. The latter word is introduced by Checkland to suggest that the realities of the problem situation may impose *some* limits on what is possible. It is an axiom of Ackoff's interactive planning that the stakeholders of a system do not have to accept the future that has been designed for them as inevitable; they can plan a desirable future for themselves and seek to bring this about. Churchman's systems approach rests on the power of decision makers to change social systems. The systems designer seeks to make this decision making rational by ensuring that it benefits all the customers of systems.

Theories with a subjective orientation seek detailed information about systems by getting as close as possible to the subjects under investigation, rather than by the quantitative analysis of data. Checkland's SSM is designed to allow clients to engage in a learning process themselves so that they change their appreciative systems. He employs conceptual rather than quantitative models; these conceptual models are elaborations of different Ws relevant to the system. Ackoff uses quantitative techniques only as subsidiary aids in the interactive planning process. Churchman (1979c) argues that the best method of inquiry for planning calls for "observing a lot of human behavior."

In spite of Ackoff and Churchman's occasionally positivist language, and although they claim that their philosophical mentor E. A. Singer has overcome the objective–subjective dichotomy, it seems apparent that the social theory to which soft systems thinking corresponds is subjectivist in Burrell and Morgan's terms. This is an argument, of course, that Checkland enthusiastically embraces with respect to his own methodology. And to those such as Burrell (1983) who might question whether Checkland's commitment to phenomenology was pure enough, one can reasonably respond by asking what a problem-resolving methodology based on a "pure" subjectivist social theory would look like. I find it difficult to see how it could be much different to what Checkland has produced.

I am trying to demonstrate that soft systems thinking rests upon interpretive social theory and have so far shown it to be subjectivist in nature. The other defining feature of the interpretive paradigm is that it is oriented to regulation. The concern of interpretive sociologists and organization theorists is to understand how order and cohesion are achieved and maintained. I have to argue that soft systems thinking is similarly more suitable for preserving the status quo than going beyond it.

The sociology of regulation concerns itself with understanding the status quo. By probing the different points of view of the actors in social systems, the soft systems approach can be seen as contributing to this end. It enables us to understand how social order is maintained at the ideological level. It does not greatly assist in the search for those structural contradictions that might be the cause of radical change. From the point of view of the sociology of regulation, social systems are seen as being basically consensual. As the reader has witnessed, the critics contend that soft systems thinking seems to rest upon this assumption too. All the soft methodologies admit that differences of opinion exist among actors in social systems. To be effective, however, they all depend ultimately on bringing about a genuine consensus or accommodation so that changes can be agreed upon. This would appear a forlorn hope to theorists adhering to the assumptions of the sociology of radical change and seeing social systems as riven by contradiction and structural conflict. Finally, there is a tendency to accept at face value, and work with, existing perceptions of reality. No attempt is made to unmask ideological frames of reference or to uncover the effects of "false consciousness." And there is a willingness to take as given compromises and accommodations achieved within the confines of prevailing power structures. Soft systems thinking has failed to take account of the possibility of systematically distorted communication and to develop in support of the emancipatory interest.

For all these reasons—and disappointingly, given the truly radical aspirations of the soft systems thinkers—our conclusion must be that the social theory underlying soft approaches is regulative, and this severely limits their ability to bring about radical change. To make this case final, however, we have to deal with Checkland's claim (noted earlier) that the social theory to which his methodology corresponds is not simply interpretive (subjective/regulative) but must occupy as well some of the radical humanist (subjective/radical) quadrant of Burrell and Morgan's map. There is nothing therefore, according to Checkland, preventing the methodology being used as an instrument for radical change. It will be remembered that Checkland bases this claim on an article by Mingers (1980) that reveals some apparent similarities between the social theory of Habermas (which possesses a radical aspect, in Burrell and Morgan's sense) and SSM. If these similarities are fundamental, then Checkland's argument that his methodology can be used as a radical social instrument is greatly enhanced. I will argue, however, that—though there are similarities—it is the differences between the work of Habermas and Checkland that are more significant.

Let us take in order the similarities identified by Mingers and accepted by Checkland.

> Firstly, both take seriously the problem of human action—at the same time purposive/radical (hence capable in principle of being engineered) and natural, or unchangeable, as a result of the characteristics of the human animal. (Checkland, 1981a, p. 283)

Unfortunately, as I have argued, Checkland offers no way of deciding what are the unchangeable attributes of the human animal and what are the historically contingent characteristics. Because it is wedded to hermeneutics, the methodology must take the common *Weltanschauungen* that occur as permanently fixed. It is incapable of understanding the social structure that conditions these Ws and of postulating alternative social arrangements in which they may change. Habermas's social theory, because it retains positivism as a necessary method in social analysis, is able to understand the dependence of certain Ws on the social structure. And because it possesses a critical aspect, it is in theory capable of discovering which Ws are historically contingent and which are permanently fixed because of the attributes of the human animal:

> The systematic sciences of action, that is, economics, sociology and politics, just like the natural sciences, serve the purpose of producing nomological knowledge. A critical social science, however, is obviously not content with this; it tries in addition to discover which (if any) theoretical statements express unchangeable laws of social action and which, though they express relations of dependence, because they are ideologically fixed, are in principle subject to change. (Habermas, 1970, p. 46)

Secondly, both Checkland and Habermas are said to recognize the weakness of systems analysis. Systems analysis (and other functionalist systems thinking, for that matter) fails to recognize the unique character of its subject matter—human beings. This is true enough. Both writers stress the importance of the subjective aspects of social life. Checkland has developed a methodology that embodies a hermeneutic social theory, and Habermas insists on the value of hermeneutics in his own social theory.

Thirdly, "both aim to unite theory and praxis and develop a rational approach to the realm of communicative interaction in order to bring about change in the world and help people solve their own problems" (Mingers, 1980). But Habermas can go much further in helping people to solve their own problems, since he can provide a theory of distorted communication and a theory of the kind of social structure that brings about distorted communication. This gives people a chance to get to the root of their problems:

> Just as dialectics eludes the objectivism under which societal relations of historically acting people are analysed as the law-like relations between things, so too it resists the danger of ideologizing which exists as long as hermeneutics naively measures the relationships solely in terms of that which they subjectively regard themselves to be. The theory will adhere to this meaning, but only in order to measure it—behind the backs of subjects and institutions—against what they really are. (Habermas, 1976b, p. 139)

For Habermas (1974), the mediation of theory and praxis is more complex than Mingers suggests. He certainly would not countenance the collapsing of theory into practice that SSM endorses.

So the fact that Habermas is prepared to offer a social theory that takes account of the objective features of the social world (even while accepting that these result from the actions of human beings) makes a fundamental difference to the way in which his work should be regarded. Mingers and

Checkland seem to believe that the major difference between soft systems methodology and critical theory is the latter's overt political stance: "Habermas is a political radical" (Mingers, 1980). But this is not the case; the major difference is theoretical. Habermas recognizes that although the social world is created by the interaction of people, it is not transparent to them. It escapes human beings, takes on objective features, and constrains them. Humans are still in the grip of unconscious forces, and their actions still have unintended consequences. In these circumstances hermeneutics cannot be the sole method appropriate to the social sciences. There must also be a moment in social inquiry in which the objective features of the social world—when people do appear to act as things—can be studied. There is need, too, for a critical moment (corresponding to the emancipatory interest). The hope is to reduce the area of social life where people act as things and to increase the realm of the hermeneutic, where rational intentions become realized in history. Though the major difference is theoretical, it *does* have a political result. Habermas's work opens up the possibility of political action to accomplish real change; it is potentially radical. Checkland's methodology confines itself to working within the constraints imposed by existing social arrangements; it is regulative.

Soft methodologies, therefore, are subjective and regulative in orientation. They embody the important aspects of the interpretive paradigm in the way they attempt to bring about change in the real world. For other compatible accounts of the relationship between soft systems thinking and interpretive social theory, the reader can consult Mingers (1984) and Oliga (1988).

I turn now to the issue of which metaphors soft systems methodologies employ in seeking to understand and intervene in organizations. The work of Churchman and Mason and Mitroff seems to privilege the metaphor of the organization as a culture. Different value positions are used as the basis for dialectical debate out of which a synthesis, a stronger and more unified organizational culture, should emerge. As was noted, the cybernetic dimension of problem solving is ignored in this dialectical systems approach, and so the metaphors of organism and brain are not to the fore.

Ackoff, by contrast, makes use of a wide range of metaphors in considering how to address problems in the systems age. Indeed, much of the power of interactive planning stems from its ability to respond to diverse organizational problems as revealed by a number of images of organization. Ackoff is not happy that looking at corporations as machines or organisms is very productive in the modern era. He wants to replace this thinking with the idea that organizations are purposeful systems, containing other purposeful systems and being part of wider purposeful systems.

This new perspective seems to combine much of the best that can be gleaned from the brain metaphor with considerable input from the culture metaphor as well. The idea of the organization as a brain leads to and supports the emphasis upon learning and adaptation as encapsulated in the responsive decision system. The purpose of idealized design is to enthuse the participants with a vision of what their organization might be like and to endow them with a mission to create a desirable future. The process should generate consensus, mobilize the stakeholders with a crusading zeal, and reveal that only the participants' limited imaginations prevent them getting the future they most desire right now. This is all about developing a strong organizational culture that is shared by all the participants and that encourages creativity. It should also be remembered that, though Ackoff distances his own contribution from the machine and organism metaphors and builds interactive planning on more sophisticated views of the organization, he is still willing to make use of what the earlier thinking has to offer in support of his own preferred approach.

Still missing, though, is a willingness to view the organization as a coercive system. According to this metaphor, organizational stakeholders do not share common interests, their values and beliefs are likely to conflict, and they cannot agree upon ends and means, or reach a genuine compromise, under present systemic arrangements. The only reason the system holds together is because of coercive forces binding the less powerful to it. It is Ackoff's inability to look at organizations this way that has led to the persistent line of critical attack launched at his work.

Checkland's SSM is becoming increasingly dominated by the cultural perspective (Davies, 1988; Checkland, 1989). Organismic thinking lives on at the pure systems thinking stages when root definitions and conceptual models are constructed and/or tested on the basis of CATWOE and the formal systems model. The logic of the organismic metaphor sits uneasily with cultural conclusions, however, and loses out completely at the later debate stages.

Atkinson (1984) has argued that almost all systems thinking rests upon an "adaptive whole system" metaphor, a sort of amalgam of organismic, brain, and cultural thinking, and he and Checkland (1988) have shown an interest in extending the metaphor system and building models of "combative," "contradictive," "syndicalistic," "host/parasite," and other systems to map onto reality. No doubt the hope is that such conceptions will lead to more challenging root definitions and more radical changes. But this work cannot change the essentially regulative nature of SSM because it remains locked in interpretive thinking and leaves untheorized and unchallenged prevailing power structures. The same might be said of attempts to strengthen SSM by including references to culture and power in Analyses 2 and 3, respectively (see the earlier section on SSM). Only impoverished notions of culture and power can survive in the dominant interpretive climate of the methodology. It is not possible with interpretive ideas to think that culture might be engineered to serve the interests of a dominant group or that power is differentially distributed according to sex, race, status, and class. That would require looking at organizations using the coercive-systems metaphor and adopting the assumptions of another sociological paradigm.

The system of systems methodologies indicates that Churchman's social systems design and SAST will be most useful for tackling problems that lie in mechanical–pluralist contexts. In unitary contexts SAST's strengths as an adversarial, participative, and integrative methodology will be redundant. Its suitability for systemic–pluralist contexts is, however, also doubtful, for although it will help in tackling the pluralist aspect of such contexts, it has little relevance to the systemic because it possesses no cybernetic awareness. In coercive contexts it will be impossible to achieve the adversarial and participative debate necessary for the proper application of SAST. Integration is achieved in such contexts by power and domination rather than through consensual agreement. Any employment of SAST is likely to get distorted and to provide benefit only to those possessing power in the organization. Mason and Mitroff (1981) see the main weakness of SAST as being its dependence upon the "willingness of participants to lay bare their assumptions." Kilmann (1983) points out that assumptional analysis "assumes that the participants want their assumptions exposed." In coercive contexts, the powerful are unlikely to want their assumptions revealed. SAST is most appropriately used, therefore, in mechanical–pluralist contexts. In such contexts it can assist in structuring the exploration of different world views and help to bring about a synthesis, or at least accommodation, among participants so that action can be taken.

Ackoff is an exemplary representative of the systemic–pluralist view of problem contexts. To tackle adequately the complexity found in and around organizations in the systems age, Ackoff has long argued that we must abandon the predict-and-prepare paradigm that dominates operations research. The emphasis has to be on learning and adapting; it is for this reason that Ackoff puts forward his responsive decision system. This should improve the decision makers' power of control over what can be controlled, while increasing responsiveness to what is uncontrollable. Pluralism is accepted as unavoidable by interactive planning and is managed through the participative involvement of all stakeholders at all stages of the planning process. Idealized design seeks to minimize petty differences of opinion between diverse groups by asking them to focus on the ultimate ends they would like to see an organization pursuing. At the same time, it allows different stakeholders to incorporate their own aesthetic values into the idealized design. Interactive planning is an ambitious attempt to handle simultaneously both the complexity of the problem situations facing modern organizations and the pluralism that inevitably follows from their serving diverse stakeholders.

Checkland's methodology certainly addresses pluralism, inviting different individuals and groups to participate in a cyclic learning process. However, it is necessary to be careful in arguing it embraces systemic assumptions. Checkland strongly opposes the idea of "systems in the world," although he confesses to an epistemological commitment to the use of systems ideas to learn about an apparently densely interconnected real world. Then there is the argument that his use of organized systems thinking, at Stages 3 and 4, becomes something of an irrelevant appendage when subordinated to the logic of the methodology as a learning system. Perhaps, therefore, SSM has more in common with SAST than it does with Ackoff's social systems sciences. Checkland, like Churchman and Ackoff, fails to give attention to coercive problem contexts.

Finally, we should consider soft systems thinking in the light of the modernism-versus-postmodernism debate. Here it is probably most accurate to identify soft systems thinking as a rather underdeveloped form of critical modernism, based upon Kant's program of enlightenment and seeking the progressive liberation of humanity from constraints. Churchman and Ackoff are the most effusive contributors to this tendency in the soft approach. The reader will remember Churchman's Singerian inquirer pushing teleology to the ultimate in the heroic mission of increasing or developing purpose in human society, so that "man becomes more and more deeply involved in seeking goals." Ackoff (1974c) wants to change the future through the idea of interactive planning. He wants "man" to take over God's work of creating the future. But even Checkland (1981a) has his moments, seeing SSM as "a formal means of achieving 'communicative competence' in unrestricted discussion which Habermas seeks" (p. 20). At the same time, because it is so underdeveloped a version of critical modernism for all the reasons we have been detailing in this chapter, soft systems thinking is particularly prone to slipping back into becoming no more than an adjunct of systemic modernism, readjusting the ideological status quo by engineering human hopes and aspirations in a manner that responds to the system's needs and so ensures its smoother functioning. Some of the examples we are given of the use of soft methodologies support the systemic rather than critical modernist interpretation (e.g., Checkland, 1985b).

Although there are no grounds currently for linking soft systems thinking to postmodernism, it is just possible to conceive of SSM being developed in a postmodernist direction. This would need to build on SSM's denial of objective truth and acceptance of multiple language games yielding multiple interpretations of the world. Such a move would disarm the critics and put SSM back into the vanguard of fashion in the systems movement. But it would also be deeply cynical and deeply despairing, in the way that postmodernism is.

I have analyzed and assessed soft systems thinking at length and with good reason. Soft methodologies represent a genuinely new direction in management science. Theoretically, a new paradigm has been opened up for exploration by systems thinking. In practice, Churchman, Ackoff, and Checkland have massively extended the area within which management science can be used to help with real-world problems. Work on messes and ill-structured problems can be confidently undertaken using the approaches outlined in this chapter. Because of some of the claims made for soft systems thinking, however, it is vital to emphasize the weaknesses as well as the strengths of the soft approach. Soft systems thinking has a limited range of problem situations for which it is clearly the most appropriate approach, just as do all the other strands that make up the systems movement. The hope is that what soft systems thinking can achieve and what it cannot achieve are both now much better understood.

Critical Systems Thinking

Introduction

Critical management science began to emerge as a distinctive tendency in the 1970s. Inevitably, the first steps in its evolution consisted of radical attacks upon other forms of management science. Traditional management science, already under fire from the soft systems thinkers, came under further attack from Marxist-inclined scholars such as Hales (1974). The thrust of this assault, as Wood and Kelly (1978) summarized it, was that traditional management science or hard systems thinking accepted existing structures of inequality of wealth, status, power, and authority as given, and indeed helped to buttress the status quo. Wood and Kelly thought that any critical management science should consider the origins of values, the relations between organizations and society, the historical development of organizations, and the relationship between management science and developments within capitalism. During the 1980s, Rosenhead (1982), Rosenhead and Thunhurst (1982), and Tinker and Lowe (1984) sustained this critical barrage against the traditional approach. Tinker and Lowe, for example, accused traditional management thinkers of being dominated by a technocratic consciousness and of having created a one-dimensional discipline. They advocated a "two-dimensional" management science that recognized the social as well as the technocratic side of the discipline. They also saw the need to understand the dialectical interplay between the technocratic and social aspects. It is necessary to grasp the social and institutional pressures that allow technocratic thinking to dominate.

As has been discussed, it is not only hard systems thinking that has been attacked by radical critics. Other approaches explored in earlier chapters—such as soft systems thinking and organizational cybernetics—have also come under fire as not being radical enough. Ulrich (1981a) has argued that the tools employed in organizational cybernetics work against social and democratic progress, whatever the intentions of their designers. Thomas (1980), too, has warned of authoritarian implications in implementing cybernetic models directly. Soft systems thinkers have been accused of basing their work upon a consensus view of society and as being essentially managerialist and reformist by critics such as Rosenhead (1976), Bryer (1979), Thomas and Lockett (1979), and Jackson (1982, 1983).

All this energy invested in assaulting other positions can certainly be justified given the lack of self-reflection in the discipline and given that critical management science was a relatively new development still seeking to establish itself. At some stage, however, the emphasis had to shift from critical questioning, which was insightful but not clearly grounded, to the creative construction of a well-theorized and coherent critical alternative in management science. The source and inspiration for the development of this alternative has again proved to be systems thinking, and the name given to the newly emerging movement of thought is critical systems thinking. Critical systems thinking was a child of the 1980s (see Flood and Jackson, 1991b), but its mature texts are beginning to emerge in the 1990s (e.g., Flood, 1990a; Flood and Jackson, 1991a) and its major impact will be felt in the 1990s and beyond. It is from critical systems thinking that the ideas are now flowing that will finally allow the foundations to be laid for a fully fledged critical management science.

Because I have previously dealt with many of the critical assaults on other positions within systems thinking, I shall concentrate discussion in this chapter on the constructive contributions made to the emerging critical systems tradition of thought. Before I can do that, however, certain assertions must be made about the philosophy and principles upon which critical systems thinking is based. This is necessary to show what is different about critical systems thinking, and in particular to separate out what I shall call "emancipatory systems thinking" from critical systems thinking itself. These two developments are sometimes confused, and it is extremely important to be clear about their differences. That done, I shall still consider emancipatory systems thinking in this chapter because it has had such a significant effect upon the growth of critical systems thinking. After looking at emancipatory systems thinking and critical systems thinking, I analyze and assess both. By that time the assertions made in the next section can be reviewed by the reader in the light of all the available evidence.

The Main Features of Critical Systems Thinking

Critical systems thinking embraces five major commitments (see Oliga, 1989a; Schecter, 1991 for compatible arguments). It seeks to demonstrate critical awareness; it shows social awareness; it is dedicated to human emancipation; it is committed to the complementary and informed development of all the different strands of systems thinking at the theoretical level; and it is committed to the complementary and informed use of systems methodologies.

Critical awareness comes from closely examining the assumptions and values entering into actually existing systems designs or any proposals for a systems design. Critical systems thinking aims to provide the tools for enhancing this type of critical awareness, as for example, in Ulrich's (1983) critical systems heuristics. Another form of critical awareness concerns understanding the strengths and weaknesses and the theoretical underpinnings of available systems methods, techniques, and methodologies. As this book hopes to demonstrate, critical systems thinking is relentless in its pursuit of appropriate means of interrogation and in using these on the various systems approaches. Fuenmayor's (1991) "interpretive systemology" aims to promote critical awareness in both of the above senses by providing an interpretive systems theory. It is precisely because it lacks such a theory, Fuenmayor argues, that SSM is noncritical and lends itself to instrumental and regulative usage. However, because Fuenmayor's interpretive systemology shows no commitment to the other four features of critical systems thinking, it should not be regarded as part of that movement.

Social awareness involves recognizing that there are organizational and societal pressures that lead to certain systems theories and methodologies being popular for guiding interventions at particular times. For example, it was inconceivable that soft systems thinking could ever flourish in Eastern European countries dominated by the bureaucratic, "rational" dictates of the one-party system. With the move towards free-market capitalism and political pluralism, however, the circumstances that allowed hard and cybernetic approaches to succeed are changing, and softer methodologies are likely to be more useful and used. Social awareness should also make users of systems methodologies contemplate the consequences of use of the approaches they employ. For example, the choice of a hard or cybernetic methodology implies that one goal or objective is being privileged at the expense of other possibilities. Is this goal general to all organizational stakeholders, or is it simply that of the most powerful? Similarly, the use of soft systems methodologies, which are dependent upon open and free debate to justify their results, might have deleterious social consequences if the conditions for such debate are absent.

Critical systems thinking is dedicated to human emancipation and seeks to achieve for all individuals the maximum development of their potential. This is to be achieved by raising the quality of work and life in the organizations and societies in which they participate. Methodologies that serve the technical interest assist material well-being by improving the productive potential and the steering capacities of social systems. Methodologies that serve the practical interest aim to promote and expand mutual understanding among the individuals and groups participating in social systems. Methodologies serving the emancipatory interest protect the domain of the practical interest from inroads by technical reason and ensure the proper operation of the practical interest by denouncing situations where the exercise of power, or other causes of distorted communication, are preventing the open and free discussion necessary for the success of interaction. All human beings have technical, practical, and emancipatory interests in the functioning of organizations and society. So a systems perspective that can support all these various interests has an important role to play in human well-being and emancipation; and this is exactly what critical systems thinking wants to achieve. It wants to put hard, organizations-as-systems, and cybernetic methodologies to work to support the technical interest, soft methodologies to work to assist the practical interest, and emancipatory methodologies to work to aid the emancipatory interest.

This dedication to human emancipation requires an equal commitment to the complementary and informed development of all varieties of systems approaches. Different strands of the systems movement express different rationalities stemming from alternative theoretical positions. These alternative positions must be respected, and the different theoretical underpinnings and the methodologies to which they give rise developed in partnership. Further, the claim of any one theoretical rationality— whether functionalist, structuralist, interpretive, or emancipatory—to absorb all others must be resisted. This should not lead the systems community to fragment. As this book's "Analysis and Assessment" sections are partly designed to show, the existence of a range of systems approaches, each driven by a different theoretical position, can be seen as a strength rather than a weakness of the systems movement. All that is required is the guidance offered by complementarism, so that each systems approach is put to work only in problem situations for which its theoretical rationality is appropriate.

Finally, critical systems thinking is committed to the complementary and informed use of systems methodologies in practice. This requires a methodology (or perhaps metamethodology) that respects all of the other four features of critical systems thinking and employs these, together with a full understanding of each individual systems approach, to describe procedures that critical systems practitioners can follow in trying to translate their thinking into action in the real world. Obviously, such a methodology is difficult to construct and will be demanding of its users. Flood and Jackson (1991a) call their attempt at such a methodology "total systems intervention" (TSI). This is redolent of the ambition of their endeavor and the prospects (and problems) the methodology holds out for critical systems practitioners and clients.

I can now distinguish, as promised, between emancipatory systems thinking and critical systems thinking. Emancipatory systems thinking seeks to embrace the first three commitments described above, but fails to give attention to the last two. It is therefore narrower than critical systems thinking. It has concentrated on providing methodologies that, through critique and the engineering of particular social arrangements, can assist with the emancipation of human actors, putting them more in control of their own destiny. To anticipate the following discussion a little, the domain of effective application of emancipatory methodologies is organizations as coercive systems or coercive problem contexts. But not all problem situations are usefully regarded as coercive; some are better seen as unitary or pluralist. Emancipatory systems thinking, therefore, just like the hard, organizations-as-systems, cybernetic, and soft approaches, possesses a limited domain for which it is the most appropriate approach. Critical systems thinking is about putting *all* the different systems approaches to work, according to their strengths and weaknesses and the social conditions prevailing, in the service of a more general emancipatory project. Despite this distinction, emancipatory systems thinking has contributed considerably to the development of critical systems thinking, and I shall discuss it first in this chapter.

Emancipatory Systems Thinking

I deal initially with Ulrich's critical systems heuristics, and then with other contributions to emancipatory systems thinking.

Critical Systems Heuristics

Ulrich's book *Critical Heuristics of Social Planning* (1983) is the greatest achievement of emancipatory systems thinking to date. It filled a major gap in the literature since it described for the first time a systems approach that responded to the possibility that problem situations might be coercive. The aim of the book was nothing less than to set out an appropriate philosophy for an emancipatory systems approach, and to develop a method that could be used by planners and concerned citizens alike to reveal the "normative" content of actual and proposed systems designs. By normative content, Ulrich meant both the underlying value assumptions that inevitably enter into planning and also the social consequences and side effects for those affected by the planning. Thus critical heuristics was designed to be emancipatory and to be critically and socially aware. I discuss this approach at length here.

In setting out his emancipatory systems approach, Ulrich distances himself from the currently dominant use of the systems idea in what he calls "systems science" (OR, systems analysis, systems engineering, cybernetics). In systems science, which is dominated by limiting mechanistic and organismic analogies, the systems idea is used only in the context of instrumental reason to help us decide *how to do things*. It refers to a set of variables to be controlled. Ulrich's purpose is to develop the systems idea as part of practical reason, to help us decide *what we ought to do*. To this end he argues for "critical systems heuristics," using each of these three words in the sense given to them by Kant. To be *critical,* one must reflect upon the presuppositions that enter into both the search for knowledge and rational action. A critical approach to systems design means planners making transparent to themselves and others the normative content of designs. All designs and proposed designs must be submitted to critical inspection and not presented scientistically as the only objective possibility.

Ulrich takes the *systems* idea in Kant to refer to the totality of the relevant conditions upon which theoretical or practical judgments depend. These include metaphysical, ethical, political, and ideological aspects. In attempting to grasp the "whole system," we are inevitably highly selective in the presuppositions we make. Ulrich follows Churchman ("every world view is terribly restricted") in seeing Kant's systems idea as an admonition to reflect critically on the inevitable lack of comprehensiveness and partiality of all systems designs. It is by reference to the whole systems concepts entering into these partial presuppositions that critique becomes possible. Finally, *heuristics* refers to a process of uncovering objectivist deceptions and of helping planners and concerned participants to unfold problems through critical reflection. It also signals that Ulrich is not going to attempt to ground critical reflection theoretically, but to provide a method by which presuppositions and their inevitable partiality can be kept constantly under review.

These arguments are further developed in a debate with the ideas on social systems design present in or inferred from the writings of Popper, Habermas, and Kant. Popper's primary concern is with the logic underpinning theoretical reason—with how we find out what is. The only rational application of theoretical reason, for Popper, is in instrumental reason, which helps us to decide how to do things. As far as social systems design is concerned, therefore, reason can only help us with technical questions such as the most efficient means to achieve predetermined ends. Rational discussion about ends, and even about the value content of means, is apparently not possible. The central question of practical reason—"What ought we to do?"—is placed by Popper beyond the scope of critical reflection. It is therefore left to "decision" and enacted without rational guidance. Practical reason, as far as it is admitted at all, is reduced to instrumental reason. This same attitude still pervades systems science. The goals served by systems science go unexamined as all the effort is put into finding the most efficient means for achieving predetermined ends. Ulrich wishes to make the question of what we ought to do subject to critical reflection.

Habermas's work is much more useful to Ulrich's enterprise because he recognizes that instrumental reason is not the only legitimate application of reason. Practical reason and emancipatory reason (aiming at freedom from oppression) are, as we know, equally important to Habermas, and each possesses its own proper object domain. All three forms of reason are capable of being critically reflected upon. In order that questions such as what ought to be done can be properly decided, according to Habermas, a process of rational argumentation must be established. All citizens, or at least all those affected by a planning decision, must be allowed to participate in the argument surrounding that decision. And the debate must be so arranged that all ideological and institutional constraints on discussion are eliminated, so that the force of the better argument persists. Through an analysis of the structure of actual speech situations, Habermas determines, as discussed earlier, what this ideal speech situation free from all constraints must be like—a theory of undistorted communication.

Ulrich regards Habermas's work as providing a useful theoretical boundary experiment but as having little practical application. In order to enter into Habermas's debate, speakers must be willing and able to exhibit communicative competence. This tends to presuppose the very rationality the debate was designed to ensure. Habermas, in attempting to ground his critical reflection theoretically, cuts himself off from the real world in which personal and group interests inevitably contaminate any such debate. Far better, Ulrich argues, to ground critical reflection on practice *heuristically*; to provide a method by which practical judgments can be constantly reflected upon and their partiality revealed by ordinary everyday accounts of the nature of social experience.

It is on a reconstruction of Kant's philosophy that Ulrich attempts to build his critical heuristics on a systems basis. Kant hoped to justify the kind of knowledge we have about the world; he was particularly concerned about what he called synthetic a priori concepts. These concepts are deeply implicated in the production of knowledge but are little understood and difficult to justify. Kant proceeded critically to reflect upon the necessary conditions for thought. He attempted to show the *theoretical* necessity of three sets of synthetic a priori concepts. First are two "pure forms of intuition"—space and time—present in the very possibility of things as appearances. Second are the twelve "categories," pure concepts of understanding necessary to connect perceptions together. Finally, there are three "transcendental ideas"—the World, Man, and God. These transcendental ideas reveal to us the necessarily conditional character of our understanding of the totality. Kant then tried to show that these synthetic a priori concepts contributed valid knowledge about the world.

Ulrich builds on Kant's work but subtly transforms it in order to make it applicable to planning and systems design. Certain presuppositions, in the form of boundary judgments, inevitably enter into any social systems design. These boundary judgments reflect the designer's "whole systems judgments" about what is relevant to the design task. They also represent "justification break-offs" since they reveal the scope of responsibility accepted by the designers in justifying their designs to the affected. Thus boundary judgments provide an access point to the normative implications of systems designs. The task is to find a means of interrogating systems designs to reveal the boundary judgments being made. Ulrich proceeds by reflecting on which of the synthetic, relatively a priori concepts inevitably entering into a social systems design have heuristic necessity. Concepts are heuristically necessary if only by making them explicit does it become possible to reflect critically upon the presuppositions entering into planning and social systems design.

The concepts meeting this criterion are arranged according to the pattern set out by Kant. To Kant's space and time, the concept of purposefulness is added as an extra dimension necessary to map social reality. Twelve critically heuristic categories are established around a fundamental distinction between those involved in any planning decision (client, decision maker, planner) and those affected but not involved (witnesses). Three quasitranscendental ideas are developed—the systems idea, the moral idea, and the guarantor idea—as critical standards against which the limitations of particular social systems designs can be compared. These concepts should enable any existing social system to be examined with a view to discovering the norms, values, and so forth that went into its design. They should enable any potential systems design to be interrogated as to its presuppositions.

The 12 critically heuristic categories are the most important for our purposes here. They arise from four groups of questions based on the client, decision maker, planner, and witnesses distinctions. The questions relating to the client concern the sources of motivation flowing into the design; they are about its "value basis." The questions relating to the decision maker examine sources of control; they are about the design's "basis of power." The questions relating to the designer seek the sources of expertise employed in the design; they concern its "basis of know-how." And the questions relating to the witnesses reflect on the sources of legitimation considered in the design; they ask for its "basis of legitimation."

There are three questions asked of each of these four groups, giving the complete set of 12 boundary questions. The first question is about the social roles of the involved or affected; the second refers to role-specific concerns; and the third refers to key problems surrounding the determination of boundary judgments with respect to that group.

The power of the 12 questions to reveal the normative content of systems designs is best seen if they are put in both an "is" mode and an "ought" mode, and the answers are contrasted. For example, compare the answer to the question, "Who is the actual client (beneficiary) of the systems design?" with possible answers to the question, "Who *ought* to be the client of the systems design?" The 12 questions in the "is" mode can be summarized (after Ulrich, 1987) as follows:

1. Who is the actual *client* of the systems design?
2. What is the actual *purpose* of the systems design?
3. What is its built-in *measure of success?*
4. Who is actually the *decision maker?*
5. What *conditions* of successful planning and implementation of the system are really controlled by the decision maker?
6. What conditions are not controlled by the decision maker (i.e., are in the *environment*)?
7. Who is actually involved as *planner?*
8. Who is involved as *expert*, and of what kind is the expertise?
9. Where do the involved seek the *guarantee* that their planning will be successful?
10. Who among the involved *witnesses* represents the concerns of the affected? Who is or may be affected without being involved?
11. Are the affected given an opportunity to *emancipate* themselves from the experts and to take their fate into their own hands?
12. What *world view* is actually underlying the design of the system? Is it the view of (some of) the involved or of (some of) the affected?

Ulrich has shown the heuristic necessity of certain concepts for understanding social systems design. He now has to demonstrate how, making use of these concepts, particular social system designs can be validated and accepted for implementation. Here, Ulrich follows Habermas rather than Kant and requires some sort of participative debate to provide the final justification for practical knowledge. He regards Habermas's forum of speakers exhibiting communicative competence, however, as being impracticable. Ulrich suggests instead a dialectical solution to the problem. It is not enough that the involved, making use of the heuristically necessary concepts, be self-reflective about the partiality of their social system designs. They must be subject also to a dialogue with the witnesses—in practice, representatives of those affected but not involved.

In order to put recalcitrant planners into a position where they have to enter into dialogue, Ulrich advocates the polemical employment of boundary judgments. This idea stems from Kant's discussion of the "polemical employment of reason." For Kant, an argument is polemical if it is used with a solely critical intent against a dogmatically asserted validity claim. Affected citizens can employ boundary judgments against planners in this sort of way. They can assert alternative boundary judgments in the full knowledge that these reflect only personal value judgments. This is quite good enough to shift the burden of proof onto the planners and to leave them floundering to prove the superiority of their own boundary judgments. It should become clear that only agreement among all affected citizens can finally lead to conclusions about what ought to be done. Ulrich's dialectical solution, therefore, is to bring the systems rationality of the planners directly into contact with the "social rationality" of those who have to live in and experience the social systems designs.

It might be useful at this point to consider Ulrich's critical systems heuristics in relation to Checkland's SSM. Apart from Churchman's writings, which Ulrich makes use of throughout his book, it is Checkland's work that is nearest to Ulrich's in terms of orientation and intent. Checkland recommends exploring problem situations by drawing up root definitions of relevant systems and constructing conceptual models from these. Well-formed root definitions should express the six elements of CATWOE, and defensible conceptual models should incorporate the management components set out in the formal system model. The six elements and components together roughly correspond to the various concepts Ulrich believes need to be made explicit if we are to be able to reflect upon social system designs. Since Ulrich goes to some lengths to demonstrate the heuristic necessity of his concepts to purposeful systems design, some interesting results might be obtained by comparing and contrasting Checkland's and Ulrich's lists. Later in SSM, Checkland sees "feasible and desirable" changes emerging from a debate in which conceptual models are compared with the real-world problem situation as it is perceived. Ulrich would insist that this debate include not only the involved, but the witnesses as well. The legitimacy of the designs emerging from the debate would depend upon this.

The originality and significance of critical systems heuristics as a methodology for generating critical awareness has now been demonstrated. A degree of social awareness is also shown by Ulrich's insistence that the systems rationality of planners should always be tested against the social rationality of the affected. The emancipatory potential of the methodology can hardly be in doubt. In terms of this book's earlier definitions, therefore, critical systems heuristics is an example of emancipatory systems thinking. It would be wrong to see Ulrich's approach as advancing critical systems conclusions, however, for two reasons. First, it is not committed to the complementary and informed use of all varieties of the systems approach at the theoretical and methodological levels. And second, it is only partially "socially aware."

The first point can be illustrated by considering Ulrich's criticisms of systems science and its usefulness in social systems design. These criticisms are somewhat overplayed, and the important role that instrumental reason (for example, in the guise of organizational cybernetics) can play in planning tends, therefore, to get neglected. This is unfortunate since rational social action will depend on what it is possible to do and on the choice of efficient means (matters of instrumental reason) as well as upon what we ought to do (a matter of practical reason). I should not labor this point; experts do have a role in Ulrich's systems approach. It may simply be a matter of emphasis. Nevertheless, the impression is conveyed that systems science approaches are more dangerous than useful when applied to questions of social systems design. Perhaps a better view, which is endorsed in critical systems thinking, is that systems science is all right in its place, and it does have a place in social systems design. In developing the role of the systems idea as part of practical reason, Ulrich forgets just how essential and useful it is as part of instrumental reason.

Ulrich's limited social awareness derives from the fact that he takes his notion of critique from Kant and fails to enlarge it by drawing upon any of the conclusions reached by Marx. Critical systems heuristics is critical in terms of the idealism of Kant, Hegel, and Churchman, but is not critical in terms of the historical materialism of Marx and the Frankfurt school sociologists. Ulrich's work allows us to reflect upon the ideas that enter into any social systems design, but it does not help us to reflect upon the material conditions that, more objectivist thinkers believe, give rise to those ideas and that lead to certain ideas holding sway. Obviously, an analysis conducted according to Ulrich's recommendations will help point to such material conditions. What it cannot do is provide an examination or explanation of the nature and development of those conditions. Material conditions that lead to particular ideas prevailing and to particular designs winning acceptance have to be introduced by Ulrich as "commonsense" explanations of what is occurring.

This same neglect of the structural aspects and development of social systems means that Ulrich's recommendations are ultimately just as utopian as Habermas's. The question remains: Why should the involved bother to take account of the views and interests of those who are affected but not involved? The issue of which class, group, or agency has the power, the will, and the interest to bring about a rational society has bothered critical theorists throughout the twentieth century (e.g., Marcuse, 1968). No consensus has been reached, but at least it has been treated as an important question. Ulrich rather neglects this type of issue, a neglect that provides Willmott (1989) with grounds for doubting the efficacy of his methodology.

These critical comments do not detract from Ulrich's main achievement. Prior to critical systems heuristics, there was no emancipatory systems approach. Ulrich's singular accomplishment has been to rectify that omission by providing a rigorous emancipatory methodology. At the same time, of course, he has contributed considerably to making possible critical systems thinking by detailing an approach suitable for problem situations in which previously existing systems methodologies would flounder.

Other Contributions

Before passing on to critical systems thinking itself, a number of other contributions to the emancipatory strand of work are worthy of attention. Jackson's (1985d) paper "Social Systems Theory and Practice: The Need for a Critical Approach" shows an early critical systems awareness of the need to apply different systems methodologies based on alternative rationalities to different problem situations. Its primary purpose, however, was to argue in an emancipatory manner for an appropriate systems approach to be fashioned for social systems in which there are great disparities in power and resources between participants, and that seem to escape the control and understanding of the individuals who create and sustain them. In constructing such a methodology, Jackson advocated following some suggestions of Habermas on the relation of theory and practice. Thus he believed, like Habermas, in the need for a theoretical solution to the problem of practical reason rather than a heuristic solution as put forward by Ulrich. In explicating the relationship between theory and practice, Habermas (1974) wrote:

> The mediation of theory and praxis can only be classified if to begin with we distinguish three functions, which are measured in terms of different criteria: the formation and extension of critical theorems, which can stand up to scientific discourse; the organization of processes of enlightenment, in which such theorems are applied and can be tested in a unique manner by the initiation of processes of reflection carried on within certain groups towards

which those processes have been directed; and the selection of appropriate
strategies, the solution of tactical questions, and the conduct of the political
struggle. (p. 32)

Jackson discusses these three functions and relates them to systems
thinking. The first function involves professional scientists in the formulation of explicit theories about the social world. These theories must be
corroborated according to the usual rules of scientific discourse. The construction of explicit social theories must therefore be an essential part of
any social systems science. The second function involves the authentica-
tion of the knowledge produced by the first stage. Theoretical validation
is not enough; knowledge must also be validated by the social actors at
which it is aimed in a process of enlightenment. Only if the theory helps
these actors to attain self-understanding, and they recognize in it an acceptable account of their situation, can the theory be said to be authenticated. To explain this phase, Habermas turns to the psychoanalytic encounter (readers will remember a discussion of this in relation to
Habermas's work in Chapter 2). The actors in the social world, Habermas
believes, are very often in the same position as the neurotic patient undergoing psychoanalysis: They suffer from false consciousness and do not
truly comprehend their situation in the social world. It is incumbent,
therefore, on the critical theorist to employ a social theory capable of
explaining the alienated words and actions of oppressed groups in society:

> The theory serves primarily to enlighten those to whom it is addressed about
> the position they occupy in an antagonistic social system and about the in-
> terests of which they must become conscious in this situation as being objec-
> tively theirs. (Habermas, 1974, p. 32)

This, of course, is the point of the first function outlined by Habermas—the formation and extension of critical theorems. If the social actors
involved come to recognize themselves in the interpretations offered, that
theory is then authenticated. The social actors previously deprived of
self-understanding in the course of distorted communication are able to
take an equal role in the dialogue. The conditions for an ideal speech
situation are approximated in respect of this particular enlightened social
group. This is a precondition for Habermas's third function—the selection
of appropriate strategies. A rational consensus can now be reached over
the appropriate strategies to be adopted. As with the soft systems approach, the "clients" have complete autonomy in the matter of what
changes to make to the system and its objectives. Now, however, they
possess a social theory that enables them to comprehend fully their position in the social world and the possibilities for action that this affords.
Jackson argues, therefore, that Habermas's suggested approach is more
appropriate for a certain class of social systems than hard or soft systems
methodologies. These are social systems characterized by inequalities of

power and resources among the participants and by conflict and contradiction. They are the products of thinking and acting human beings, but at the same time are not transparent to them. These systems can escape both the understanding and the control of humans and take on objective features that constrain them.

Much of Oliga's work can also be seen as making an important contribution to emancipatory systems thinking by fulfilling the requirements of Habermas's first function and supplying social theories to support social systems science. This is true of his critical exegesis of the many conceptions of power as a social phenomenon (Oliga, 1989b). Ten faces of power are examined, the ideological understandings of power contained in hard and soft systems thinking are critiqued, and a "contingent, relational" view of power appropriate to emancipatory systems practice is presented. Another paper (Oliga, 1989c) proceeds similarly to set out nine conceptions of ideology, to highlight a critical view of ideology suitable for the project of enlightenment, and to use this analysis to unmask the ideological underpinnings of the different systems approaches. A third article (Oliga, 1990) examines systems stability and change as the outcome of an interaction between power and ideology. These significant theoretical statements have yet to be absorbed and translated into emancipatory systems practice.

Finally, but of first-ranking importance, I should record some attempts to apply an emancipatory systems perspective to real-world situations. The Open University's Co-operative Research Unit has for some time been involved with using systems approaches to assist workers' cooperatives and democratic social management (Spear, 1987). A more recent initiative was launched in 1986 by the Operational Research Society (U.K.) inspired by its president at the time, Jonathan Rosenhead. This "community OR" initiative was designed to extend awareness and use of OR to new sections of the community and to enrich OR methodology as a result of bringing it into contact with novel problem types (Rosenhead, 1986). Following this initiative, a Community OR Unit was established at Northern College and a Centre for Community OR set up at Hull University in the U.K. (see Carter et al., 1987). Currently, both Unit and Centre are flourishing and other community OR work is being coordinated by a "Community OR Network." The community OR initiative and its links to emancipatory systems thinking are more fully discussed in Chapter 9.

Critical Systems Thinking

In seeking to describe critical systems thinking, and to show how it came to embrace all five commitments set out earlier in this chapter, it will be best to give a kind of historical account of its development. In doing so we must be aware of the inevitable bias that enters into the construction of any historical record, and so the following should be read as my own account of how I came to accept and now perceive the main ingredients of the critical systems approach. To eliminate some of the bias, a further subsection presents more of an organized literature review of current developments in critical systems thinking.

Historical Origins

A reasonable starting point in history is Checkland's (1978, 1981a) critique of the pretensions of hard systems thinking. Briefly, Checkland argued that the assumptions made by the hard approach severely limited its domain of effective application. Making explicit reference to Burrell and Morgan's work on sociological paradigms, Checkland (1981a) showed that hard systems thinking is guided by functionalist assumptions. The world is seen as made up of systems that can be studied objectively and that have clearly identifiable purposes. Thus decision makers can be presented with the means to regulate better the systems under their command. The problem for the hard approach, Checkland argued, is that very few real-world problem situations present themselves in terms of systems with clearly defined goals and objectives. At best, therefore, hard systems thinking will prove ineffective in the great majority of problem situations. At worst there will be a temptation to distort situations so that they "fit" the demands of the methodology.

Although not a critical endeavor in the sense of the term used in this chapter—Checkland's aim being to make the case for soft systems thinking—his critique opened the door for work that was self-consciously critical. Taking Checkland's lead, I embarked upon a critique of the ambitions of soft systems thinking (Jackson, 1982) as expressed in the work of Churchman, Ackoff, and Checkland. It was argued that the assumptions made by these authors about the nature of systems thinking and social systems constrained the ability of their methodologies to intervene, in the manner intended, in many problem situations. Soft systems thinking, too, had a limited domain of application. Using Burrell and Morgan's framework, it was shown that soft systems thinking was based upon interpretive assumptions. With Churchman, Ackoff, and Checkland, system thinking becomes much more subjective, and the emphasis shifts from attempting to model systems "out there" in the world toward using systems models to capture possible perceptions of the world. In Checkland's methodology, for example, systems models of possible human activity systems are used to structure and enhance debate among stakeholders so that a consensus or accommodation about action to be taken can emerge. The recommendations of soft systems thinking remain regulative because no attempt is made to ensure that the conditions for genuine debate are provided. The kind of open, participative debate that is essential for the success of the soft systems approach, and is the only justification for the results obtained, is impossible to obtain in problem situations where there is fundamental conflict between interest groups that have access to unequal power resources. Soft systems thinking either has to walk away from these problem situations, or it has to fly in the face of its own philosophical principles and acquiesce in proposed changes emerging from limited debates characterized by distorted communication.

By 1982, therefore, the emerging critical systems perspective had, with the help of Burrell and Morgan's work, gone some considerable way to developing the necessary critical and social awareness specified earlier. The next step on the journey to critical systems thinking was the creation of a classification of systems methodologies that would allow for their "complementary and informed" use. Burrell and Morgan's framework might have helped with this task as well; however, as was noted in Chapter 2, it was not the easiest of devices to apply in interrogating systems approaches. Jackson and Keys (1984) sought therefore to provide, in their system of systems methodologies, an alternative framework that would serve the critical purpose mentioned and at the same time be suited to the language, concerns, and internal development of management science. The system of systems methodologies attempted to reveal what was being assumed in terms of systems and decision makers (later, participants) in using each type of systems methodology. This, it was felt, would enable potential users of systems methodologies to assess their relative strengths and weaknesses for the task at hand and to be fully aware of the consequences of employing each approach. The dimensions of systems and participants were chosen because they seemed to bring the greatest insight to the matter of distinguishing systems approaches. And, conveniently for the argument, systems methodologies did seem to make up a "system of systems methodologies" when allocated according to the matrix of problem contexts produced by combining these dimensions.

The system of systems methodologies opened up a new perspective on the development of systems thinking and management science. Previously it had seemed as if these disciplines were undergoing a "Kuhnian crisis" as hard systems thinking encountered increasing anomalies and was challenged by other approaches (Dando and Bennett, 1981). By questioning one of the underlying assumptions of this analysis—that management science has a well-defined and somewhat uniform subject matter—an alternative future was opened up. Instead of being seen as different strands of systems thinking competing for exactly the same area of concern (as per Dando and Bennett), alternative approaches can be presented as being appropriate to the different types of situations in which management scientists are required to act. Each approach will be useful in certain defined areas and should only be used in appropriate circumstances. If this perspective is adopted, then the diversity of approaches heralds not a crisis but increased competence and effectiveness in a variety of problem situations. Thus the system of systems methodologies represented the relationship between different systems methodologies as being complementary in nature and provided informed guidance about the assumptions that were necessarily being made in using any one systems approach.

The system of systems methodologies also prepared the ground for an appropriate welcome to be given to Ulrich's emancipatory systems thinking. As was stated in the original 1984 article, the unitary–pluralist dimension could be extended to embrace coercive contexts as well (an extension later made by Jackson, 1987c, 1988b, 1988c). At the time, Jackson and Keys did not know of any systems methodologies that assumed and acted as though problem contexts might be coercive. From the critical point of view, this was obviously a weakness in the capabilities of systems thinking and made the construction of such approaches imperative. Thus, although Ulrich's (1983) critical systems heuristics represented an independently developed strand of critical thinking (really, emancipatory systems thinking) deriving from Kantian idealism and Churchman's reflections on systems design, when the approach became known in the United Kingdom it was like the discovery of an element that filled a gap in the periodic table. Critical systems heuristics was arguably capable, where soft systems thinking was not, of providing guidelines for action in certain kinds of coercive situation. It enabled system designs or proposed designs to be carefully interrogated as to their partiality and set down criteria for genuine debates between stakeholders, which had to include both those involved in systems design and those affected by the designs but not involved.

It was unfortunate for the development of critical systems thinking that the system of systems methodologies did not, while it was demonstrating how systems methodologies could be used in a complementary and informed manner, spend more time on the issue of how the rationalities underlying different strands of the systems movement could also be employed in a complementary and informed way. Unfortunate because, in some hands, the system of systems methodologies lost its original critical intention and was used as the tool of just one rationality (see Jackson, 1990a). Banathy (1984, 1987, 1988) and Keys (1988), for example, both present entirely functionalist interpretations of the system of systems methodologies. They recommend proceeding by identifying the "true" nature and dynamics of the real-world problem situation faced, so that it can be fitted into some abstract classification of systems or problem contexts. Then, because they presume to know the appropriateness of different design methods (Banathy) or the respective strengths of different systems methodologies (Keys) in terms of their abstract classifications, it becomes a relatively simple matter to choose the correct methodology for the real-world problem they are confronting.

This objectivist orientation is accompanied, in the manner of functionalism, by a regulative bent. The Banathy and Keys interpretation of the system of systems methodologies seeks to help decision makers achieve better regulation of the systems they command. This is signaled by the complete lack of attention to issues such as structural inequality, economic and political contradiction, power, domination of some groups over others, and false consciousness. All conflict that goes beyond the pluralist— differences of values and preferences—has to be ignored. The coercive aspect of the participants dimension, introduced in the original Jackson and Keys (1984) paper and crucial to its critical intent, is apparently dismissed as not relevant. So, if coercion exists—if some systems are best seen as characterized by conflict and contradiction, and by the domination of some groups over others—this will go unrecognized by Banathy and Keys.

The functionalist reading of the system of systems methodologies is, of course, subject to many criticisms. From the interpretive standpoint, critics such as Kijima and Mackness (1987) argue that a functionalist system of systems methodologies ignores the possibility of different interpretations of problem situations. For interpretive thinkers, systems and problem contexts are in the mind of the observer and not in any real world "out there." Flood and Carson (1988) and Ellis and Flood (1987) argue that for soft systems thinkers such as Checkland, the system of systems methodologies (in its functionalist guise) can have no use, since there is no real-world structure to any problem situation that can act as a guide for methodology choice. This critique from the interpretive perspective is indeed a damning one for Banathy and Keys, for it reveals not only the practical difficulties of using their approaches but, at the same time, a deep internal contradiction in their work. While they seem, through the system of systems methodologies, to be advocating the use of soft approaches when appropriate, their functionalist vision denies the very principles upon which the soft approaches are based. Only extremely denatured versions of the soft approaches can survive in the functionalist climate of Banathy and Keys's system of systems methodologies. Equally damning criticisms can be raised from the point of view of radical sociological paradigms. Viewed from a radical position, Banathy and Keys clearly fail to meet the challenge provided by coercive systems, and so their work lends itself to authoritarian usage by powerful decision makers.

Banathy and Keys locate the system of systems methodologies squarely in the functionalist paradigm. From this position, inevitably it is possible to offer only an impoverished understanding of the insight and power provided by methodologies based on interpretive thinking (such as soft systems methodologies), and it is all too easy to neglect the needs of coercive contexts. The whole point of the system of systems methodologies should be that it draws upon the strengths of all versions of the systems approach, whatever the assumptions on which they rest and the paradigm within which they are located. The system of systems methodologies will always fail to fulfill its potential if it is associated too closely with any one paradigm. This point is forcefully made by Flood (1989a), who as part of an epic argument on the future of systems problem solving works through the implications of an interpretive reading of the framework. While this initially seems more promising than the functionalist version, it inevitably has to denature functionalist methodologies and to provoke anomalies when considering coercion and conflict. A radical or emancipatory reading of the system of systems methodologies would be equally distorting. The system of systems methodologies, to realize its proper potential, requires support from above the paradigms: support capable of marshaling the various systems approaches, whatever their theoretical assumptions, on the basis of a metaunderstanding of their capabilities.

So far I have done little more than reiterate the need for the system of systems methodologies to be combined with an understanding of how the different rationalities underlying the different strands of the systems movement can themselves be employed in a complementary and informed way, and shown the consequences of ignoring this. It is now time to tackle the problem head on. The main difficulty, as Flood (1989a) notes, in accepting that systems methodologies based upon competing epistemological and ontological presuppositions can be brought together in one pluralist or complementarist endeavor is that the arguments in favor of "paradigm incommensurability" are so strong. For Kuhn (1970), paradigm incommensurability occurs when "two groups of scientists see different things when they look from the same point in the same direction" (p. 150). Burrell and Morgan (1979) support the notion of incommensurability between their sociological paradigms. It would seem inconceivable for proponents of paradigm incommensurability that different systems methodologies, based upon irreconcilable theoretical assumptions, could ever be employed together in some complementarist way. There is the insurmountable difficulty of how it is possible to stand above the paradigms and work with them in this manner. How could such a privileged position be attained?

While it is not possible to quell all doubts at this time, it is clear enough in what direction critical systems thinking is looking for answers. The preferred vehicle to support critical systems thinking's complementarism at the theoretical level (and, therefore, to give coherence to the system of systems methodologies) is Habermas's theory of human interests. There is a remarkable convergence in the way that three critical systems thinkers have used Habermas's ideas in developing their own approaches. Jackson (1985b, 1988c) has linked the technical interest to the concern systems methodologies show for predicting and controlling the systems with which they deal, and the practical and emancipatory interests with the concern to manage pluralism and coercion. It follows that the two dimensions of the system of systems methodologies can be justified from Habermas's work and the different systems methodologies represented as serving, in a complementary way, different human species imperatives. Oliga (1986, 1988) argues that Habermas's interest-constitution theory is an important improvement over the interparadigmatic-incommensurability position of Burrell and Morgan, since

> whereas Burrell and Morgan merely explain the different paradigmatic categories, Habermas explains and reconciles the interest categories in terms of their being individually necessary (although insufficient) as human species, universal and invariant (ontological) forms of activity—namely labour, human interaction, and authority relations. (Oliga, 1988)

Oliga then goes on to conduct his own survey of how well the technical, practical, and emancipatory interests are served by systems methodologies. Ulrich (1988) similarly uses Habermas's taxonomy of types of action—instrumental, strategic, and communicative—to specify three complementary levels of systems practice, roughly parallel to the requirements of operational (or tactical), strategic, and normative planning. Different systems approaches can then be allocated as appropriate to service operational, strategic, and normative systems management levels.

Enough has been said to suggest that Flood's concern about paradigm incommensurability can be resolved at the level of human interests. I have, therefore, established the possibility of the complementary and informed use of different systems rationalities at the theoretical level. In the process, of course, I have made it possible to rescue the system of systems methodologies from adherence to any one paradigm or rationality. Complementarism at the theoretical level provides the justification and basis for complementarism at the methodological level. Understood in terms of critical systems thinking, and not chained to functionalism, interpretivism, or radicalism (in Burrell and Morgan's sense), the system of systems methodologies becomes theoretically coherent and an exceptionally powerful tool for guiding practical interventions (see Jackson, 1990a). It can point to the strengths and weaknesses of different strands of systems thinking, both in terms of problem-solving capacity and social consequences of use, and can put them to work in a way that *respects and takes advantage* of their own peculiar theoretical predispositions in the service of appropriate human interests.

The theoretical shortcomings that dog Banathy and Keys's functionalist version of the system of systems methodologies are thus overcome. The aim is not to establish the exact nature of some real-world problem context so that an appropriate problem-solving methodology can be used. Rather, it is to reveal the particular capabilities of available systems approaches and to make explicit the consequences, because of the assumptions each makes about systems and the relationship between participants, of using any of these. Attention is also drawn to the need to be aware of the social context within which a methodology is to be used, because this will condition the purpose to which it is put. In particular, the prospect of authoritarian or conservative usage of existing regulative methodologies is highlighted by drawing attention to the potential existence of coercive contexts and the need for approaches suited to the peculiarities of these situations.

I have been discussing how critical systems thinking came to build in the commitments to complementarism specified earlier in this chapter (at least according to my own viewpoint). Critical systems thinking, resting upon Habermas's theory of human interests as mediated through the system of systems methodologies, can adequately support a complementarist vision of the future of systems thinking and management science at both the theoretical and methodological levels. In this, all strands of the discipline are employed in an informed and complementary manner to facilitate the management task. It remains to consider the commitment to human emancipation; in fact, this has found expression in two ways. First, it is noticeable that those involved in the creation of critical systems thinking have also been influential in seeking to develop emancipatory systems approaches. Jackson, Oliga, and Ulrich have all sought to facilitate the emergence of new, emancipatory methodologies to tackle problem situations where the operation of power prevents the proper use of soft systems thinking. Second, there is the adherence to the broader emancipatory project enunciated in Habermas's theory of human interests and in his social theory, as detailed toward the beginning of this chapter.

By about 1990, therefore, critical systems thinking had begun to take on some sort of form, at least in my view. It seemed to be built upon the five pillars of critical awareness, social awareness, dedication to human emancipation, complementarism at the theoretical level, and complementarism at the methodological level.

Current Overview

In order to allow readers to develop a less personalized view of events and to permit them to explore more fully for themselves the unfolding of this exciting new movement in systems thought, I shall now review the five commitments again. This will allow me to mention some other contributions to progress in critical systems thinking to date and, particularly, to give a little attention to some new developments.

Critical awareness is encouraged both at the level of systems thinking as a whole and at the level of particular methodologies. At the general level are Jackson's (1988c) review of systems methods for organizational analysis and design, Oliga's (1988) look at the methodological foundations of systems methodologies, Ulrich's (1988) program for systems research, and Flood and Ulrich's (1990) examination of the epistemological bases of different systems approaches. Related to specific methodologies are the soft systems thinker's assaults on hard systems thinking (Checkland, 1978; Ackoff, 1979a; Churchman, 1979b); Jackson (1982) and Mingers (1984) on soft systems thinking; Ulrich (1981a), Jackson (1986, 1988a), and Flood and Jackson (1988) on cybernetics; and Jackson (1989b) on SAST.

Social awareness involves, as one of its aspects, considering the organizational and societal climate that determines the popularity, or otherwise, of particular systems approaches at particular times. Here some contributions from "critical management science" have fed into critical systems thinking. Hales's (1974) and Rosenhead and Thunhurst's (1982) analyses of the evolution of management science in terms of the historical and material development of the capitalist mode of production are particularly worthy of mention.

According to Hales, management science under capitalism takes on a profoundly ideological character. It misrepresents the nature of the systems with which it deals, seeing them as consisting of objects to be controlled and denying the possibility of their free development as the conscious expression of the social nature of their members. This misrepresentation takes place primarily because of the social, political, and economic pressures under which the discipline evolved. Management science must be understood as an ideology in relation to the development of the capitalist society that it is its major concern to serve. Essentially, it has evolved in response to the changing demands imposed on twentieth-century capitalism by the need to control the work force.

Rosenhead and Thunhurst offer, specifically in relation to OR, a similar "materialist" analysis. OR is studied not simply in terms of the internal development of the subject; this internal development is further related to wider social processes and to the history of capitalism as a whole. In particular, the rapid growth of OR after World War II is seen as resulting from the demands of the postwar crisis of British capitalism. OR assisted the more efficient extraction of surplus value from the workers and so helped overcome the crisis. Furthermore, as one element of scientism, OR contributed to the mystification of the work force. It was presented as the only source of rational answers to organizational problems. Thus it contributed to the subjective as well as the objective subjugation of the workers.

For Rosenhead and Thunhurst, as for Hales, the ultimate solution to management science's problems lies largely outside its own sphere of influence. Only by joining in the wider struggle of labor against capital can management science hope to overcome its contradictions and speed the day when it becomes "self-management science," aiding active decision making by all rather than helping an elite to maintain control. Having said this, Rosenhead and Thunhurst do see some role for a critical OR in advancing the wider struggle and suggest some tasks it could perform. They also hint at the form the new self-management science, or "workers' science" (Rosenhead, 1987), might take after the necessary transformation in society has taken place.

Flood and Gregory (1989; Flood, 1990a, 1990b) would regard the Hales, and Rosenhead and Thunhurst, accounts of the history of management science as structuralist in character. In a useful contribution, they set out four ideas on the nature of the history and progress of knowledge— linear sequential, structuralism, worldviewism, and genealogy—and relate these to accounts of the development of systems thinking. The linear sequential model sees knowledge building chronologically and cumulatively; my account of the rise of critical systems thinking would fit into this category. Structuralism represents deeper processes as being at work in history, and uses the "scientific" approach to unearth these and build cumulative knowledge of them. Worldviewism rejects the unilinear perspective and accepts the existence of contrasting and even contradictory knowledges, although there may be periods of settled or "normal" science (Kuhn, 1970). Dando and Bennett (1981) offer a worldviewist account of the situation in management science. Genealogy, deriving from Foucault's writings, puts emphasis on the effect power at the micro level can have on the formation and development of knowledges. Localized power relations outside of discourse can effect the success or lead to the subjugation of knowledges. In Flood and Gregory's opinion the first three ideas on the history of knowledge are well represented in accounts of progress in systems thinking, but the genealogical view has not yet been exploited. The result has been a neglect of the effect of power at the micro level on the way the subject has unfolded. Obviously, a properly conducted genealogical study could contribute significantly to the social awareness of critical systems thinking.

The other side of social awareness is giving full consideration to the social consequences of use of different systems methodologies. This has been a guiding principle of Jackson's research (1982, 1985d, 1988a, 1988c, 1989b), has led Oliga (1989c) to seek to unmask the ideological foundations of the different systems approaches, and provides the rationale for Ulrich's (1983) demand that the systems rationality of planners always be exposed to the social rationality of the affected.

Critical systems thinking recognizes its overall emancipatory responsibility and seeks to fulfill this by adequately servicing, with appropriate systems methodologies, each of Habermas's human interests (Jackson, 1985b, 1988c; Oliga, 1986, 1988; Ulrich, 1988). At the same time it perceives a special need, because of previous neglect, to nurture the development of emancipatory systems thinking. In theory, this means encouraging the use of specifically emancipatory systems methodologies suitable for coercive contexts (Ulrich, 1983; Jackson, 1985d). In practice, it includes supporting initiatives such as community OR (see Chapter 9) and attempting to liberate the critical kernel in Beer's work so that cybernetics can be used to promote democratic organizational forms (Schecter, 1990).

Flood (1990a), following Foucault's logic, has argued persuasively enough that the project of liberating systems theory must include additionally the emancipation of suppressed knowledges in systems theory itself. Critical analysis must focus as much on revealing lost or suppressed knowledges as on the examination of those that have survived and become dominant. Since the rise of some knowledges to prominence and the subjugation of others depends upon localized contexts and struggles governed by power in the nondiscursive realm, and since there is no overall rationale to any of this (a postmodernist position), the only way to counter dominant knowledges and release the suppressed is through "oppositional thinking." Such thinking is for fighters and resisters rather than those who already know the answer, and it focuses on the extremities and the nonroutine.

As an example of a subjugated knowledge in systems thinking, Flood and Robinson (1989) provide general system theory (GST). GST has lost favor in the systems movement, but the reasons can hardly be entirely scientific, they argue, because the criticisms leveled against GST (which have become generally accepted) simply do not stand up to close examination. Presumably, we are supposed to gather from this that GST has had power withdrawn from it in the course of various nondiscursive engagements. However, Flood and Robinson provide no analysis of how or why this might have happened, and so the example is ultimately unconvincing. This does not detract from Flood's conclusions about the usefulness of

Foucault's writings for critical systems thinking. Oppositional thinking needs developing as a means of liberating both people and knowledges, even if we should choose to guide its use with a modernist emancipatory rationale. This, indeed, seems to be the position adopted by Flood. In *Liberating Systems Theory* (Flood, 1990a), Foucault's arguments are contained within a basically Habermasian framework.

In a later article (1990c), Flood compliments and comments on Oliga's studies on control, power, and ideology in social systems. These phenomena are seen by Oliga as functioning not to maintain systems as a whole but to benefit certain members of systems. At the same time, they give rise to contradictory pressures and resistances. Flood argues that these can be used to raise the consciousness of those subject to domination and so empower them with the capacity to transform their situation.

Critical systems thinking's adherence to complementarism at the theoretical level rests upon its acceptance of Habermas's arguments for human-species-dependent knowledge-constitutive interests (Jackson, 1988c; Oliga, 1988; Ulrich, 1988). I shall deal further with the arguments in favor of taking a complementarist position in systems thinking in Chapter 10. Here, however, I take up a consequence of this that allows the introduction of another significant input to critical systems thinking. Since Habermas is seen by postmodernists as guilty of most of the major sins of modernism, it follows that critical systems thinking must also be open to the postmodernist critique. In *Liberating Systems Theory* and other writings, Flood (1990a, 1990b, 1990c) has attempted from a critical systems perspective to come to terms with postmodernism, particularly as it is expressed in the works of Foucault. Flood argues that despite their differences, Habermas and Foucault can be seen as contributing to a position opposed to theoretical isolationism (especially of the technocratic kind) and in favor of theoretical pluralism. Habermas provides a basis for accepting three types of rationality, for promoting the development of each, and for criticizing the limitations of each. However, he is naive in the way he conceptualizes power, believing that power can be made to follow knowledge (to issue forth from the force of the better argument). Foucault sees power as immanent in all aspects of social life and as intimately linked to knowledge, so that—for example—it determines what the better argument is. Various localized forces (which cannot be grasped through some grand narrative such as Habermas's social theory) decide which discourses should be dominant and what knowledges subjugated.

Flood argues, therefore, that in order to achieve the maximum diversity in systems approaches (so that the fullest support can be provided to Habermas's human interests), it is necessary first to follow Foucault's method to reveal subjugated knowledges. Foucault provides the understanding and the means necessary to liberate suppressed knowledges so that a diversity of approaches is achieved. These can then be subject to critique according to the principles set out by Habermas for assessing the theoretical and methodological legitimacies and limitations of different knowledges. An "adequate epistemology for systems practice" (Flood and Ulrich, 1990; Flood, 1990a) can be established on essentially Habermasian foundations, but with support from Foucault's conceptualization of power. These notions of "liberate" and "critique" were later (Flood, 1990c) joined by those of "empower" and "transform" (already mentioned) to provide the basis for Flood's critical systems thinking.

In Flood's (1990c) view, the establishment of the complementarist position in systems thinking in opposition to isolationist tendencies represented a first-stage redefinition of the management and systems sciences. The setting up of a tension with complementarism by confronting it with postmodernist arguments, and the extension to embrace "empower" and "transform," leads to a second-stage redefinition and the proper establishment of critical systems thinking. In reality, no great second-stage redefinition takes place. Foucault is robbed of most of the essentials of postmodernism in order to make his arguments fit with those of Habermas, and other postmodernist writers are hardly considered at all. So critical systems thinking remains tied to Habermas's project of enlightenment. The ideas of "empower" and "transform" find their natural home in emancipatory systems thinking, where they are already implicitly recognized. Nevertheless, it cannot be doubted that even the adulterated version of Foucault's thinking incorporated by Flood into his critical analysis does strengthen critical systems thinking.

There remains complementarism at the level of methodology. This commitment originates from Jackson and Keys's (1984) system of systems methodologies, since taken in different directions by the two authors (Keys, 1988; Jackson, 1990a). It was made explicit in Jackson's (1987b) argument for pluralism in management science. The suggestion is that pluralism cannot be attained by mixing methodologies in any pragmatist way; to get the most out of each methodology, they have to be used in ways that are true to their theoretical underpinnings, and significant differences divide advocates of the alternative strands of systems thinking. However, this should not lead us to accept the full implications of the doctrine of paradigm incommensurability. Because at a metalevel different strands of management science can all be seen as offering complementary support for the anthropologically based cognitive interests of the human species, so too can the methodologies be employed in a complementary fashion. This argument receives greater attention in Chapter 10. I shall also devote another chapter (11) to the metamethodology recently developed by Flood and Jackson to help realize in practical application the benefits that can be gained from accepting complementarism in theory and practice. This "total systems intervention" (TSI) approach requires another book, however, in order to do it full justice (Flood and Jackson, 1991a).

Critical systems thinking is a relative newcomer in the systems tradition of thought, yet it is now developing more quickly than any other part of systems thinking. I have treated it as an evolving body of work, taking first my own impressions of its development and then classifying the published literature associated with critical systems thinking according to the five commitments established earlier. It would be premature to make any long-term predictions about the effect that critical systems thinking will have upon systems thinking and management science. It is not too presumptuous, however, to follow Schecter (1991) in setting down a number of significant contributions it has already made to the field. Schecter notes that it has brought greater theoretical depth to discussions and produced some strong original work in metatheory; it has produced challenging critiques of earlier systems work; it has put issues of power and human emancipation on the agenda and put its commitment to emancipation into action; it has produced a framework for the complementary development of all the different systems approaches; and it has championed a commitment to careful, critical, self-reflective thinking.

Analysis and Assessment

The "Analysis and Assessment" section needs to be a little bit different in this chapter since it has to deal with emancipatory systems thinking and critical systems thinking. However, this does not mean that it has to be extended. I shall deal with both together, but briefly.

Critical systems heuristics seeks to make the systems idea relevant to the problem of practical reason. It has little to say about systems methodologies supporting the technical interest and, in fact, downplays the importance of the technical interest in a way that Habermas would never do. In terms of the practical interest, and satisfying the requirements that it develop through free and open debate, Ulrich decides to pursue a heuristic rather than a theoretical route. He provides a method by which practical judgments can be reviewed and their partiality revealed by ordinary everyday accounts of social experience. This decision yields as a major gain an emancipatory systems methodology. However, it can also be held responsible for the weaknesses of critical systems heuristics identified by the critics. Ulrich is unable to reflect upon the conditions that would guarantee free and open debate and how these might be brought about.

Critical systems thinking wants to give due attention to all three human species imperatives as identified by Habermas. It recognizes critical systems heuristics as an important contribution to achieving rationalization in the sphere of the practical interest, but continues with Habermas to seek theoretically justifiable standards against which the degree of communicative competence attained in any actual debate, and the social conditions under which debate takes place, can be evaluated.

From the discussion that has taken place on emancipatory and critical systems thinking, it is apparent that the concerns addressed include some that are entirely foreign to those of other types of systems thinking, whether organizations-as-systems, hard, cybernetic, or soft. Let us recall Wood and Kelly's contention, mentioned at the beginning of the chapter, that the common thrust of the critical challenge lies in a refusal to accept as preordained (which traditional management science does) existing inequalities of wealth, status, power, and authority, and in a refusal to act simply as legitimization and support for the status quo. To take this stance, emancipatory and critical systems thinking must be based on entirely different assumptions about the nature of society from those accepted in more traditional approaches. Other systems approaches rest on a belief in social order and consensus and aim to promote integration so as to improve existing social systems, from which all are seen as benefiting. They help buttress the status quo. Emancipatory systems thinking specializes in, and critical systems thinking accepts the strong possibility of, contradictions in social systems, the existence of conflict, and the domination of some groups over others. Where these conditions exist, the aim is to promote radical change and to emancipate the deprived majority.

These differences amount in the case of emancipatory systems thinking—and in Burrell and Morgan's terms—to a difference between adherence to the sociology of regulation and adherence to the sociology of radical change. This distinction is a fundamental one that means that emancipatory systems thinking operates from a different paradigm than other forms of systems thinking. Of course, Burrell and Morgan recognize two different paradigms that share the assumptions of the sociology of radical change. In radical humanism, the critique is focused on the presently existing consciousness of people. In radical structuralism, the emphasis is on the contradictions and conflicts present in social systems. Critical systems heuristics is more akin to radical humanism. If one were to propose an emancipatory methodology based on Hales's or Rosenhead and Thunhurst's materialist accounts of how society and ideas interrelate, the result would be closer to radical structuralism. In the case of critical systems thinking, the aim is to harness knowledge gained of social reality appropriately by viewing it through all of the sociological paradigms, and to make use of systems methodologies based on the assumptions defining each of the paradigms.

As was seen in the discussion of the philosophy of critical systems heuristics, Ulrich rails against the limitations of the machine and organismic analogies that dominate systems science. It is the influence of the culture metaphor and especially, perhaps, of the idea that social situations can become coercive systems when planners do not submit their designs to rational argumentation that is most easily traced in his work. The effect of this, mentioned previously, is that Ulrich neglects the importance of instrumental reason in social systems design but is highly original in the matters of promoting informed and challenging debate and safeguarding his methodology from the possibility of authoritarian usage. Critical systems thinking wants to use all the metaphors to understand problem situations. Flood and Jackson's (1991a) TSI employs an understanding of a range of systems metaphors, as well as the system of systems methodologies, to interrogate problem situations creatively and to guide the choice of appropriate problem-resolving approaches.

Emancipatory systems thinking is positioned towards the coercive end of the participants dimension of Jackson and Keys's system of systems methodologies (see Figure 2.3). This should be taken as more an indication of the unique contribution of the approach than of its limitations in dealing with pluralism. In particular, it should not be read as suggesting that there will be few opportunities to use emancipatory systems thinking in the real world. Many situations can be seen as exhibiting aspects of coercion, and most pluralistic debates could benefit from the kind of clarification Ulrich's approach provides. If one were forced to place critical heuristics in the mechanical–coercive or systemic–coercive box, the argument would go in favor of the former positioning. Critical heuristics does not seek to assist with complexity management along the systems dimension. More evidence for this can be adduced from the distinction Jackson (1987c, 1990b) makes between these two contexts. Mechanical–coercive contexts are those in which only the first dimension of power, as defined by Lukes (1974), operates and the sources of power imbalance are relatively obvious. In systemic–coercive contexts, the complexity of the system(s) of concern is likely to hide the true sources of power and domination, and to support the operation of Lukes's second and third dimensions of power. Coercion that is, in the realist sense, embedded structurally in organizations and society cannot be addressed using Ulrich's approach.

This relates closely to the criticism that critical heuristics is critical in the sense given to that word by Kant, Hegel, and Churchman, but not in terms of the historical materialism of Marx and the Frankfurt school sociologists. Since critical systems thinking is committed to the complementarism at the level of methodology expressed in the system of systems methodologies, I hardly need to detail again its intention to make informed use of methodologies corresponding to all the combinations of assumptions set out in that framework.

Although the belief in multiple language games—and the acceptance that the differences between these cannot be resolved in a forum of speakers exhibiting communicative competence—might give us a moment's pause, critical heuristics is properly assigned to the category of critical modernism. Its affiliation to Kant's and Churchman's enlightenment philosophies determines that Ulrich's work has the fundamental modernist features. Critical systems thinking was, until Flood made his contributions, an advanced form of modernism that did not reflect on this fact. It now has the opportunity to be reflectively critically modernist. There is little except fashion that might lead it to want to go any further in the postmodernist direction than, say, Flood and Jackson's (1991a) TSI has already gone. Critical systems thinking has always been implicitly aware of many of the issues raised by the postmodernists. Knights (1989) argues that those who criticize OR and aim to reformulate the discipline of management science need to be aware of their own power. Intervention methodologies always involve the exercise of power over human subjects, and so critically inclined management scientists especially need to ask themselves what kind of subjects they would feel "morally, politically, and socially justified in producing." To this kind of social awareness, of course, critical systems thinking is already heavily committed.

It was suggested in Chapter 4 that one way of reading Chapters 5, 6, and 7 of this book was as responses to the failure of hard systems thinking to tackle extreme complexity, subjectivity, and its own conservatism: organizational cybernetics aiding the management of extreme complexity, soft systems thinking helping with multiple perceptions of reality, and critical systems thinking designed to free the discipline from serving the status quo. As far as this simplification has any validity, we can see that emancipatory systems thinking and critical systems thinking do fulfill their assigned purpose—though, of course, critical systems thinking goes much further as well. I shall be taking up some of the key aspects of critical systems thinking in future chapters: community OR in Chapter 9, complementarism in Chapter 10, and TSI in Chapter 11. Thus there will be an opportunity for readers to learn more of this most significant development in modern systems thinking. For the moment though, I turn to the practical application of systems methodologies. One thing that will emerge is that the birth of critical systems thinking owes as much to real-world experience as it does to theoretical speculation.

III

Practical Applications

8

Illustrative Case Studies

Introduction

In this chapter, I provide case studies to illustrate the use of each of the broad categories of methodological approaches outlined in Part II of the book. These cases are meant to draw out the strengths of the different approaches and, at the same time, hint at their weaknesses. In order to consolidate understanding of the strengths and weaknesses of the various methodologies, each case is analyzed according to the theoretical schemata set out in Chapter 2—to see, for example, what metaphors are being employed to understand the organization in that intervention. The first two cases are well-known and documented in the literature; the other three stem from my own consultancy experience, and the names of the organizations and some of the circumstances of these interventions have been changed. In all instances, the space available makes it impossible to give a detailed account of what actually happened. The purpose of the chapter, in any case, is to demonstrate the logic of use of the methodologies rather than to seek to provide a thorough and "accurate" exposition of the events that took place. What the reader gets lies somewhere between description of actual interventions and what Ackoff (1989) calls "fables."

Organizations as Systems—Shell's New Philosophy of Management

The following account of this sociotechnical systems intervention of the 1960s comes from Hill (1971) and Blackler and Brown (1980). Some of the background has already been provided in Chapter 3. Essentially, in the early 1960s, Shell UK was a company faced with some very pressing internal and external problems. Internally, the main problems were of an industrial-relations nature, with a multiplicity of unions confusing wage negotiations, frequent demarcation disputes, overmanning, excessive overtime working, and supervisors who felt they were losing control to the shop stewards. A 1964 "rundown" of the company, including some dismissals, had created even more bad feeling among some employees. Shell was, therefore, hardly in a position to respond flexibly to the need for rapid technological change as required by the turbulent environment it faced. Nor was it likely to be adaptive enough to adjust to other external threats to companies in the oil industry in the era that followed Suez and saw the beginnings of OPEC, as well as the birth of the ecological lobby. In 1965, a special study group headed by Hill proposed to top management some radical solutions for getting the company out of the difficulties it faced. These involved, firstly, promulgating a new "philosophy of management" throughout the company that would help change attitudes; and secondly, attending to the conditions of work of employees, improving these as part of productivity deals with the unions that would require greater flexibility and less demarcation on the employees' side. As soon as these recommendations were accepted by top management, sociotechnical researchers from the Tavistock Institute were brought in to help develop the philosophy and to consider how it could best be diffused. To these researchers, the Shell problem situation was ideal for trying out their ideas on how organizations should be managed to deal with turbulent field environments. They were committed to the need to encourage new values, to introduce flexible structures, and to use particular methods of diffusion practiced during the Norwegian Industrial Democracy Project.

The philosophy of management, as described in Chapter 3, sought to combine the pursuit of profit with various social objectives, such as treating Shell's resources as "community" resources, developing employee potential through appropriate job design, paying particular attention to employee and public safety, and minimizing pollution of the environment. It also embraced the principle of the joint optimization of the technical and social systems, although certain features of the technical system were regarded as fixed for the foreseeable future. The philosophy was diffused throughout the organization in a series of conferences, held between 1965 and 1967—first for top management, then for senior staff, and finally for lower staff levels, foremen, supervisors, and union officials. To give some indication of the effort that went into this, the philosophy conferences for senior staff were two-and-a-half-day events involving around 20 people from the same location. At the time, Hill believed that the conferences were getting across the message of the philosophy and its implications.

To complement and reinforce the lessons of the conferences, four further channels of implementation were opened. Three demonstration projects were set up aiming to show the power of sociotechnical thinking in action. Success was patchy, but the simplified nine-step method of sociotechnical analysis resulted, and other experiments started on this basis. Departmental managers were charged with the task of acting as change agents. They were supposed to enthuse their staff with the philosophy and to encourage spontaneous job-design experiments. Early reports gave the impression of great activity in this area, but it seems that enthusiasm soon waned. One initiative, in the wax department at the Stanlow refinery, was played up to be a great success story of this part of the implementation process but came later, unfortunately, to be seen as something of a disaster and got the philosophy a bad name in certain quarters (Blackler and Brown, 1980).

The third leg of implementation was the productivity deals with the unions, which offered improvements in working conditions in tune with the philosophy (including staff status for all workers) in exchange for increased efficiency, greater flexibility, and less demarcation. These were eventually successfully negotiated in 1968, the philosophy playing a very significant part in ensuring agreement and easing introduction. Finally, the design of a new refinery at Teesport was heavily influenced by sociotechnical thinking. At this green-field site, genuine joint optimization of the social and technical systems was possible, the job design criteria for satisfying work were observed, and single-status employment was introduced.

Looking back at the experiment in 1980, Blackler and Brown concluded that earlier accounts of what happened at Shell (such as by Hill) were somewhat rosy. Accepting the enthusiasm of those involved, they nevertheless felt that the philosophy had only moderate success and in most important respects did not take off as expected. Nothing could be made of the notion of Shell stewarding "community resources," and so implementation turned out to be entirely inward looking. The conferences were very top-down events with at least implicit pressure on all present to conform and accept a philosophy developed by experts and ratified by senior management. The philosophy was sold rather than argued out. Many no doubt were convinced, but many others—especially at more junior levels—just went along with it as the easiest thing to do. The initial pilot projects, according to Blackler and Brown, raised and then dashed expectations and were not imitated. Activity at departmental-manager level soon declined, and a task force had to be sent in to sort out the wax plant at Stanlow. The philosophy helped passage of the productivity agreements, but the idea of collaboration gradually gave way to manipulation as negotiations proceeded, and management drove a hard bargain as the deals took on the character of ordinary bargaining over cash. By the time of the follow-up study, the predeal orthodoxy in terms of conditions for ordinary staff had largely returned. Even at Teesport, where more of the spirit of the philosophy survived, there was some return to traditional working conditions and arrangements.

In general, Blackler and Brown believe that the philosophy failed as an attempt to forge a new role for Shell in the world and as a means of creating a long-term partnership with its work force. However, from the point of view of top management, it succeeded in the short term since it did something to restore the legitimacy of the company in the eyes of its employees and helped the firm get through a period of industrial-relations difficulties and negotiate new productivity deals. In this sense, Blackler and Brown see sociotechnical thinking of this kind as manipulative—whatever the best intentions of those using the ideas. Such thinking appeals to managers because it presents all stakeholders as benefiting equally from company success. It neglects conflicts of real interest between, say, managers and unions, and fails to recognize the power of some groups over others. Sociotechnical thinking is seen as misguided in believing that such problems can be overcome by better human relations. In reply (in Blackler and Brown, 1980), Foster, of the Tavistock Institute, and Hill defend the philosophy experiment. Foster regards it as remarkable for its day and as making a positive and worthwhile contribution. Hill sees Blackler and Brown's conclusions as negatively biased, narrow, and academic. Although the philosophy was not sufficiently embodied in the organization to prevent setbacks, it brought many positive changes and provided great learning opportunities from which other projects benefited. For example, Shell Canada's Sarnia plant in western Ontario was built in 1978 on sociotechnical principles after a "collective contract" had been agreed with the unions.

Reaching a balanced assessment of the Shell experiment is not easy. It certainly was remarkable for its time, both for the sophistication of the sociotechnical ideas employed and the considerable and genuine enthusiasm generated among many involved. On the other hand, it seems true that a lasting transformation in management style and considerable and permanent improvements in working life for ordinary employees were not achieved. It is hoped that the theoretical considerations set out in Chapter 2 can now help us to reach a broader perspective on what was done at Shell during the 1960s and what can be attained using sociotechnical systems thinking.

The intervention in Shell was focused primarily on the technical interest and sought to assist managers to predict and control better the sociotechnical systems for which they had responsibility. The more efficient development of the forces of production was to be ensured by tackling the firm's major industrial-relations problems through the productivity deals. At the same time, broader steering issues were addressed by the philosophy, which restated Shell's overall corporate purpose and aimed through the conferences and other methods of diffusion to marshal employees behind that purpose. According to Blackler and Brown, the conferences were top-down events at which the philosophy was handed down from on high rather than subjected to thorough debate and discussion. The guiding ethos was indoctrination and not mutual understanding. Whatever the intentions of the Tavistock researchers, therefore, the practical and emancipatory interests were subordinated in the real world to the technical interest.

This outcome is hardly surprising given the functionalist character of the sociotechnical thinking employed to guide the intervention. Sociotechnical theory is objectivist in nature, endorsing various principles of organization that it believes enterprises should adopt to make them more efficient, effective, flexible, and adaptive. Although attention is given to human beings, the tendency is to treat them mechanistically and to see them as becoming motivated if a series of psychological needs are met. All humans are supposed to respond favorably to appropriately designed jobs, group working, and an organization that provides them with a clear sense of purpose. People are not treated as self-conscious, autonomous actors capable of reading different meanings into the situations they face. Further, sociotechnical theory adheres to the sociology of regulation and emphasizes consensus, cooperation, and the status quo rather than conflict and contradiction between opposed interest groups. Hence in the eyes of Blackler and Brown, who perceive Shell in the 1960s as a company facing massive industrial-relations problems, the philosophy was ideologically manipulative because it tried to cover real disputes with a gloss of common interest. In reality, the negotiations over the productivity deals soon reduced to bargaining over cash. But in a sense, the manipulation worked in that the deals were put in place.

Sociotechnical thinking is dominated by the organismic metaphor, which represents the organization as an open system seeking to adapt to the turbulent environment it is confronting. Within this general orientation, consideration is also granted to improving the machinelike propensities of organizations through the sociotechnical redesign of productive processes. By the time of the Shell experiment, as the philosophy attests, the idea that successful "organisms" need a shared culture was also fully accepted. The coercive system view remains absent.

Sociotechnical thinking is based upon systemic–unitary assumptions, although it is recognized that work may have to be done before the unitary consensus emerges. It is an example of a systemic modernist approach, combining a commitment to increasing the performativity of systems with a recognition of the need to reduce environmental uncertainty.

The reader may wish to use the organismic, systemic–unitary, and systemic modernist categorizations of sociotechnical thinking to reinterpret what happened in the Shell intervention.

Hard Systems Thinking—Improving Blood Availability and Utilization

The illustrative case for hard systems thinking is a systems analysis study of blood distribution and utilization in the Greater New York area, reported in the literature by Brodheim and Prastacos (1979) and Prastacos (1980), and described by Miser and Quade (1985). Miser and Quade regard it as an outstandingly successful example of systems analysis in use, exhibiting all the main stages of a proper systems analysis approach.

The problem was essentially one of maintaining satisfactory levels of blood availability at hospitals so that it was there when and where needed, while attempting to reduce the high levels of blood that had to be discarded because it had passed its legal lifetime of 21 days without being used. At the time the study began, the "outdate rate" (the proportion of blood that had to be discarded) was around 20% of the total collected.

The sociotechnical system of concern involved human donors, collection points such as Regional Blood Centers (RBCs) where the blood was collected from donors, Hospital Blood Banks (HBBs) storing the blood in each hospital, the patients, and the medical and administrative staff engaged in various activities. The blood was collected at the RBCs, typed, screened, and processed (if necessary) before being distributed to the HBBs and used according to random patient demand. This system attained a degree of complexity due to the uncertainties of supply and demand; variations in the size of hospitals and therefore their blood banks; the relative occurrences of the eight major blood groups in the population (ranging from 39% for the most common to 0.5%); the need for processed as well as pure blood; the difficulty of estimating some costs (e.g., costs of unavailability); the need to keep actors at both the regional and hospital levels happy; and fundamentally, of course, the requirement to maintain high levels of availability balanced against the desire to operate efficiently, cutting waste and maintaining the implicit commitment to donors to make the best use of their gift.

The management of the system as it existed was decentralized and reactive. HBBs placed daily orders with RBCs designed to keep their inventories at what each considered a safe level. Historically, inventories were high because emphasis was placed on ready availability and low utilization was accepted. The RBCs responded to orders placed, making on average 7.8 deliveries to each hospital per week, while attempting to keep their own buffer stocks. The outcome of the way the system was managed was satisfactory availability but high delivery costs and, as mentioned, high wastage rates.

The systems analysis began with a phase when the researchers familiarized themselves with the Long Island blood distribution system, which was to be the test bed for the analysis. Patterns of supply and demand were established by a combination of statistical analysis and Markov-chain modeling. Acceptable availability levels at hospitals were ascertained by asking HBBs to provide estimates of what they felt to be adequate stocks of each of the eight blood types. Relatively simple mathematical models were constructed simulating the system first at the hospital, then at the regional level.

In consultation with the HBBs, various alternatives for managing the system efficiently were then considered. Decentralized (as now) and wholly centralized options were entertained, but the optimum solution was obtained from a centralized management system combined with some rotation of stocks between HBBs. There was to be centralized management at the regional level with prescheduled deliveries to HBBs supplemented by emergency deliveries as necessary. In addition, blood would be collected from HBBs at the time of scheduled deliveries (if it looked as though it would not be used) and passed onto other HBBs where that type was in short supply. A final model was constructed that achieved set targets for availability and utilization, met all HBB requirements, and specified desired inventory levels for each HBB, frequency of necessary delivery to each HBB, and the size of the retention and rotation shipments to each. At the RBC level, inventory is evaluated and adjusted daily on the basis of anticipated regional blood flow. This Programmed Blood Distribution System (PBDS) was implemented initially for four hospitals in the test region and later for others who volunteered to join the scheme. Finally, the analysts began adapting the PBDS to make it applicable to other regions.

The results of this systems analysis were impressive. Wastage of blood was cut from around 20% of the total collected to 4%. Instead of 7.8 unscheduled deliveries to each hospital per week on average, 4.2 deliveries were necessary, with only 1.4 unscheduled. This led to a reduction of approximately 64% on delivery costs, in part because the scheduled deliveries could be made at times of low traffic density. Availability of blood to patients was also improved, with the result that there were fewer cancellations in prescheduled surgery.

The success of the PBDS provides a good example of the ability of hard systems thinking to support the technical interest in prediction and control. Following empirical analytic procedures, a model of the system was built that captured the interactions going on within it to such good effect that the system became predictable. Thus it was possible to conceive of a management system making use of prescheduled deliveries—the innovation from which most of the benefits were obtained. The fact that implementation brought the expected benefits can be seen to verify that the model accurately reflected the nature of the real-world system. It is taken for granted by the systems analysts, and by Miser and Quade, that what we have here is a legitimate use of hard systems thinking. The question of what ought to be done appears obvious, and so the problem is seen to be clearly defined, with adequate measures of performance available against which to judge system effectiveness. Such a stance is possible when, as in this case, the "client" is taken to be a relatively homogeneous group of decision makers relatively free from political pressures and sympathetic to analysis. It is legitimate, as again in this instance, when the main concern is with the technical aspects of an agreed-upon transformation process. Impressively, there was constant reference back to the HBBs to check that the system would meet expectations.

The methods used in this systems analysis study confirm that hard systems thinking is functionalist in nature. The system of concern is taken to exist in the world, the interactions within it are studied, and human behavior is fed with other data into a mathematical model that is then used to ensure improved regulation of the existing system. The machine metaphor is dominant. The goals of the controllers of the system are taken as given, and the system parts are logically arranged to achieve maximum efficiency and effectiveness. The assumptions made about the problem context in the blood availability and utilization study are that it is mechanical–unitary. It is taken, and this seems to have been confirmed by events, that there is general agreement about the objectives to be achieved so that effort and imagination can be turned to the best means of achieving those objectives. The system with which the analysts have to deal exhibits aspects of complexity but remains simple enough to permit its essence to be represented in mathematical models. Finally, the case shows systems analysis as an example of systemic modernism. The system is reprogrammed to achieve increased performativity.

Organizational Cybernetics—Humberside Window Systems Ltd.

Humberside Windows is a leading Humberside and Lincolnshire window company manufacturing, selling, and fitting uPVC double glazed doors and windows. Founded in 1978, it grew dramatically and by 1989 was employing some 105 people, including 45 in the factory, 15 sales consultants, and 25 fitters. In 1989, the founder of the firm sold out to Spartan International Ltd. The new owners commissioned a study to look at the company's structure and information flows, which they felt could be improved. The systems consultants, with the agreement of management, decided to make use of Beer's VSM as a means of looking into the problems of Humberside Windows. Here I shall concentrate on the recommendations made for restructuring the firm in order to make it more viable and effective.

Having taken over the firm, Spartan International decided to rely, for the time being at least, on the skills of the existing technical director to manage its overall activities. This director had worked in several departments in Humberside Windows and understood the organization well, but inevitably found it difficult to adjust to his new role while continuing to fulfill his old duties overseeing purchasing, scheduling, fitting, and manufacture. He began to experience considerable work overload, exacerbated by the tendency of all other managers to come to him for advice and guidance. The ex-owner's interventionist style of management had not encouraged others to make decisions for themselves, and indeed there were no clear job descriptions that indicated individual spheres of discretion.

The most important roles in the organization directly responsible to the technical director were the works manager, the chief surveyor, and the scheduling officer. The works manager controlled the factory making the uPVC windows and doors and the glass shop. Things generally ran smoothly in this part of the business, although there were periods of considerable slack if the sales force could not sell enough of the product. The chief surveyor with his assistants was responsible for measuring openings for windows and doors and providing manufacturing specifications. His main concerns were the failure of many managers to take the initiative and make decisions, the tendency of sales people to try to please the customer even to the extent of selling items the company could not make, and the failure to convey proper standards of work to the fitters. The scheduling officer had to schedule jobs for the 12 fitting teams working from headquarters. He also had to handle the numerous customer complaints and to deal with remedial work. His was a very stressful job, dealing with irate customers and often unable to find senior managers willing and able to take responsibility for problems and sort them out.

On the sales side of the business were a commercial manager and a sales director. The commercial manager's duty was to secure new large commercial contracts with local authorities, regional hospital boards, builders, factories, and the like. Having recently been recruited from another company, he was acutely aware of just how chaotic management was in Humberside Windows and commented particularly on the lack of coordination between departments. The sales director's main responsibility was to increase sales to private householders. He had four sales managers under his control, each responsible for a showroom and salesmen in a particular geographical area. The sales director apparently made centralized decisions about such matters as advertising campaigns. He suffered from the same problem as all other senior managers, with other people in the firm constantly coming to him for advice about things that were not his concern.

Looking at this problem situation from the viable-system point of view, it was possible to identify three levels of recursion. Spartan International resides at recursion level 0. Recursion level 1 encompasses the headquarters of Humberside Windows and all its activities. Recursion level 2 embraces the three activities of Humberside Windows that can be regarded as viable systems in their own right—production, sales, and fitting. That these could all be viable systems is clear from the existence of firms in the window business making a living from each of these operations. Diagnosis began at recursion level 2.

Sales consists of the four geographical branches, which can be regarded as System 1 operations. Each of these has its own manager but is in reality controlled by the sales director. The sales director also fulfills the System 2 through 5 functions. The main problem here seems to be the lack of autonomy granted to the sales managers. Recommendations were made to the effect that each sales manager should become a local marketing manager responsible for promoting as well as selling the product in his or her region. The sales director would then be freed for overall marketing activities. Attention was also drawn to the need to provide adequate training to the sales force on what products and services Humberside was actually capable of providing.

Production has two System 1 operational elements—the factory and the glass shop. The basic internal management functions of the production subsystem, Systems 1 through 3, are handled well. However, this relatively efficient part of the business is not realizing its potential because it currently has no direct links with the external environment. Its only outlet is through the sales arm of Humberside Windows. Recommendations were therefore made to capitalize on the viability of this part of the business by allowing it to sell its product to other organizations selling and fitting windows and doors; obviously, appropriate Systems 4 and 5 would have to be put in place.

Fitting consists of 12 fitting teams as System 1 elements. It is poorly controlled. The scheduling officer performs the System 2 role, but Systems 3 and 3* hardly exist. The technical director is nominally Systems 4 and 5, and because of the lack of a System 3 even finds himself getting dragged into dealing with customer complaints, but as mentioned he has too many duties elsewhere to perform these functions adequately. It was recommended that proper attention be given to the metasystemic functions 2 through 5 in fitting. What should follow is better training for the fitters, with proper standards of work being communicated and demanded from them. Fitting should be subject to checks on the quality of work. Customer complaints should be handled separately from the scheduling task. Additionally, thought might be given to appointing a senior fitter to head each team.

Turning to recursion 1, the recommendations centered on trying to establish appropriate Systems 2, 3, 4, and 5 at the Humberside Windows level. Most of the managers who should have been concentrating on these functions (the sales director, the technical director) were otherwise engaged in activities at recursion level 2. To free them to operate at the proper level, a System 3 was necessary that would oversee but not interfere unnecessarily with the System 1 elements of manufacturing, sales, and fitting. These System 1 parts should be granted greater autonomy to pursue agreed-upon goals in their own way, using resources allocated in an annual budget. Adequate control could be maintained by System 3 if it institutionalized System 2 and System 3* coordination and audit channels and generally improved information flows. Freed from the need to interfere lower down in the enterprise, managers at recursion level 1 would then need to be educated, as a first step by providing them with appropriate job descriptions, to see themselves and act as managers of the whole of Humberside Window Systems Ltd. An adequate System 4 would need to be put in place. Humberside's planning was short term when it occurred at all. There was little time or effort put into market research or the future development of the business. Spartan International would need to ensure a System 5 existed that could achieve the right balance between ongoing activities and development efforts. Frequent meetings between System 3, 4, and 5 managers would initially be necessary to coordinate managerial exertions and to develop an identity for the company and an ethos to guide its actions. These needed careful planning and feeding with appropriate information.

Some of the many recommendations put to Humberside Windows were accepted and put into effect. However, others proved not to be feasible given the history and culture of the organization at that time.

This illustrative case shows organizational cybernetics giving support primarily to the technical interest. It provides knowledge oriented to regulation in the social domain that can be used to increase the steering capacities of organizations. The recommendations made to Humberside

Windows sought to make the organization more adaptive in the face of its environment while improving control of operations at all levels of the organization. If they had been followed as a whole, they should have enhanced the organization's ability to be efficient and effective, and its capacity to change in response to environmental requirements. Of course, the practical interest is also served at least to the extent that the VSM provides a model around which mutual understanding can be developed about the purpose, identity, and organizational features of the enterprise.

The recommendations were not reached solely on the basis of empirical observation of the dysfunctions of the existing system. The cybernetic principles encapsulated in the VSM highlight particularly problematic aspects of the organization of all systems and guide the investigator to consider how these are being handled in the system of concern. The model pinpoints systemic/structural constraints that have to be observed by any organization. Similarly, the recommendations emerge from ensuring that an underlying structure and system of relationships are established in the organization that obeys cybernetic principles. The structuralist bias of cybernetic diagnosis and redesign requires that an organization be produced that respects cybernetic laws.

Organizational cybernetics rests upon the machine, organism, and brain metaphors. Humberside Windows was encouraged to improve the efficiency of its transformation process, to become more responsive to its environment, and to devolve responsibility so as to increase its overall problem-solving capabilities. Organizational cybernetics is said to make systemic–unitary assumptions about problem contexts. Humberside Windows was treated as a highly complex system that needed to be made more self-regulating and self-organizing. It was not presumed necessary to address the possibility that different value positions or conflict existed among the stakeholders in the enterprise. Neglect of the culture metaphor and the problems of pluralism may have hampered the eventual acceptance of some of the recommendations made. The aim of the intervention into Humberside Windows was to increase the rationalization of the enterprise so as to improve its functioning greatly. This is entirely consistent with the systemic modernism characteristic of organizational cybernetics.

Soft Systems Thinking—Thornton Printing Company

I take as an illustrative case for soft systems thinking a strategic assumption surfacing and testing (SAST) investigation in Thornton Printing Company. This is reported more fully in Ho and Jackson (1987).

Thornton Printing Company engages in the printing of labels for other company's products and the printing of tickets. It also manufactures label-application machines for other companies. In recent years Thornton's business environment has changed very rapidly. Printing technology has been in a state of flux, with new products frequently coming onto the market. Many small and efficient firms have managed to take advantage of this situation to establish themselves and to gain a reputation for producing and delivering labels quickly and cheaply to exact customer specifications. Thornton has been unable to adapt satisfactorily to changing circumstances, and this has shown in disappointing financial returns. It does little research and development and, in fact, has no separate department for this. Inevitably it has fallen behind its competitors in product innovation. The firm has poor communications with its market and plays no role in trying to nurture its environment. Thornton's marketing has been far too passive in the face of aggressive tactics from competitors. Its sales force lacks proper training and professionalism and does not seem motivated to establish and develop customer relations. Sales personnel are unable to service customers properly because of a simple lack of knowledge about what the company can offer. Internally, communication between sales and production planning is weak, and this causes difficulties in scheduling and in maintaining proper utilization of the diverse high-technology machines.

The situation within the production function itself was also at crisis point. Traditionally, managers and supervisors felt that employees did not work hard enough and imposed close supervision and control on subordinates. This had degenerated into management by threat, as market pressures had led to very high targets for output being set and detailed work routines and procedures being enforced. There were many errors and mistakes, leading to high levels of waste and spoiled work and low-quality products. This led to excessive overtime being worked to correct problems, and this in turn increased costs. Morale was extremely low. Workers felt they were being blamed for poor-quality work that in fact often resulted from the poor-quality materials with which they were supplied. They refused to collaborate with their supervisors, and industrial-relations problems between management and unions or shop stewards were frequent.

In the face of these external threats and internal problems, Thornton obviously could have done with a well-trained and highly aware management team. In fact this was lacking. Management jobs were specialized, and there was little team spirit. A number of senior managers failed to see the scale of the difficulties facing Thornton and were reluctant to change.

The managing director of Thornton Printing Company, alarmed by the situation, determined to put things right by introducing a comprehensive quality-management program into the company. He and his executive team formulated their own quality proposals based first and foremost on the notion of "conformance to requirements." A strong corporate culture was to be propagated and introduced from the top, emphasizing the importance of quality and conformance to requirements. There was to be a "quality coordinator" to act as a champion for the program and as a troubleshooter. The program was to be introduced with quality-management sessions for top managers and then cascaded down to the shop floor, where workers would demonstrate that they had absorbed the principles by applying them in their day-to-day work. It was recognized that for implementation to work, managers and supervisors would have to change their conception of their roles and become leaders, creating excellence and quality by motivating and educating their subordinates rather than by tightly controlling and threatening them.

"Conformance to requirements" was to apply both to relationships with customers and suppliers and to all work-related activities in the organization. With regard to customers, the aim was to learn their needs more accurately and to provide them with the best possible service. The company should innovate in cooperation with customers, developing an "enhancing" relationship with them. Suppliers were expected to contribute to quality by supplying "zero-defect" products and materials. In terms of internal activity, quality requirements were to be made clear and specific and communicated effectively. Quality targets for each process were to be set and used to establish a "prevention" approach to quality. The aim was to "get things right first time" in order that there would be zero defects. If there was a deviation from output requirements, that should be regulated immediately. Nonconformance to requirements was to be eliminated. In order to ensure that employees got it right the first time, it was important that they develop the right attitude. Employees were to be motivated to "own" quality themselves in order to ensure this. Inevitably there would have to be changes in work organization to make jobs more interesting and meaningful. The managing director was convinced that if conformance to requirements could be achieved, the organization would become more adaptive, morale would improve, there would be fewer mistakes and problems, and productivity and profits would increase.

The intervention in Thornton Printing Company began when the systems consultants were invited to observe some of the early quality-management sessions arranged for senior managers at which the program was supposed to be fully debated. Observation of these sessions revealed, alarmingly, that very little real discussion took place. There was an unstated assumption that quality management was right for Thornton, that it fitted in with the corporate culture. Managers spent most of the time trying to justify the validity of the various principles proposed, rather than challenging them. Furthermore, because the assumptions underlying the ideas put forward were not debated, different interpretations of key concepts remained. With the terminology employed continuing to mean different things to different people, no genuine communication could occur, and no real consensus could be reached.

In these circumstances, the consultants were worried that the program might flounder on various fundamental weaknesses in the company that it did not address. These could be remedied by other methods in due course, but the first task was to convince the managing director of the validity of the consultants' immediate concerns. To achieve this, SAST was chosen as a methodology that could reveal the shaky assumptions upon which the quality management program was based.

Outsiders were not able to contribute actively at the sessions (one of the problems, of course). However, it was possible to present top management with a report that was critical of the quality-management program in its existing form. First, all the stakeholders—all those with an interest or concern in the program—were identified. Second, it was asked in relation to each of these stakeholders: What is being assumed of this stakeholder in believing that the quality management program will be successful? It was then a relatively easy matter to demonstrate how shaky many of these assumptions were. For the stakeholder "senior management," it was assumed that they had a shared vision of where the company was going and could communicate this to subordinates with ease. In fact, no clear vision existed. It was expected that sales staff would play a key role in nurturing customers. It was doubtful, in reality, whether they had a full understanding of what Thornton could offer to customers. Workers were assumed to be motivated to do things right the first time simply by remembering the core concepts of quality management. Workers in fact seemed unlikely to do things right the first time unless they knew something of corporate strategy and trusted their supervisors. Suppliers, it was hoped, would supply zero-defect raw materials, but the incentive for their doing so remained unclear.

This critique of the assumptions underpinning the existing program led to suggestions for an enhanced quality-management program based on different assumptions, and a comparison of how the existing and enhanced versions would address the problem situation confronting the firm. Suggestions were also made to Thornton about how other systems approaches might help alleviate problems not dealt with in the quality-management program. Specific uses were proposed for cognitive mapping, Checkland's SSM, dialectical debate, the VSM, and the system of systems methodologies (Ho and Jackson, 1987). Thus the study anticipated the informed use of different methodologies in combination, which is now a hallmark of critical systems thinking (see the next section).

Further, the consultants continually entertained for their own purposes the possibility that this particular business organization might be most appropriately viewed as providing a systemic–coercive context. The owners liked to regard it as a family firm with a genuine concern for the work force. However, this image was in danger of shattering in the face of increasing industrial unrest. Managers were eager to paper over the cracks that were emerging with appropriate human relations techniques. The consultants were asked to see the industrial disputes as a result of a short-term breakdown in communications. In fact, from the systemic–coercive perspective, the firm actually operated in a very traditional manner and employed autocratic control procedures; the coercion had at last come to the consciousness of the work force. This entertaining of different views of the organization was another anticipation, this time of the total systems intervention (TSI) methodology discussed in Chapter 11. In this case it led to questions of consultant obligations coming to the fore.

The employment of SAST in Thornton Printing Company was in support of the practical interest in promoting intersubjective communication. The quality-management sessions taking place were not being very successful in securing mutual understanding. It was felt that introducing an element of dialectical debate would help draw out different interpretations of the concepts of quality management, and different perspectives on the purpose of the program, so that the discussion would become much richer and the consensus reached would be more soundly based. Of course, like all soft systems methodologies, SAST is inhibited in the support it can offer the practical interest because of its failure to recognize the effect of structural inequalities and power relationships on the kind of debate that takes place. It lacks an emancipatory dimension and therefore will acquiesce in consensus derived from systematically distorted communication.

SAST rests upon subjectivist rather than objectivist assumptions about systems thinking. As can be seen from the Thornton intervention, the concern is with understanding and engineering the way people view the world. If the way people perceive things alters, then it is assumed they will have the will and power to bring about desired changes to social systems. The methodology makes no use of quantitative techniques. SAST is regulative in the approach it adopts to social systems. It assumes an underlying order and consensus and seeks simply to readjust this at the ideological level. Making subjectivist and regulative assumptions amounts to an adherence to the interpretive sociological paradigm in Burrell and Morgan's terms.

The culture metaphor is privileged in SAST, the purpose of its use in Thornton being to create a stronger and more uniform corporate culture. Other metaphors take a back seat. SAST handles pluralism well, first surfacing and making use of it to generate creative discussion and then managing its resolution in a new synthesis. It pays little attention to systemic complexity. The consultants in Thornton had to suggest other systems approaches to deal with problems of organizational structure. SAST, therefore, responds to mechanical–pluralist problem contexts. As an underdeveloped representative of the critical modernist tradition of thought, SAST has some potential for assisting humans in the self-conscious pursuit of goals and ideals. However, because of its underdevelopment, it easily slips into becoming an adjunct of systemic modernism. In Thornton it sought to contribute to engineering human perceptions and actions so as to facilitate the smoother functioning of the overall sociotechnical system.

Critical Systems Thinking—West Newton Council for Voluntary Service

Examples of critical systems heuristics in use as an emancipatory systems approach are provided in Ulrich (1983). I concentrate here on critical systems thinking itself and the way it enables the complementary and informed use of various systems methodologies. This illustrative case is therefore an example of how to employ the TSI approach described more fully in Chapter 11. The study was undertaken for the West Newton Council for Voluntary Service. It employed SSM as the dominant methodology throughout but with the VSM in a strong supporting role. The coercive-system metaphor also helped to illuminate the nature of the problem situation, although it did not become necessary to translate this into the use of any additional systems methodology. A much fuller account of this project is given in Flood and Jackson (1991a).

Councils for Voluntary Service act as umbrella organizations for the wide variety of other voluntary bodies they have in their membership. They are local development agencies that are non-profit making and non-governmental. There are about 200 such Councils for Voluntary Service in England and Wales. Councils for Voluntary Service aim to promote more and better voluntary action in their areas. West Newton is a large Council for Voluntary Service (CVS); it was founded in 1980 and grew rapidly in size and influence. By the time of the study it had more than 300 voluntary and community organizations under its umbrella and employed around 80 staff.

West Newton CVS had a number of problems, but the one on which the project came to focus concerned certain difficulties faced by its executive committee. This committee was experiencing problems trying to oversee and control what was a rapidly expanding organization in a turbulent environment. It continued to operate as it did when the CVS was first founded, meeting every six weeks for a programmed two hours. The committee did not possess the flexibility or means to respond to the needs of the CVS West Newton had become, and was widely perceived to be ineffective. From a series of interviews with committee members and staff, and other gathering of information, it seemed that the following were very significant issues that had to be addressed:

- Providing more time for the executive committee to deal with policy issues
- Increasing the professionalism of the committee's handling of management issues
- Improving the handling of committee business
- Generating mutual respect between committee members and staff
- Making the committee more aware of staff work
- Increasing committee contact with staff
- Increasing staff confidence in the committee

On the basis of the information obtained on West Newton CVS, it would have been easy to think of it as an organism trying to grow at the same time as adapt in a highly turbulent environment. Our attention had, however, become focused on the "brain" of that organism—the executive committee. In cybernetic terms, the committee did not possess the variety to manage the organization. It somehow had to be equipped with the various functions of management exhibited by Beer's VSM. Presenting a report based upon the VSM might well, therefore, have provided some useful solutions to the executive committee's problems. It would, however, have ignored other very significant aspects of the problem situation, for the CVS was nothing if it was not a coalition of different groups with somewhat different interests and ways of perceiving the situation. A way had to be found to generate a consensus for change among the elements of this coalition. And what was surely needed was a change in the culture of the organization so that it was ready to accept change and particularly to rethink the way the executive committee functioned. If these matters were not tackled, then any rationalistic report might fail to achieve improvements because of the opposition it generated, or because it failed to gain the commitment and enthusiasm of the most involved agents. The project, therefore, had to generate a culture for change in the organization—and change that did not offend any of the groups in the coalition. At the same time, of course, the eventual design had to meet cybernetic criteria of viability. The executive committee had to become an effective "brain."

This led to the choice of SSM as the dominant methodology. SSM articulates particularly well the concerns raised by the culture metaphor and is highly suitable for contexts exhibiting pluralism. There was also going to be a role for organizational cybernetics as a supporting methodology, backing up SSM in dealing with systemic complexity because of its understanding of "brain"-related problems. Finally, it seemed as well to be aware of the significant political aspects to the problem context; these at times threatened to take the situation beyond the pluralistic toward the conflict-and-coercion end of the participants dimension. There was conflict between some on the executive committee and some staff, and on the committee itself between those happy to leave responsibility for running the show to the staff and those who tended to suspect the motives of the key officers. Particular attention had to be paid to the most influential individuals associated with the various interest groups in order to gain their support and trust. However, in this case, the political aspect could be handled informally within the bounds of SSM.

Embarking on the project using SSM, the first task was to build a "rich picture" of the problem situation. The next step was to draw from all the information gathered (and incorporated in the rich picture) some insightful ways of looking at the work of the executive committee and the problems it faced. Six relevant systems were in fact proposed and subject to systemic investigation. The executive committee was defined and modeled as a representative body for the voluntary sector; a policy development committee; a need-seeking system; a classical management committee; a committee accountable to CVS members for CVS staff work; and a staff-supporting body. Interestingly enough, these relevant systems, uncovered and refined during lengthy discussion and debate with CVS staff and executive committee members, mapped well onto the kinds of concern that would have emerged had executive committee structures and procedures been compared with Beer's VSM.

The fact that our choice of relevant systems had this additional cybernetic legitimacy gave us confidence. We were clearly thinking along the right lines if we wanted to provide the executive committee with the requisite variety to manage the organization. Throughout the study we continued to employ this cybernetic rationality in a subordinate role, thinking about what functions had to be performed in Beer's VSM and how they could be carried out in West Newton CVS. From the outside, indeed, it might have looked as though we could have taken a shortcut through all the information gathering and interviews by using Beer's VSM directly to pinpoint cybernetic faults. This would be a mistaken impression. We had to change the culture of the organization to create a momentum for change, and we had to hold together the various factions in the coalition, securing the support of each for the proposals. At the same time we had to sidestep and manage the political problems. Only constant working with the people in the organization, so that they were fully involved in generating proposals and came to own the suggested solutions, could address these issues. SSM had to remain dominant if anything was going to change in West Newton CVS. The brain-driven logic could not be allowed to take over from the culture emphasis supplied by SSM.

The implications of the root definitions and conceptual models deriving from the relevant systems were fully discussed with the most important members of the executive committee and the staff. A comparison was then made between the conceptual models and the real-world situation. Recommendations gradually began to emerge. Eventually, through a long, drawn-out, and time-consuming process of going back and forth between important committee members and staff and constantly modifying the recommendations, we arrived at proposals we believed had general support. They also met the minimum cybernetic specifications that we felt any changes should attain in order to make the organization viable. We were rewarded for this hard work when the recommendations were presented at an executive committee meeting. The significant actors had come to own them as their own, and there was no opposition to the setting up of a subcommittee charged to oversee their implementation. The recommendations included moving management and auditing tasks down to specialist committees, thus leaving time for policy discussion at executive committee meetings; setting up committee "support groups" for CVS staff in important areas of work; and providing induction and training sessions for new executive committee members. The operating procedures of the CVS executive committee were substantially restructured with the help of these recommendations.

The West Newton case study demonstrates most of the facets of critical systems thinking and practice. It was conducted with constant critical reflection upon the relative strengths and weaknesses of the systems tools being used and with full attention given to the social consequences of their use. Different systems approaches were employed in a complementarist manner at both the theoretical and methodological levels. The project was emancipatory in the outward sense that it was assisting an organization committed to helping the most disadvantaged members of the community. It will be easy enough for the reader, therefore, to relate this illustrative case to the theoretical schemata of Chapter 2 following the same arguments that were set out for critical systems thinking in Chapter 7. A critical systems approach employs methodologies that cater for all the human species imperatives as identified by Habermas. The technical and practical interests are respected, and the latter is guarded by emancipatory reflection and action from adverse social conditions that might preclude any approximation to communicative competence among the involved and affected actors. Rationalities emerging from all the sociological paradigms are used; critical systems thinking being different from other systems approaches in accepting the strong possibility of contradiction, conflict, and domination in social systems and accepting the need to respond to this possibility. Critical systems thinking uses all available metaphors to gain a better understanding of problem situations. In the West Newton case the organismic, brain, culture, and coercive-system metaphors were all found to be insightful. Problem contexts will be observed from all the perspectives highlighted by the system of systems methodologies during the course of a critical systems study in order to make an informed choice of dominant and subordinate methodologies. Finally, although critical systems thinking responds to the postmodernist critique and accepts and welcomes alternative rationalities, it proclaims itself unashamedly to be reflectively critically modernist in orientation.

Conclusion

I have tried, in this chapter, to show how each of the categories of methodological approaches to which a chapter was devoted in Part II of this book is used in practice. Obviously, I have only been able to take examples from each of the categories—asking systems analysis to stand in for the whole of hard systems thinking, SAST for the whole of soft systems thinking, and so on. Nevertheless, the reader should now have a greater appreciation of the relative strengths and weaknesses of each of the methodological types and a sense of the wide range of different problem situations that can be addressed using systems methodologies. If the reader is also beginning to get a feel for how reflection upon the underlying philosophical and sociological assumptions made by different methodologies can assist with the choice of appropriate approach for the problem situation confronted, then the chapter will have served all its purposes.

9

Community Operational Research

Introduction

If the last chapter provided examples of how each type of systems methodology is used, this chapter has the somewhat different aim of demonstrating how the integrated use of different systems methodologies can support a particular project. The project in question is community operational research (COR), a relatively recent development in management science. COR aims to make appropriate operational research expertise available to organizations whose main purpose is to serve the community rather than to make a profit or to perform some government function. Community organizations are often small, lack a clear managerial hierarchy, show a commitment to participative decision making, and possess few tangible resources. They pose different challenges to OR methodology. It is argued in this chapter that the use of an integrated set of systems methodologies, with an awareness of the strengths and weaknesses of the different approaches, is the best way to pursue COR. The background to COR and the purposes of the initiative are first described. Jackson and Keys's system of systems methodologies is suggested as a possible support for COR practice. Some examples of problems encountered by community clients and the responses that can be made by choosing appropriate systems methodologies are then outlined. This chapter draws on work first reported in Jackson (1987d, 1988b).

Background

The usual impression of operational research held by other systems researchers is of a hard systems approach that seeks to use quantitative techniques to solve tactical problems in pursuit of goals specified by management in large organizations. This view of OR, and especially as it is not a wholly unfair characterization of much contemporary practice, should make us pause in considering the prospects for COR. For OR of this type (let us call it "impoverished OR") would appear, for many reasons, to be unsuitable for the different context of community and cooperative organizations. It is as well to be aware, therefore, that OR began not as a mathematical but as an interdisciplinary science, and that the creation of interdisciplinary teams was seen as one of the most important elements of OR practice in the early textbooks (Churchman et al., 1957; Ackoff and Sasieni, 1968). I should also note that these same textbooks emphasize that OR is a "systems approach," aiming to be relevant to strategic as well as tactical problems, and we should appreciate that many of the pioneers of OR were socialist scientists who believed that OR should be used for public rather than sectional interests, and that only under socialism could science realize its full potential for increasing human well-being (Rosenhead, 1987).

Given the aspirations of early OR theorists and practitioners, the way the discipline and profession actually developed and was employed came to many as a major disappointment (as discussed in Chapter 4). Some within OR, however, did keep faith with its original intentions. Cook (1973), for example, lamented that its current methodology has led OR to move from the position of "science helping society" to that of "science helping the establishment," and sought to develop new methods with clients outside the normal power structure. Others remained true, but felt obliged to change the disciplinary banner under which they worked— Ackoff, Beer, and Churchman, for instance. We can, therefore, reasonably talk in terms of an "enhanced OR" based on the spirit of the early pioneers of OR and drawing upon the work of those (either in OR or on the fringe of the subject) who have continued to develop the discipline according to its original intentions. This kind of OR is an interdisciplinary science employing rational methods to alleviate ill-structured and strategic (as well as tactical) problems arising in social systems, for the benefit of society. It is not unreasonable to associate enhanced OR with critical systems thinking and to suggest that critical systems thinking can provide to this form of OR the theoretical support that it has hitherto lacked and that can help its progress and development.

On the basis of enhanced OR, the idea of community OR begins to look much more plausible. Furthermore, a long tradition of thought upon which community OR can build is identified. Of particular significance, from this point of view, must be Ackoff's work with the leaders of the black ghetto of Mantua (Ackoff, 1970, 1974c), work carried out under Cook's guidance with inner-city community organizations (Luck, 1984), Beer's project with the Allende government in Chile (Beer, 1981a), and various projects undertaken from Bath University in the United Kingdom with charitable and community groups (Jones and Eden, 1981; Sims and Smithin, 1982).

The recent surge in COR activity in the United Kingdom—including the setting up of the Community OR Unit at Northern College, Barnsley; the Centre for Community OR at Hull University; and a national COR network (see Carter et al., 1987)—can, however, be more immediately traced to the community OR initiative launched by the Operational Research Society in 1986 and inspired by its then-president, Jonathan Rosenhead. In his presidential address to the society, Rosenhead (1986) set out the route he believed OR had to follow if it was to carve out for itself a significant role in society, and if future progress in the discipline was to be facilitated. This involved expanding the range of OR's clients beyond the managements of large organizations and, on the basis of the challenges arising in assisting "alternative" clients, developing available themes and methodologies to make them more appropriate to new problem situations. Rosenhead's preferred vehicle for traveling this route turned out to be COR, and the announcement of the Operational Research Society initiative followed.

Two assumptions underpin Rosenhead's conception of COR. The first is that OR, as an interdisciplinary, systems-based subject with a modeling orientation, can be of great assistance to a range of alternative clients. The second is that, in trying to help such clients, the OR approach can be enriched in ways that will increase its capacity to aid decision making in society at large. The following will, it is hoped, lend support to these assumptions by considering in turn the purposes that COR can serve, a possible theoretical framework to underpin the activity, and some examples of COR practice.

The Purposes of COR

During the course of inviting proposals from institutions to house a community OR unit, the steering group for the Operational Research Society initiative stated (Steering Group, 1986) the aims of COR to be:

1. To extend awareness of OR to new sections of the community, thus broadening the range of clients
2. To demonstrate the relevance of OR to a wider range of problem situations
3. To enrich OR methodology and revitalize intellectual life through involvement in novel types of problems

4. To contribute to improving the quality of discussion and decision making in society at large

It is also possible to interpret COR as having a more critical and radical dimension. This interpretation will be followed here and can be summarized under two more headings:

5. To help redress the resource imbalance that exists under capitalism by assisting those underprivileged in this respect
6. To develop decision-aiding and problem-solving methods appropriate to a more democratic and socialist milieu

The implications of these possible purposes will now be explained as a prelude, in the following sections, to suggesting how they might be realized.

(1) The intention to broaden the range of OR's clients implies that the present set of customers is seriously limited. Rosenhead (1986) argues that the customers of OR have been

> almost exclusively . . . the managements of formally established and legally entrenched organizations disposing of substantial resources (capital, equipment, buildings, supplies), including the labor power of their employees.

Following Rosenhead's writings and Cook (1973), with some additions, the list of excluded groups will number, among others, patients' associations, community health councils, trade unions, consumer groups, political parties, charitable bodies, citizen groups, residents' associations, Councils for Voluntary Service, voluntary organizations, and workers' cooperatives. As Rosenhead (1986) suggests, some of these have been ignored because they lack the funds to pay for OR consultants, while others, such as trade unions, have been neglected because of mutual suspicions regarding aims and intentions and because of fears of alienating OR's traditional clientele of managers.

In order to extend the range of organizations served, OR consultants will have to accept the enhanced version of OR, be prepared to sympathize with the more varied concerns exhibited by "alternative" clients, and be willing to provide services at reduced cost to needy clients—as suggested long ago by Ackoff (1974b). To extend awareness of the usefulness of OR to new groups will entail publishing relevant work done through the various networks that link nontraditional clients. It will also help if methods and techniques suitable for community OR are taught on degree courses and as a specialist provision to alternative clients.

(2) As has already been suggested, to demonstrate the relevance of OR to a wider range of problem situations will require the abandonment of "impoverished OR" and a commitment to the creation of an "enhanced

OR," drawing upon the spirit of the original pioneers of the discipline and upon the work of those who, whether calling themselves operational researchers or not, have developed OR or "systems" according to that spirit. The kind of impoverished OR that became the norm in the 1960s, and which still remains in the ascendancy, is unsuitable for the great majority of problems found in the community context. In large part this is because, as Rosenhead (1986) argues, it evolved and was fashioned according to the needs of large bureaucratic organizations with a tendency toward centralization, an emphasis on controlling their members' activities, and an interest in deskilling their workers. Traditional OR methodology reflects the need for a hierarchically organized decision-making system that can dictate the goals to be pursued and can ensure implementation of recommended procedures using autocratic control devices. In these circumstances human elements could be regarded as passive, and quantitative and optimizing techniques employed.

In doing community OR, there will be fewer situations where a clearly defined goal can be agreed upon or can be enforced through the managerial hierarchy, and many more situations where debate and consensus building will be necessary before action can be taken. Wide involvement of personnel in decision making is necessary if satisfactory results are to be obtained and implementation achieved. Fortunately, during the 1970s and 1980s a number of "softer" approaches were developed in OR (e.g., Eden, Jones, and Sims, 1983) and systems thinking (Ackoff, 1981a; Checkland, 1981a; Mason and Mitroff, 1981) that encourage and facilitate participation and debate. An enhanced OR can utilize these methods in assisting alternative clients to come to terms with the "messes" (Ackoff, 1981b) with which they are constantly confronted.

(3) Just as the OR methods wrought in the service of large corporations took on a specific form tuned to the needs of these enterprises, so the OR fashioned in the community context will take on characteristics that, it is hoped, will make it adept in these circumstances. Thus the experience of doing OR for alternative clients should enrich OR methodology and revitalize the intellectual life of the discipline and profession. The organizations that community OR will serve usually lack the resources of traditional clients, may be wedded to democratic decision-making procedures, and may lack a clear managerial hierarchy that can delimit preferences and ensure the implementation of recommended changes. The usual props supporting the success of impoverished OR will therefore be missing, and practitioners will be forced in a different direction if their work is to prove useful. Rosenhead (1987) has listed some of the characteristics that an "alternative OR" will have to take on. Six features of alternative OR are arrived at by taking each of six characteristics he sees as underpinning

"managerialist OR" and replacing it by its opposite or "deadly enemy." The dimensions of alternative OR are then:

- A "satisficing" approach that permits different objectives to be measured in their own terms
- The use of analysis to support judgment with no aspiration to replace it
- The treatment of human elements as active subjects
- An acceptance of conflict over goals and the development of transparent methods that clarify conflict and facilitate negotiation
- Problem formulation on the basis of a bottom-up process in which decisions are taken as far down the hierarchy as there is expertise to resolve them
- The acceptance of uncertainty as an inherent characteristic of the future, and a consequent emphasis on keeping options open

A number of soft OR and soft systems thinking approaches already demonstrate some of these characteristics and can provide a good foundation for the further enrichment of OR methodology.

(4) The tools and techniques developed to aid alternative clients should, of course, contribute to improving the quality of discussion and decision making in the sectors of society in which these clients operate. This, however, is not the only benefit to emerge for society. It can be argued that in many other sections of society, too, methods capable of alleviating "messes" will be welcomed. For example, strategic problems in organizations and social issues facing governments are of a type with those confronting COR's clients—ill-structured, involving many stakeholders with multiple perceptions, and embedded in an uncertain environment. The work conducted by Ackoff (1970) and his colleagues with leaders of the Mantua black ghetto illustrates the point. The project revealed the need for continuous, adaptive, participative planning in the situation faced by the ghetto leaders—a situation characterized by uncertainty, lack of hierarchy, and the need for active intervention. The idea that planning should be continuous, adaptive, and participative later became the cornerstone of the interactive planning methodology recommended by Ackoff (1981a) to corporate executives facing turbulent environments. So, in exposing itself to alternative clients and learning from the experience, OR may become more relevant to the strategic and social concerns from which it has been effectively excluded because impoverished OR is only deemed suitable for resolving tactical questions.

(5) It has been argued by Ackoff and Churchman that OR has a social responsibility to serve all the stakeholders of the systems in which it intervenes, and all segments of society. For Ackoff (1974b), OR practi-

tioners, if they are to deserve the title "professional," must ensure that the interests of those not participating in a decision but affected by it are considered. And they should make provision for all those who might benefit from OR but cannot afford it. Ackoff has given detailed consideration (1974c, 1981a) to how planning can be made more participative, involving more of the interested parties, and how resources to assist with planning can be made available to the more underprivileged of these groups. Churchman (1970) similarly argues that the primary responsibility of OR as a profession must be to serve all the "customers" of the system it is supposed to be benefiting, and not just the powerful decision makers.

Both Ackoff and Churchman seem to believe, however, that the resource imbalances that are admitted to exist under capitalism—and that prevent full participation by those underprivileged in this respect—can be sidestepped by good OR practice that persuades the powerful that they, too, have something to gain by admitting the powerless into decision making (Ackoff, 1982; Jackson, 1982, 1983). While this is worth a try, self-respecting community OR practitioners on occasion will have to take sides. They will come across conflicts of interest that cannot be simply resolved through debate with the powerful. To challenge resource imbalances, the community OR practitioner may be called upon to help develop methods of struggle against the advantaged group or groups.

(6) Rosenhead (1986) has argued that there is nothing inherently capitalist about OR and that

> despite the market/control bias of the dominant methodology which it has actually accreted . . . it could be argued that OR prefigures a planning mechanism for a society whose impetus does not come from the dynamic of capital accumulation.

Community OR workers of a radical bent will be hoping to show the truth of this and will certainly content themselves with the opinion that the tools and techniques perfected with alternative clients are those that will be most useful in some democratic, non-exploitative, socialist society of the future. Various methods already developed in the tradition of enhanced OR show potential in this respect. Checkland (1981a) has suggested that his soft systems methodology can help enrich and structure debates approximating to the model of communicative competence that Habermas believes must underpin any rational society. Beer's (1981a) work in Chile illustrated how organizational cybernetics could be used to design a form of economic coordination that might prove more acceptable than the market mechanisms employed in capitalist countries and the centralized bureaucratic planning that, until recently, dominated in East European communist states.

A Theory to Guide COR

Consideration of the purposes outlined above suggests that COR practitioners need to engage in action research. The purposes embrace a commitment both to practical problem alleviation and to science. These two commitments can, to a large extent, be realized together through action research. Existing knowledge will be employed in the choice and use of appropriate OR and systems methodologies and techniques to help clients for whom, at present, little OR gets done. This experience will then become the basis for learning to what extent and in what ways existing knowledge needs to be modified to provide better guidance and more effective practice in the future. Successful action research demands a set of integrated and clearly formulated theoretical hypotheses and a closely monitored program of practical intervention. In this section of the chapter I will concentrate on the first of these requirements.

In order for any action-research program to realize its aims it needs to be built upon theoretical premises that can guide practice and against which the results of practice can be interpreted. The idea that it is possible to start with pure observation on practice and, drawing upon this, to construct theory is not defensible. All observation and all practical intervention is already and always premised upon some theoretical assumptions—whether made explicit or not. Science and technology progress best if theoretical and methodological assumptions are made clear at the outset. This permits other scholars and practitioners to carry out falsification tests and to learn and contribute to knowledge in a discipline. A body of work and an intellectual literature can develop around the original contributions. The process of incrementally building up knowledge in the field of interest is set in motion.

We need, therefore, some theoretical guidelines on which to base COR practice. In order that our search is not linked to any preconceptions about the current nature of OR, these should initially be very broad. To this end Jackson (1987d) has offered a very general account of organizations as systems, derived from the work of Habermas and from the notion of organizations as sociotechnical systems. His argument from this is that problems arise for the human species if the *systems* with which they deal become difficult to predict and control and/or if there is a lack of genuine agreement among *participants* about the objectives they wish to see attained through organizational systems. This allows us to develop a theoretical codification of the problems likely to arise within organizations for OR practitioners, from which it is a short step to specifying the nature of an enhanced OR suitable for steering COR work. The theoretical codification is, of course, Jackson and Keys's (1984) and Jackson's (1987c) ideal-type classification of problem contexts.

As outlined earlier, Jackson and Keys classify problem contexts along two dimensions, according to the nature of the systems of concern and the relationship between the relevant participants. Systems stretch from the mechanical (relatively simple) to the systemic (complex); participants can be in a unitary (agree upon goals), pluralist (have differences), or coercive (fundamental divergencies, bound together by power) relationship to one another. The six-celled matrix of Figure 2.2 emerges, with problem contexts labeled mechanical–unitary, systemic–unitary, mechanical–pluralist, systemic–pluralist, mechanical–coercive, and systemic–coercive. If the ability of COR to help alternative clients is not to be restricted, then it should possess the facility to operate in each of these problem contexts.

From the point of view of impoverished OR, this is an impossible standard to meet. There will be times, when confronted with mechanical–unitary contexts, that the techniques of classical OR will be useful because a system can be modeled and optimized in pursuit of agreed-upon goals. The optimal way to deliver services to members of a trade union may not differ from the optimal way of carrying out the same activity in a private business organization. But, as will be easy to appreciate, it is reasonable to expect a shift in the balance of problem contexts found when serving nontraditional clients, away from the unitary and toward the pluralist and coercive. There will be more situations where debate and consensus building are necessary before action can be taken, and more situations where the client needs to be supported in the face of powerful opposing interests. It is fortunate that there is the tradition of enhanced OR, to which I have referred and which provides a variety of OR-related, systems-based methodologies corresponding to many of the ideal-type problem contexts outlined.

If, therefore, we abandon the narrow scientism of impoverished OR and work with enhanced OR, embracing approaches such as cybernetics and soft systems thinking, we can see that we have already gone some way toward developing the necessary range of methods that will be required in doing OR work in the community situation. Jackson and Keys's complementarist system of systems methodologies demonstrates this case (see Figure 2.3). It can also be used to help further enrich the methods available to community OR. It insists on the continual development of the theoretical side of the work and hints at the areas from which theoretical support might be forthcoming. For example, once pluralism and coercion are encountered, the social sciences become the obvious source of insight, however underdeveloped they may be at present. Increased dialogue between operational researchers and social scientists is to be encouraged. The classification can also help on the practical side, giving cohesion to the work undertaken, guidance on the choice of appropriate tools and techniques, and criteria for the choice of projects. It is to the practice of COR that we now turn.

COR Practice

I attempt to show in this section how the theory and the methodological procedures mentioned can be utilized in COR practice. The examples that follow are meant to illustrate the sorts of problems that can arise in COR and the kind of enhanced OR approach that can be adopted if the system of systems methodologies is used for theoretical guidance. They are drawn from projects I and others have undertaken at the Centre for Community OR at Hull University, but are not intended to be accurate reports of these projects. The examples are arranged in order according to whether the context was defined as unitary, pluralist, or coercive.

The first example concerns a project with a small "entertainments group" (Jackson and Alabi, 1986). We can take this as a community organization because of its commitment to the local area and strong orientation to conservation. The converted warehouses it used for some of its activities were highly regarded by conservationists and had won five major awards. The organization, which had begun originally as one club, had grown considerably in size and had plans for further expansion. The directors felt the need to move toward a more formal structure with proper planning, control, and information-handling procedures. At the same time, they did not want to lose the informal management style that had created a particular atmosphere within the company. It was decided to treat the problem context as systemic–unitary (there were other possibilities) and to try a cybernetic approach to the problem based upon Beer's work. The group was modeled at three levels of recursion, and the structures and information flows actually in place compared with those suggested by the VSM. Focusing on the middle level of recursion, recommendations were made about how the functioning of Systems 1 through 5 could be improved and appropriate information flows designed. The proposals supported an essentially decentralized structure of decision making, with more autonomy granted to the parts of System 1, overall control being maintained through the strengthening of System 3 and the development of efficient information channels. The intention was to maintain informality at the human level while formalizing routine business processes.

The majority of problem contexts encountered in dealing with small community and cooperative organizations are probably best defined as pluralist. Though there will be strong divergences of opinion on the exact aims to be pursued and the best means of achieving these, there is usually an underlying shared value system that can be tapped as the basis for a temporary consensus around a particular issue. There will often be, as well, some commitment toward democratic decision making. Two examples might suffice to give an indication of this type of situation.

The first example involved an assumption-surfacing exercise using Mason and Mitroff's (1981) SAST approach. The aim was to give the development workers in a Co-operative Development Agency insights into their behavior as a collective and to help them in decision making in the future. The particular focus of the exercise was a disagreement in the agency over the relative merits of top-down (as against bottom-up) co-operative development work. The top-down approach, which involves identifying business opportunities and then recruiting individuals to form worker cooperatives in these fields, is usually viewed with great mistrust in cooperative circles. The preferred approach is bottom-up, essentially encouraging and assisting groups already thinking about starting cooperatives in particular fields. Group formation, stakeholder analysis, assumption surfacing, and synthesis sessions were staged in accordance with the approach, and the exercise helped clarify where differences of opinion lay and produced consensus on the need for experiments with a modified top-down approach. This intervention is described much more fully in Jackson (1989b) and Flood and Jackson (1991a).

The second example involved assisting the staff of a Council for Voluntary Service to establish some criteria for evaluating the performance of the council (Clemson and Jackson, 1988). In accordance with SAST principles, a wide cross-section of individuals with an interest in the problem was assembled. It was recognized that the established goal and system models of organizational effectiveness were inappropriate given the multitude of different viewpoints about what success for the council would mean. Using stakeholder analysis, it was possible to draw up a list of relevant, interested parties. This list was used to ask questions about how each of these parties would see success for the council and made it possible to build up an extremely rich picture of the potential expectations held of the council. Surveys were then conducted to establish the actual views of these groupings, and an evaluation system designed that allowed continuous feedback to the council of changing attitudes and expectations toward its activities.

The above two examples were relatively short interventions as part of longer projects. They did not themselves involve any sophisticated redesign of procedures and structures and can therefore be perceived as taking place within mechanical–pluralist contexts. The Co-operative Development Agency provides another example (Chung and Jackson, 1987), this time of a problem context defined to be systemic–pluralist. The agency was disappointed with the number of cooperatives being set up, by the number of inquiries received from the public, and by the number of people coming to the agency to ask for help. It was presumed that something was wrong with the marketing strategy, and Checkland's soft systems methodology was employed to look into this activity. Various possibilities for improving marketing were considered in systems terms—planning, organizing, and controlling marketing activities; mobilizing potential support for marketing; using more appropriate techniques; a more aggressive top-down strategy; and ways of improving the image of the agency and the idea of workers' cooperatives. Recommendations were made asking for a more positive attitude to marketing, a division of labor to ensure that marketing was not neglected (structural change), and regular marketing audits (procedural change).

The context facing a voluntary organization, a community furniture venture, was also considered to be systemic–pluralist. This organization collects furniture from people who no longer need it and provides it, after refurbishment if necessary, to those in need. Demand for the services of the venture was decreasing, and problems loomed associated with the possible end of funding. Checkland's methodology was again used to investigate advertising strategy and possible income-generating activities, including selling surplus furniture.

Another project was in a distinctly coercive setting, and—since the sources of power imbalance were relatively clear—might be regarded as being within a mechanical–coercive context. This involved the proposed development of a piece of land as a nuclear waste disposal site. Test drilling had already begun on the site. The resources available to the company concerned, and the government, were clearly much greater than those of the local protest group and the local councils that were opposing the development. An attempt was made using Ulrich's (1983) critical systems heuristics to clarify the value judgments embedded in different proposals for the site, with a view to securing more meaningful debate on the issue. Fortunately, because of a change in government policy, it was possible to abort this project.

As a final example, reference can be made to an ongoing project that is taking a critical direction and keeping its options open as to how its problem context might best be defined. This intervention is being undertaken for the National Association of Councils for Voluntary Service and is being funded by the Leverhulme Trust. It concerns the design of appropriate evaluation systems for Councils for Voluntary Services (CVS).

While it is tempting to define all CVS as being in pluralist contexts and to recommend "multi-actor" systems of evaluation (see Jackson and Medjedoub, 1988) there are stages in the life cycle of CVS and situations in certain CVS that are more appropriately understood using some alternative appellation. In these circumstances, the goal and system methods of evaluation retain considerable usefulness when converted into practical tools that can be used by CVS. The research is likely to recommend a contingency approach to evaluation resting upon complementarist principles.

The purpose of this section has been to give some examples of COR work using enhanced OR, and to show how the theory outlined in the last section can both guide community OR practice and assist reflection on it.

Conclusion

In this chapter, COR has been introduced and an attempt made to show how it links with a long tradition of "enhanced OR" work. The purposes of pursuing COR were outlined and a framework provided that can assist in realizing those purposes by linking theoretical and practical endeavors. Finally, some examples of COR projects were given, showing how these relate to the classificatory framework. The argument is that the use of an integrated set of systems methodologies is the best way to pursue COR. The integration suggested in the chapter was obtained by using Jackson and Keys's system of systems methodologies. However, a similar result could have been obtained using any of the theoretical schemata provided by Habermas, Burrell and Morgan, or Morgan as outlined in Chapter 2. What is important is that there is some means of distinguishing between different OR and systems methodologies according to their strengths and weaknesses. Once this can be done it becomes possible to recognize circumstances in which one approach is more appropriate than others. This book is dedicated to the belief that this is a useful thing to do. COR provides a small demonstration of the point.

IV

Future Prospects

An Argument for Complementarism

Introduction

In this part of the book, some unresolved theoretical and methodological issues are surfaced and discussed. The present chapter argues the case for complementarism in systems thinking against three possible alternative futures that might be followed in the discipline, those being labeled "isolationism," "imperialism," and "pragmatism." Chapter 11 concerns itself with how complementarism can be turned into a set of methodological recommendations that can be followed by those who wish to use a complementarist and critical systems approach in practice. The methodology recommended is called *total systems intervention*, or TSI. This is an approach to combining systems methods that promotes creativity, guides the choice of appropriate methodologies, and ensures effective implementation.

The first task is to argue for complementarism in systems thinking. I do this initially by sketching out a brief history of management science, pointing out the fragmentation in the discipline that occurred in the 1970s and particularly the 1980s. On the basis of the history I then chart four possible developmental strategies for management science and systems thinking, and seek to demonstrate that the complementarist strategy is the most coherent and fruitful. Finally, the key point in question is addressed. This is about whether systems thinking is in the throes of a "Kuhnian crisis" or whether a complementarist version of the situation, with different methodologies contributing to increased overall competence in the discipline, can be made to appear a feasible alternative.

Traditional and Modern Management Science

For the purposes of this discussion, I leave aside the organizations-as-systems version of systems thinking. That has had its main impact on another of the branches of the management sciences—organization theory. The focus here is on management science (without the *s*), which is a discipline concerned with the development and appropriate utilization of rational methods of intervention in human affairs. Traditional management science, on the basis of this definition, can be taken to embrace such related approaches as operations or operational research (OR), management science/operations research (MS/OR), systems analysis, planning-programming-budgeting systems (PPBS), systems engineering, decision science, and policy science. In other words, it is coextensive with hard systems thinking. Modern management science must be taken to include, in addition, more recent systems trends such as soft systems thinking, organizational cybernetics, and critical systems thinking.

The origins of management science are lost in history, although it is reasonable to date its emergence as a discipline to the early twentieth century and the scientific-management movement of Frederick Taylor (1947). Full flowering, however, did not occur until World War II and its aftermath. This development grew out of the work on military problems undertaken by scientists from many different disciplines. During the 1950s and 1960s, management science experienced very rapid growth. It was increasingly used in civilian organizations and became institutionalized with the foundation of professional societies and journals. Today, societies such as The Institute of Management Sciences (TIMS) and the Operations Research Society of America, in the United States, and the Operational Research Society in the United Kingdom continue to function successfully. Journals like *Management Science, Interfaces, Operations Research, Journal of the Operational Research Society, European Journal of Operational Research,* and *Omega* publish articles by management-science theoreticians and practitioners.

During the period of rapid growth and development, there was considerable unanimity about the nature and function of management science and general optimism about future prospects. To use the popular Kuhnian terminology (Kuhn, 1970), the dominant paradigm—the set of ideas, assumptions, and beliefs—guiding the activity of management scientists went unchallenged, and facilitated the practice of "normal science." This paradigm, as was argued in Chapter 4, is based upon functionalism, serves the technical interest, uses the machine metaphor, rests on mechanical–unitary assumptions about problem contexts, and is systemic modernist in orientation. It advocates a transfer of the methods of research felt to operate in the natural sciences to human affairs. On the basis of this paradigm, a typical methodology emerged. The problem of concern is formulated according to the objectives to be realized. The system in which it is located is represented in a quantitative model. Experimentation on the model suggests an optimal solution. This solution is then tested in the real world. The success or otherwise of the implementation becomes the verification or falsification of the hypotheses built into the model. Use of this methodology brought considerable success over a relatively narrow range of management problems. Problems of allocation, inventory, replacement, queuing, sequencing, routing, and so forth could be tackled with great confidence. It also allowed a considerable amount of knowledge to be built up about the operation of systems of a limited sort.

In the 1970s, however, the confidence that management scientists had in their discipline and its purpose began to wane. Failures began to accumulate as researchers started to push beyond the narrow range of problems of initial concern, to tackle problems with strong behavioral and social aspects. Hoos (1972) has documented the many difficulties that arose in trying to apply systems analysis to public policy issues. Further, the belief held by, for example, Ackoff and Sasieni (1968) that OR would be able to extend its scope of operation from tactical to more strategic problems was disappointed. The reader has heard Churchman's (1979b) view that the original intention of a holistic, interdisciplinary, experimental science addressed to problems in social systems was betrayed as OR degenerated, in the 1960s, into little more than mathematical modeling.

The failure of traditional management science to come to terms with the "softer" problems found at the strategic level in organizations and in social systems led to the spate of criticisms of the approach documented in Chapter 4; the main faults identified being summarized by Jackson (1987c) and Keys (1987) as an inability to cope with multiple perceptions of reality, to handle extreme complexity, and to escape from conservative bias. By the late 1970s, because of obvious failings and as a result of the critical assault, considerable uncertainty and even pessimism became apparent among at least some sections of the management-science profession. Dando and Bennett (1981) trace this loss of firm assurance in a survey of articles published in the *Journal of the Operational Research Society*. In 1963 and 1968, articles published in this journal reveal little sign of crisis. By 1973, a degree of uncertainty has begun to set in. By 1978, about one-quarter of the major papers published contain significant criticism of the conventional approach. Dando and Bennett conclude that the certainty and optimism about the role and prospects of management science existing in 1963 had largely evaporated by 1978 and had been replaced by considerable uncertainty and pessimism among at least some sections of the profession.

The feeling of something akin to a crisis was reinforced by the increasing influence of various alternative systems approaches that challenged the traditional functionalist orientation in management science. During the late 1970s and 1980s, organizational cybernetics, soft systems thinking, and critical systems thinking were successful in establishing themselves as significant inputs to the discipline. This book has studied, in previous chapters, the very different foundations upon which each of these approaches to management science is built. In terms of sociological paradigms, the functionalism of traditional management science is complemented by the structuralism of organizational cybernetics, the interpretivism of soft systems thinking, and the radical perspective of emancipatory systems thinking. Modern management science must, therefore, be taken to embrace these newer elements as well as the traditional approach. Given the uneasy relationship that currently exists between the various strands of the discipline, creative thinking is required if management science is to develop and progress as a cohesive field of endeavor.

This is, indeed, the reason for this chapter. Accepting that management science and systems thinking are now much more diverse areas of work than in the 1950s and 1960s, I shall concentrate on the relationships that currently exist, and could potentially exist, between the different perspectives that contribute to them. How can these relationships best be theorized and employed so that management science can make the most beneficial contribution to organizations and society?

Developmental Strategies

Four strategies will be discussed, each of which offers a different way forward and, it is argued, widely differing prospects for the future well-being of management science as a discipline and profession. The strategies are labeled *isolationist, imperialist, pragmatist,* and *complementarist.* The idea of looking at possible lines of development in this way, and two of the labels used (isolationist and imperialist), have been taken from Reed's (1985) account of possible "redirections in organizational analysis." However, the terms have been given a somewhat different meaning in making them relevant to the situation in management science, and only a few of Reed's specific arguments have survived unaltered the transfer to this new domain. From Flood's (1989a, 1989b) reworking of my ideas I have learned the important lesson that it is necessary to specify whether each strategy is being pursued at the theoretical or methodological level or both. For example, is isolationism a stance advocating isolationism at the theoretical level *and* the methodological level? This helps to clarify the arguments below. However, having absorbed this lesson, I still find myself with four strategies rather than Flood's six scenarios. The reason is that I can find no compelling differences between Flood's "theoretical isolationism," "methodological imperialism by subsumption," and "methodological imperialism by annexation." I therefore include all these under my label of imperialism.

Isolationism

Isolationism would promote the separate development of the different strands of management science—each isolated in its own paradigmatic enclave. This is because the isolationist offers no alternative to the different strands of management science continuing to go on their own way, developing independently on the basis of their own presuppositions and with minimal contact among the strands. This is the implicit position adopted by those who see their own approach to management science as being essentially self-sufficient. They believe that there is nothing to learn from other perspectives, which appear to them not to be useful or, perhaps, even sensible. In these circumstances, attempts to incorporate ideas from alternative tendencies could weaken and, therefore, threaten the preferred position. It will be clear that isolationists are isolationist in both theory and practice, although the usual expression of this isolationism is adherence to one methodology, with an equally strong support for the theory assumed by that methodology being implicit.

Despite the criticism leveled at its theory and practice, and in spite of the emergence of fully fledged alternative trends, traditional management science retains its hold over the majority of theoreticians and practitioners. Even a cursory glance at the contents of journals such as *Management Science, Operations Research, Journal of the Operational Research Society, European Journal of Operational Research,* and *Omega* reveals the extent to which the functionalist approach remains in the ascendancy. And it is among those management scientists who cling to the orthodoxy that the isolationist strategy finds its greatest support. The majority of contributors to these journals are content to pursue, with little self-doubt and little reference to other positions, the traditional type of analysis. Organizational cybernetics, however, also has its fair share of isolationists. Although organizational cybernetics is a recent development, cybernetics itself has almost as long a history as a recognized field of study as traditional management science. It has quite naturally, therefore, become institutionalized, with its own societies and journals. Further, the limited range of concepts employed in cybernetics (feedback, black box, variety, etc.) both sets it apart from other perspectives and seemingly makes it an attractive home for those who wish to talk about social issues but fear the arduous task of getting to grips with the vast literature of the other organizational sciences. Isolationist thinking is much less prevalent among soft systems thinkers and critical management scientists. This is only to be expected.

Since these approaches emerged almost as a reaction against traditional management science, they had to engage with other perspectives from the start. Even the in-house journal of U.K. soft systems thinking, the *Journal of Applied Systems Analysis,* shows a refreshing acceptance of pluralism.

There is, in fact, a profound intellectual justification for isolationism, although it is rarely adduced by those who pursue the strategy. This justification rests upon the notion of paradigm incommensurability. The word *paradigm,* as employed by Kuhn, refers to the world view of a scientific community—the set of ideas, assumptions, and beliefs that guide its scientific activity. Talking about the most fundamental aspect of incommensurability, Kuhn (1970) says that "the proponents of competing paradigms practice their trades in different worlds. . . . the two groups of scientists see different things when they look from the same point in the same direction" (p. 150). If, then, it can be shown that the proponents of the different strands of management science inhabit different paradigms, it is scarcely worthwhile for them to attempt to communicate with one another. Even with the best intentions in the world, the different philosophical/sociological assumptions on which they draw will mean that they talk past one another, and no fruitful dialogue can occur. To take one example, Beer (1983b) has attested to the difficulty he felt in dealing with criticisms leveled by Ulrich (a representative of emancipatory systems thinking) against the VSM and its use in Chile, because communication seemed to be needed between two paradigms.

Giving further support to the argument from paradigm incommensurability is the article by Dando and Bennett (1981). They argue that OR is presently going through a period of crisis similar to the kind of crisis Kuhn describes as occurring from time to time in the natural sciences. This crisis is signaled by a number of competing paradigms based upon irreconcilable assumptions. Their thesis is, in many respects, supported by the analyses earlier in this book. It has been argued that traditional management science rests upon functionalist foundations, while soft systems thinking is more interpretive in orientation, organizational cybernetics is more structuralist, and emancipatory systems thinking takes a radical view of the social world as riven by conflict and contradiction.

I shall tackle the notion of management science in a Kuhnian crisis in the next section. Apart from this argument, isolationism has little to commend it. The isolationist strategy gives up the possibility that management science can develop as a cohesive discipline. It is inconceivable that rival strands will wither away and leave the field open to one undisputed perspective. All the various strands represent important contributions that should be incorporated as part of the discipline. The prospect held out, therefore, is of a multiplicity of approaches developing in isolation. This inevitably forestalls the possibilities for learning that could arise if some dialogue were established between the different tendencies. Even allowing for a degree of paradigm incommensurability, there are important benefits to be gained from "reflective conversation" (Morgan, 1983b) involving adherents of alternative approaches. Further, if isolationism prevails, enthusiasts for particular tendencies will continue to use their favored methods in all circumstances, and with frequently deleterious results. This can only help to discredit the profession in the eyes of clients already confused by the competing claims of rival approaches.

Imperialism

The imperialist strategy assumes that one or another of the strands of management science is fundamentally superior and can provide suitable foundations for the development of the discipline, but at the same time is willing to incorporate aspects of other strands if they seem to be useful and to add strength in terms of the favored approach. Insights from other tendencies will be integrated into the edifice of the favored approach as long as they do not threaten its central tenets. Imperialists believe that they can explain the existence of alternative approaches, and analyze the limited sphere of application of these alternatives, in terms of the approach to which they grant hegemony. The usual expression of imperialism finds one theoretical position being favored (and so the strategy is isolationist at the theoretical level), with the methodology most closely associated with that theoretical position also preferred. However, versions or bits of other methodologies corresponding to alternative theoretical standpoints are used in a manner that corresponds to the implicitly or explicitly favored theoretical position. This obviously denatures them and turns them away from the purposes they are best able to serve.

Traditional management scientists tend to prefer isolationism to imperialism, but occasional imperialist aspirations are heard. Cook (1984), writing in 1964, provides a framework that could become the basis for a coherent imperialist platform for the traditional approach. In his view, the development of OR is being held back because it cannot incorporate human behavior into its models, anticipate human resistance to its rational recommendations, or supply an understanding of the environment in which it works. Thus clear space is made within the OR framework for the contribution of other approaches in a subordinate role. More recently, in the OR community, the work of Checkland and Eden is being hailed as an important contribution to "problem formulation." So emasculated, it is easily incorporated into traditional methodology.

The imperialist strategy is more strongly represented in soft systems thinking, organizational cybernetics, and critical management science. This is not entirely surprising since all three of these tendencies had, to some degree, to think through their relationship with the preexisting traditional orthodoxy and to represent themselves as an important advance on that way of thinking. Checkland (1983, 1985a) divides the area of the systems movement relevant to management science into two parts—hard systems thinking and soft systems thinking—and regards the hard approach as a special case of the soft. The traditional hard approaches, developed in the 1950s and 1960s, are only useful in those rare circumstances when a consensus already exists about what needs to be done. With most significant problems, no such consensus will exist, and a soft systems approach that attempts to bring about consensus or accommodation will be required. This soft systems "imperialism" is discussed further in the next section. Beer (1959a) sets out the imperialist manifesto for organizational cybernetics, reserving the most significant control problems—such as those arising in exceedingly complex, probabilistic systems like economies, brains, and companies—for the province of cybernetics. Lesser control problems can be addressed using applied statistics and operational research. The emancipatory version of an imperialist strategy sees all other approaches as serving the interests of capitalist society; they offer various solutions to the perennial problem faced by capitalism—the need to control the work force. Emancipatory systems thinking is seen as exposing the ideological character of the other tendencies and laying the foundations for a genuine self-management science.

The imperialist strategy holds out the hope of a unified management science discipline if one particular approach is able to dominate by incorporating into its mode of operation useful aspects of other tendencies. This would have to be done in such a way as to convince adherents of alternative positions that their unique insights were being fully respected. However, to believe this is possible would seem to ignore the difficulty of breaking down fundamental divergencies between what can reasonably be presented as positions emanating from different philosophical/sociological paradigms. This imperialist scenario seems, therefore, unlikely to come to pass as a result of natural developments in the discipline. Perhaps it could come about if extradisciplinary, broader societal influences favored one approach at the expense of the alternatives. For example, it might be that the traditional hard systems approach, with its respect for managerial prerogatives, will become even more favored in the future. If so, the result would hardly be beneficial to management science, which would lose much of its diversity and become even more strongly associated with the technical interest in prediction and control.

Pragmatism

The pragmatist strategy is to develop management science by bringing together the best elements of what may appear to be opposing strands, on the criterion of what works in practice. Pragmatists are distrustful of theory, believing that the wranglings to which it gives rise distract attention away from management-science practice. Theory is, in any case, deemed too underdeveloped to be of much help with the complex social problems managers face (Naughton, 1979; Vickers, 1978). Management science is presented as being essentially a technology; theoretical development must wait upon technological success and not vice versa (Tomlinson, 1987). Pragmatists, therefore, do not worry about "artificial" theoretical distinctions. They concentrate on building up a "tool kit" of techniques that can be used as required in the real-world situation. Proven techniques from different strands of management science are employed together in the course of problem solving if the situation warrants it. The choice of techniques and the whole procedure is justified to the extent that it brings results in practice. Obviously, pragmatists are eclectic at the methodological level, and (following the argument that all methodologies must rest upon theoretical assumptions) they must also be, by implication, eclectic at the theoretical level—even though they do not themselves make reference to theory.

The pragmatist or tool-kit strategy seems to arise most naturally from a traditional or soft systems base. Organizational cybernetics and critical management science are more theoretically oriented and are therefore unlikely to give birth to pragmatist inclinations. Tomlinson (1987) admirably presents the pragmatist case from an OR standpoint, arguing that the way to develop OR is on the basis of good practice rather than abstract theory. Here, I shall concentrate on a version of the strategy put forward from the soft systems position by Naughton (1979). Naughton argues that the systems approach is best viewed as a kind of social technology. It can most easily realize its interdisciplinary aims if it becomes problem rather than theory oriented, and if it takes as its aim effective action and not understanding. Systems people should be "activist," seeking out problems that can be tackled using systems ideas. Available theory should be used pragmatically and eclectically. If no helpful theory is available, as will be the case with most of the ill-structured problems managers face, systems practitioners should rely on the craft knowledge of their discipline. The building up of useful craft knowledge should, indeed, be the major aim of systems research at its present stage of development. Where possible, this might be incorporated into methodologies so that it can more easily be accessed by other analysts. Naughton (1979) regards Checkland's soft systems methodology as an example of a craft approach, embodying the activist, pragmatist, and eclecticist principles. Checkland's (1981a, 1985a) recent concern with the theory underpinning his methodology, and the alien feel of the methodology to many other management scientists, would lead one to dispute this particular contention. This does not, however, invalidate the rest of Naughton's argument. The pragmatist strategy is discussed more fully in Flood and Carson (1988).

Pragmatism will seem a good bet to many management-science practitioners eager to keep clients happy by using whatever methods and techniques appear to work in the real world. It has, after all, brought success and stimulated the development of theory in other fields, such as engineering and design. However, in my opinion, to build management science—which is in large part a social practice—only upon technology is to court disaster and to hinder serious intellectual development. Of course, lessons would eventually be learned through practice, but at what cost? It is much less easy to conduct experiments in the social domain. Theoretical support should enable a reasoned choice of management-science method to be made that would reduce costly mistakes. Further, theory allows us to understand exactly why particular methods work and others do not, so that we can more easily adapt in the world of rapid change confronted by managers. It also allows us to pass on this knowledge to others—one of the most important tasks for any discipline. The pragmatist approach makes it difficult for management science to engage with other related disciplines and to take advantage of whatever usable knowledge is produced in, say, psychology or sociology.

Finally, the pragmatist approach employed in the social domain can lend itself to misuse in the service of authoritarian interests. In the same way that Bahro (1978) argues that authoritarian ideology "appears as 'true' and 'scientific' precisely to the extent that the compulsion functions effectively" (p. 245), traditional approaches in management science often "work" not because they are the most suitable for the situation in which they are employed, but because they reinforce the position of the powerful and implementation is therefore enforced. Theoretical understanding can allow such misuse to be identified.

Complementarism

Complementarism seeks to respect the different strengths of the various trends in management science, encouraging their theoretical development and suggesting ways in which they can be appropriately fitted to the variety of management problems that arise. The complementarist vision is, therefore, of the continued existence of a variety of strands within management science. Theoretical and practical developments will be mutually informing. Arguments stemming from the different assumptions employed by the various strands will continue but will be conducted with mutual respect, since it will be recognized that different approaches address different (if interrelated) aspects of the management task. The strengths and weaknesses of the different strands of management science will be more fully understood, and the domain of effective application of each approach will become established. A metatheory will develop that can guide theoretical endeavor and can advise analysts confronted with different problem situations as to which approach is most suitable. The diversity of theory and methodology available in management science will be seen to herald not a crisis in the discipline, but increased competence and effectiveness in a variety of different problem situations.

Jackson and Keys's (1984) system of systems methodologies is perhaps the most formal statement of this position at the methodological level—the argument being, as described previously, that the development of different strands of management science can be related to the existence of a variety of ideal-type problem-contexts. At the theoretical level, the complementarist strategy accepts that significant differences divide advocates of the alternative strands of management science. However, it does not accept the full implications of the doctrine of paradigm incommensurability. At the most fundamental level, all of the different strands of systems thinking are necessary as supports for the anthropologically based cognitive interests of the human species—the technical interest in prediction and control, the practical interest in mutual understanding, and the emancipatory interest in removing constraints imposed by power relationships (see Habermas, 1970).

Even if complementarism sometimes has difficulty in manifesting itself in practice, therefore, it is worth arguing that constructive dialogue should be possible if it is recognized that the different approaches address different aspects of what is nevertheless a unified management task. Complementarism recognizes that the management task is so complex that it is impossible at present to produce a satisfactory, unified body of thought that can assist with all its aspects. Better, then, to have a range of insightful and useful, if somewhat contrasting, methods than to risk premature theoretical and methodological closure. In contradistinction to pragmatism, the complementarist strategy insists on the continued development of the theoretical side to the discipline as a support for technological activities. The system of systems methodologies hints at the areas from which theoretical support might be forthcoming. For example, once pluralism and coercion are encountered, the social sciences become the obvious source for insight, however underdeveloped they may be at present.

As a final point, the complementarist endeavor takes heart from the fact that each of the newer tendencies in management science seems to represent an attempt to come to grips with one of the key weaknesses of the hard approach identified in Chapter 4. Soft systems thinking helps with multiple perceptions of reality and organizational cybernetics with extreme complexity, while critical systems thinking aims to free the discipline to serve interests other than the status quo. As management science has matured, a variety of different approaches has been developed, and these allow the management scientist to work with a good chance of success in the full range of problem situations found.

This, then, is the argument for complementarism. Its success rests heavily on the idea that the different strands in management science herald increasing competence and not a Kuhnian crisis. This matter should, therefore, receive further consideration.

Crisis or Increasing Competence?

The variety of approaches—hard, soft systems, cybernetic, critical—that now inhabit the management-science domain are often opposed on fundamental matters concerning the nature and purpose of the discipline. They attract different groups of adherents, put different emphases on the subject matter and key concepts of the field, and sometimes even harbor different interpretations of the role of the discipline. They rest upon different philosophical/sociological assumptions. In essence, they are based within different paradigms. In these circumstances it is possible to see management science as being in the throes of a Kuhnian crisis. Although not a happy conclusion for those who would like to see management science as a unified body of thought, this idea does at least yield some understanding of why a variety of approaches should currently coexist. It is therefore worth exploring; fortunately, this work has already been done by Dando and Bennett (1981).

Dando and Bennett (with some important reservations because OR is a technology rather than a science) suggest that OR is presently going through a period of crisis similar to the kind of crisis Kuhn (1970) describes as taking place in the natural sciences. Crisis occurs, according to Kuhn, when the dominant paradigm in a field of study is confronted by apparent anomalies with which it cannot deal. If the anomalies persist, a number of potential alternative paradigms are likely to arise. A period of crisis will ensue as the competing paradigms battle for dominance.

This scenario, Dando and Bennett argue, maps well on to the situation in OR. The functionalist approach had, in the period following World War II, become established as the dominant paradigm in management science. Much progress was made on a limited range of problems during this period of what Kuhn calls "normal science." Eventually, however, different types of problem began to assume importance, involving highly complex and strategic issues with behavioral and social aspects. Such problems were demonstrably of interest to management science but eluded the methods and techniques of traditional OR. The result was the birth of alternative paradigms challenging the functionalist approach for dominance. OR entered a period of crisis, or "extraordinary" science.

Dando and Bennett proceed to investigate the competing paradigms. Initial conclusions drawn from an analysis of debates at the 1979 Society for General Systems Research Conference suggest that three competing approaches can be identified. Transferring the argument to OR, Dando and Bennett find the same three positions represented. First, an "official" or positivist position is still held by a significant proportion of the OR community. Second, a "reformist" stance has its main champion in Ackoff and demands considerable revision of conventional OR methodology; it is still, however, based on the presumption that we live in an essentially cooperative society and that improvements made in organizations and society will benefit all. Third, from a "revolutionary" stance this is denied; instead, the belief is that the social world is riven by conflict between exploiting and exploited groups and that taking sides with the exploited is the only guarantee of genuine progress.

The argument is then extended to take in the philosophical/sociological underpinnings of the three competing positions. The conclusions reached are very similar to those unearthed in the earlier chapters of this book (Dando and Bennett do not consider cybernetics). The official position relates to the positivist view in social science with its belief in extending the methods of the natural sciences to social affairs and its interest in regulation and control. The reformist position is equated with interpretive social science; the emphasis is on overcoming barriers to successful communication and achieving a workable consensus or, at least, accommodation among concerned actors. The revolutionary position corresponds closely to critical social science and stresses conflict, contradiction, and the need to emancipate disadvantaged groups.

According to Kuhnian reasoning, a period of crisis comes to an end when one of the competing paradigms establishes itself as the new dominant paradigm and the practice of normal science resumes on this new basis. In OR, Dando and Bennett envisage that the reformist position is most likely to establish itself as the new dominant paradigm. Both the internal dynamics of the OR community and other, broader societal influences tend to point to this outcome.

The idea of a Kuhnian crisis in management science, as developed by Dando and Bennett, certainly imposes a pattern upon events in the discipline and generates some important insights. The orthodoxy within management science has clearly broken down. There is competition between advocates of alternative approaches. Extradisciplinary considerations—of career and politics—play a significant part in motivating participants in the debate and are likely to influence its outcome. The truth in the Dando and Bennett analysis should not, however, blind us to a rather different way of looking at recent developments that have taken place in management science. If one of the underlying assumptions of their analysis is, for a moment, questioned—that management science has a well-defined and somewhat uniform subject matter—then an alternative perspective opens up before us. Instead of seeing different approaches as competing for exactly the same area of concern (as Dando and Bennett do), we can see them as being appropriate to the different types of situations in which management scientists are required to act. Each approach will be useful in certain defined areas and should only be used in the circumstances where it works best. The evaluation of each different approach should be confined to assessment of its success in solving problems in such circumstances and in specifying the boundaries of the situations in which it is appropriate. If this perspective is adopted, then the diversity of approaches heralds not a crisis but increased competence and effectiveness in a variety of situations. Perhaps official or traditional management science possesses a domain in which it is still the most efficient tool. Other strands of the discipline should be examined to see if they enable good work to be done in other types of problem situations.

If this second perspective on developments in management science and systems thinking is to be given coherence, however, a classification must be produced that matches different approaches to different problem situations. Two possible classifications will now be considered that attempt to realize this aim. The first is a classification of Checkland's (1983, 1985a), the second is the classification made possible by this book.

Checkland, as was seen earlier, essentially divides the area of the systems movement relevant to management science into two parts. On one side, there is hard systems thinking, predicated on the goal-seeking model and concerned with how we should achieve known ends (with prediction and control and optimization). Then, on the other side, there is soft systems thinking, premised on a model of human behavior as oriented to maintaining relationships and concerned with what we ought to do as well as how we should do it (with participation and learning). What, then, is the relationship between these two approaches, and when should each be used?

In a 1983 article, Checkland identifies three types of entities that can be deemed to be systems. Type 1 systems are "situations or phenomena characterized by interconnections which are part of the regularities of the universe." Obviously, these systems are in the domain of the natural sciences. Type 2 systems are situations "characterised by inter-connections which derive from the logic of situations." Checkland gives as examples of such systems "arrangements to manufacture or assemble products, or situations dominated by a decision about to be taken to achieve a known objective." It seems clear that such systems can be optimized in pursuit of their goals using hard systems thinking. Type 3 systems are situations in which the "interconnections are cultural, situations dominated by the meanings attributed to their perceptions by autonomous observers." Improvements to these systems can only be brought about using a soft systems approach.

In a later paper, Checkland (1985a) takes the discussion a little further. Soft systems thinking does represent a shift in paradigm but does not simply replace hard systems thinking. The achievements of the hard systems thinkers of the 1950s and 1960s remain with us. The newer soft systems thinking of the 1970s and 1980s should be seen as complementary to the earlier work. It is therefore important to know, when dealing with a problem situation, which type of systems approach to employ. In general, the hard approach may be useful at the operational level when a consensus exists on what needs to be done and what constitutes an efficient way of doing it. The objective of the system and its nature can in these circumstances be taken as given (Type 2 systems of Checkland's earlier paper). With most problems in organizations, however, no such consensus will exist. Most real-world problems will involve Type 3 systems. In this case, a soft systems approach—which attempts to bring about an accommodation—will be required. The hard approach is therefore a special case of the soft, appropriate when *Weltanschauungen* have already consolidated into a consensus over certain objectives to be achieved.

Checkland's papers give some insight into the strengths and weaknesses of different management-science tendencies and the problem situations for which they are most appropriate. They are disappointing, however, for two main reasons. First, they fail to provide much comment on the other strands of systems thinking discussed earlier in this book—particularly organizational cybernetics and critical systems thinking. Cybernetics in general is taken to be more relevant to the development of systems ideas than to systems practice. Beer's work is apparently an exception to this, but its functionalist model of the organization and basis in control theory identifies it essentially as a hard approach. This is, as we saw in Chapter 5, an inaccurate presentation. Critical systems thinking receives no mention at all.

The second weakness of Checkland's proposed classification stems from its imperialistic soft systems perspective. It is clear that, despite his use of the word *complementary*, Checkland views the relationship between hard and soft systems thinking from a roughly Kuhnian position. This sees the recent history of systems thinking in terms of the replacement of the old hard paradigm with a new and vigorous soft paradigm. The hard paradigm, unable to deal with the anomalies arising when it is applied in complex, human-centered organizational and societal situations, has given way to a soft paradigm, which both preserves the achievements of the hard in its specialized domain of application (as Einsteinian physics accepts the limited applicability of Newtonian laws) and extends the area of successful operation of systems ideas to the behavioral and social arena. The great paradox for Checkland, of course, is that in telling this Kuhnian story from the soft systems perspective, he then has to stop the progress of science at this point. A critical systems thinker, wanting to continue the story, might well want to argue that the difficulties with which soft systems practitioners currently wrestle (in attempting to apply their approach to power, contradiction, culture, etc.) are new anomalies that will eventually lead to the dominance of the newly emerging critical systems paradigm.

For those who reject the notion that hard and cybernetic approaches are simply special cases of the soft—and that critical systems thinking is simply a soft approach coupled with a loony left ideology—another type of classification may, however, seem preferable. This is the complementarist position pursued in this book, which seeks to recognize the complementary strengths of the different systems tendencies and to align each of them with the sort of problem situation for which it should, in theory, provide the most suitable approach. Thus the problems of "logical ordering" that are the concern of hard approaches need to be seen as different in kind from the problems pursued by soft systems thinkers; similarly with problems of communication, control, and organizing that lie within the domain of cybernetics.

The difficulty remains for complementarism that once it accepts the existence of wholly different systems approaches resting upon apparently irreconcilable presuppositions (inhabiting different paradigms), how can the problem of paradigm incommensurability be overcome? Without privileging any one of the competing positions, how can a metatheory be created that respects the relative strengths and weaknesses of each and oversees their correct employment by systems practitioners? The answer pursued in this book has been to make explicit the presuppositions upon which different systems approaches are based. Different methodologies look at organizations using different metaphors, rest upon alternative paradigmatic assumptions, take for granted different views of problem contexts, have distinct relationships to modernism and postmodernism, and provide the means of serving differing interests according to Habermas's formulation of fundamental human interests. Systems thinking is rich in variety in the methodologies it has developed and offers to the management sciences. If we can understand the different strengths and weaknesses of the various approaches and impose some sort of pattern on the variety so that the methodologies can be used as an integrated set of complementary approaches, then we are putting the practitioner in a very powerful position to intervene in organizations and society. That is the purpose of this book, and the extent to which it has been achieved is discussed further in the Conclusion.

This book therefore offers a second, complementarist form of classification—one that, it is hoped, does succeed in helping to match different systems approaches to different problem situations. This form of classification thus provides the rationale for arguing that management science is gaining in its ability to demonstrate overall competence. The development of different versions of management science is related to the existence of a variety of problem contexts. This obviously places a different perspective on the "management science in crisis" debate. No crisis exists. As systems thinking has matured, a variety of different approaches has been developed, and this allows the management scientist to work with a good chance of success in the full range of problem situations found. Just one of the classificatory mechanisms described earlier is sufficient to demonstrate the point. Jackson and Keys's system of systems methodologies would argue (remembering that we are dealing with ideal-type contexts) that mechanical–unitary problem contexts require hard systems thinking. Systemic–unitary contexts require treatment from organizational cybernetics. Mechanical–pluralist and systemic–pluralist contexts are best tackled using soft systems thinking. Emancipatory systems thinking should be employed to deal with mechanical–coercive and systemic–coercive contexts.

Conclusion

The argument for complementarism took the form first of all of a brief history of management science—which, in many ways, is the history of the impact of systems thinking upon it. This showed traditional management science coming under increasing attack because of its own failures, and also the development of alternative strands of work within management science (particularly organizational cybernetics, soft systems thinking, and critical systems thinking). Four possible developmental strategies were then considered for management science, given the current state of the discipline. Pragmatism was shown not to offer a very fruitful way forward. The future prospects held out by isolationism and imperialism were also limited but might follow inevitably unless paradigm incommensurability could be overcome. Complementarism offered the best option, but it had to be shown that the different approaches to management science could be seen and used as a complementary set.

The relationship between the different systems methodologies was therefore examined next. One explanation of the diversity of approaches, supporting isolationism and imperialism, is that there is a Kuhnian crisis in the discipline. This perspective yields a number of insights. As Dando and Bennett argue, there is competition between different management-science perspectives, and extradisciplinary considerations do play a part in this. However, it is possible to challenge their main conclusion and to see the new approaches to management science that have been opened up as representing attempts to come to terms with problem areas poorly served—or left entirely alone—by traditional management science. Each of the new approaches suggests a way of getting to grips with one of the key weaknesses of the traditional approach as identified in Chapter 4. This book provides a classification that shows how different approaches possess different strengths and weaknesses and are appropriate in different problem situations.

Just as hard systems thinking provided the foundation for traditional management science, so critical systems thinking—embracing complementarism—can provide the basis for a much enriched and empowered management science in the future. Recently, a committee drawn from the larger universities and research and development laboratories in the United States published in *Operations Research* a paper on "the next decade in operations research" (Committee on the New Decade, 1988). The entire emphasis lay on the further extension of complicated technical theories to cope with technical problems. Although no one would doubt the value of such work within the narrow boundaries set, it represents a depressing and limited future for management science; an extension of what Churchman (1979b) called the "dreary sixties" of mathematical modeling into the dreary 1990s and beyond. Within the vision held out for the future of management science (and the management sciences) by critical thinking, this specialist work is allocated its proper place, but alongside much else besides. For the sake of both the intellectual excitement necessary for a discipline to flourish and the major problems facing today's organizations and societies, the route laid out by critical thinking is the one the OR/MS community must travel.

11

Creative Problem Solving: Total Systems Intervention

Introduction

In this brief chapter, I outline a methodology that can be used by those who wish to follow the philosophy and principles of critical systems thinking. This methodology is known as *total systems intervention* (TSI); it is dealt with at book length in Flood and Jackson (1991a). This account draws heavily on Chapter 3 of that book.

TSI represents a new approach to planning, designing, problem solving, and evaluation based upon critical systems thinking. It uses a range of systems metaphors to encourage creative thinking about organizations and their problems. These metaphors are linked by a framework—the system of systems methodologies—to various systems approaches, so that once agreement is reached about which metaphors are most relevant to an organization's concerns and problems, an appropriate systems-based intervention methodology (or set of methodologies) can be employed. Choice of an appropriate systems methodology will guide problem solving in a way that ensures that it addresses what are the main concerns of the particular organization involved.

From this account it can be seen that TSI employs two of the theoretical schemata set out in Chapter 2—Morgan's work on metaphors, suitably developed in a systems direction; and the system of systems methodologies. These are used both to promote creative thinking about organizations and their problems and to guide methodology choice (because they allow us to unearth the presuppositions made by different systems methodologies). It should be obvious, however, that the other schemata could also be used to enrich TSI. Habermas's formulations and Burrell and Morgan's work on sociological paradigms could equally well assist creativity and help with methodology choice. The incorporation of only two of the schemata in the "official" Flood and Jackson (1991a) version of the methodology is designed to make the approach manageable. In any case, as the

271

reader has witnessed, there is some redundancy in using all the schemata all the time. Nothing said here, however, should prevent the sophisticated TSI analyst from employing the full armory of ideas provided by this more theoretical book to enhance TSI.

TSI advocates combining the work on metaphors, the system of systems methodologies, and knowledge of the individual systems approaches in an interactive manner that is deemed to be particularly powerful and fruitful. In this chapter the logic of the combination, and hence the TSI methodology itself, is explored theoretically. This is done first by looking at the philosophy and principles of TSI and then by considering in detail the three phases of the methodology.

The Philosophy and Principles of TSI

The philosophy underpinning TSI is the critical systems thinking described in Chapter 7. As the reader will remember, this new development in the systems movement makes its stand on five positions. These are critical awareness, social awareness, complementarism at the theoretical level, complementarism at the methodological level, and a commitment to human well-being and emancipation. This philosophy should be known and respected by all who would use TSI.

There are seven principles embedded in the three phases of TSI. These are:

1. Organizations are too complicated to understand using one management model, and their problems are too complex to tackle with quick fixes
2. Organizations, their strategies, and their problems should be investigated using a range of systems metaphors
3. Systems metaphors that seem appropriate for highlighting organizational strategies and problems can be linked to appropriate systems methodologies to guide intervention
4. Different systems metaphors and methodologies can be used in a complementary way to address different aspects of organizations and their problems
5. It is possible to appreciate the strengths and weaknesses of different systems methodologies and to relate each to appropriate organizational concerns and problems
6. TSI sets out a systemic cycle of inquiry with interaction back and forth between the three phases
7. Facilitators and clients are both engaged at all stages of the TSI process

The Three Phases of TSI

The three phases of TSI are labeled *creativity, choice,* and *implementation.* I consider these in turn, looking in each case at the task to be accomplished during the phase, the tools provided by TSI to realize the task, and the outcome or results expected from the phase.

Creativity

The task during the creativity phase is to use systems metaphors as organizing structures to help managers and other stakeholders think creatively about their enterprises. The sort of questions it would be pertinent to ask are:

- Which metaphors guide current organizational strategies, structures, and control and information systems?
- What alternative metaphors might capture better what we want to achieve with this organization?
- What metaphors throw light onto this organization's problems and concerns?

The tools provided by TSI to assist this process are a set of systems metaphors. Different metaphors focus attention on different aspects of an organization's functioning, as the reader has seen. Some concentrate on organizational structure, while others highlight human and political aspects of an organization. Some examples (from Chapter 2) are:

- The organization as a machine
- The organization as an organism
- The organization as a brain
- The organization as a culture
- The organization as a coercive system

The main aspect of organizations highlighted, and those aspects neglected, by each metaphor would be disclosed in order to enhance discussion and debate. As well as the metaphors, Jackson and Keys's grid of problem contexts and the other theoretical schemata can be used at this stage to gain insight into the organization of concern and its problems.

The outcome (what is expected to emerge) from the creativity phase is a "dominant" metaphor that highlights the main interests and concerns and can become the basis for a choice of appropriate intervention methodology. There may be other, "dependent" metaphors that it is also sensible to pursue into the next phase. The relative position of dominant and dependent metaphors may, indeed, be altered by later work. If all the metaphors reveal serious problems, then the organization is obviously in a crisis state.

Choice

The task during the choice phase is to choose an appropriate systems-based intervention methodology (or set of methodologies) to suit the particular characteristics of the organization's situation as revealed by the examination conducted in the creativity phase. The tools provided by TSI to help with this stage are the system of systems methodologies (as set out in Figure 2.3) and, derived from that, knowledge of the underlying metaphors employed by systems methodologies.

Although it would be possible to link systems methodologies and systems metaphors directly, the pattern in the variety of systems methodologies is best discerned if the link is made through the system of systems methodologies. As was demonstrated in Chapter 2, the system of systems methodologies neatly unearths the assumptions underlying different systems approaches by asking what each assumes about the system(s) with which it deals and about the relationship between the participants concerned with that system. Putting these points together in the matrix of Figure 2.3, it is apparent that systems methodologies can be classified according to whether they assume problem contexts to be mechanical–unitary, mechanical–pluralist, mechanical–coercive, systemic–unitary, systemic–pluralist, or systemic–coercive. Combining the information gained about the problem context during the creativity phase and the knowledge provided by the system of systems methodologies about the assumptions underlying different systems approaches, it is possible to move toward an appropriate choice of systems intervention methodology. For example, if the problem context is characterized by there being clear and agreed objectives (unitary) and by being transparent enough so that it can be captured by a mathematical model (mechanical), then a methodology based upon mechanical–unitary assumptions can be used with every hope of success.

On the basis of the system of systems methodologies, it is possible to relate individual methodologies to the metaphors of organization previously described, as in Table 11.1. Bearing in mind the metaphors that came out as dominant and dependent during the creativity phase and the conclusions of the system of systems methodologies, an appropriate choice of systems methodology (systems methodologies) to guide intervention and change can now be made.

The most probable outcome of the choice phase is that there will be a dominant methodology chosen, to be tempered in use by the imperatives highlighted by dependent methodologies.

TABLE 11.1. *Systems Methodologies Related to Metaphors of Organization*

Systems Methodology	Assumptions about Problem Context	Underlying Metaphors
Organizations as systems	S–U	machine organism
Hard systems thinking	M–U	machine
Organizational cybernetics	S–U	machine organism brain
Soft systems thinking	M–P S–P	culture machine organism
Emancipatory systems thinking	M–C S–C	culture coercive-system

Implementation

The task during the implementation phase is to employ a particular systems methodology (or systems methodologies) to translate the dominant vision of the organization, its structure, and the general orientation adopted to concerns and problems into specific proposals for change.

The tools provided by TSI are the specific systems methodologies used according to the logic of TSI. The dominant methodology operationalizes the vision of the organization contained in the dominant metaphor. The logic of TSI demands, however, that consideration continue to be given to the imperatives of other methodologies. For example, the key problems in an organization suffering from structural collapse may be best highlighted using the metaphors of organism and brain, but the cultural metaphor might also appear illuminating, if in a necessarily subordinate way given the immediate crisis. In these circumstances a cybernetic methodology would be chosen to guide the intervention, but perhaps tempered by some ideas from soft systems methodology. Managers in another organization might wish to redesign their information systems but be held back by conflicting views about where the organization should be going, exacerbated by some political infighting. This situation might usefully be understood with the culture metaphor as dominant, but with the brain and coercive-system metaphors also illuminating. In this case, soft systems methodology might guide the intervention, but with aspects of cybernetics and critical systems heuristics also being used.

The outcome of the implementation stage is coordinated chang' brought about in those aspects of the organization currently most vital for its effective and efficient functioning.

TABLE 11.2. *The 3-Phase TSI Methodology*

Creativity

Task	To highlight aims, concerns, and problems
Tools	Systems metaphors
Outcome	Dominant and dependent metaphors highlighting the major issues

Choice

Task	To choose an appropriate systems-based intervention methodology (or methodologies)
Tools	The "system of systems methodologies" and the relationship between metaphors and methodologies
Outcome	Dominant and dependent methodologies chosen for use

Implementation

Task	To arrive at and implement specific change proposals
Tools	Systems methodologies employed according to the logic of TSI
Outcome	Highly relevant and coordinated change improving effectiveness and efficiency

---

Conclusion

The three-phase methodology of TSI is set out in Table 11.2. It is important to stress, however, that TSI is a systemic and iterative approach. It asks, during each phase, that continual reference be made, back or forth, to the likely conclusions of other phases. So, for example, during phase 1, creativity, attempts are made to anticipate the likely consequences of particular visions of the organization for the organization's structure, and information and control requirements.

I have provided one example of TSI at work in West Newton Council for Voluntary Service (in Chapter 8). The task there was to redesign the executive committee of the council. The dominant metaphor was that of the organization as a culture, although the brain and coercive-system metaphors were also illuminating. SSM guided the intervention (tempered by some ideas from organizational cybernetics and by reflecting on the coercive aspects). The executive-committee redesign corresponded most closely to the requirements of the culture metaphor as realized through SSM. Many other examples are treated in depth in Flood and Jackson (1991a).

12

Conclusion

The story is told, and there is little need for a grand conclusion. Three points only require some additional comment. First, there is the nature of systems thinking itself and what it can contribute to the management sciences; then, there is the relationship between systems methodology and the social sciences; finally, we might address the question of the form of human emancipation pursued by critical systems thinking.

One of the aims of this book is to reconstruct systems thinking as a unified approach so that it can again occupy a position at the leading edge of research and practice in the management sciences. The chosen way of doing that has been to demonstrate the complementary strengths of the different systems methodologies. An in-depth study of each of five types of systems methodologies—organizations-as-systems, hard, cybernetic, soft, and critical—demonstrates that these are each individually strong and have something to offer. Illustrative case studies of each type of methodology in use further contribute to this conclusion. At the same time, the study of the various types of systems methodology reveals that they are each based upon very different assumptions pertaining to the human interests they serve, systems thinking and social systems (sociological paradigms), the nature of organizations (metaphors), assumptions about problem contexts, and about rationality and progress as addressed in the modernism-versus-postmodernism debate. Some conclusions of the arguments that reveal the different assumptions of the various types of systems methodologies can be found in Table 12.1.

The breadth and depth of knowledge available in systems thinking is revealed by this examination. But it is still necessary to show that the methodologies make up a complementary set and can be used together in a coherent manner. In a sense, a structure is imposed by each of the theoretical schemata to which the methodologies are related. I have demonstrated, for example, that systems methodologies exist that can serve each of the human interests reflected upon by Habermas. Available to the reader, therefore, are a number of ways of imposing a pattern on the variety of methodologies. To make the point further, however, I have

TABLE 12.1. *Some Conclusions of the Argument*

Systems Methodology	Assumptions and Orientations
Organizations as systems	Technical interest (practical subordinated)
	Functionalist
	Machine, organism
	Systemic–unitary
	Systemic modernism
Hard	Technical interest
	Functionalist
	Machine
	Mechanical–unitary
	Systemic modernism
Organizational cybernetics	Technical interest (particularly steering capacities)
	Structuralist
	Machine, organism, brain
	Systemic–unitary
	Systemic modernist (critical modernism on Beer's agenda)
Soft	Practical interest (to a limited degree)
	Interpretive
	Culture, machine, organism
	Pluralist (mechanical and systemic)
	Critical modernist (underdeveloped)
Emancipatory	Emancipatory interest
	Radical (humanism and structuralism)
	Coercive system, culture
	Coercive (mechanical and systemic)
	Critical modernist
Critical	Serves all human interests
	Rationalities emerging from all paradigms allocated a role
	Uses all metaphors
	All problem contexts considered
	A developed and self-reflective form of critical modernism

constructed the argument for complementarism, ultimately resting on Habermas's work; shown how the system of systems methodologies could ensure integrated use of the methodologies in community OR; and shown how TSI uses an understanding of metaphor and the system of systems methodologies to provide a complete metamethodology for putting these insights into practice.

Systems thinking is powerful these days, therefore, both because of the strength and diversity of its various strands and because those strands can be seen as complementary and can be brought together in an integrated way in problem resolution. Systems thinking has always had a profound impact upon management science. The early development of management science was given coherence by hard systems thinking; later developments are being led theoretically by soft systems and critical systems thinkers. The sort of unity in diversity that is offered by modern systems thinking should make possible a rosy future for management science (see Chapter 10). Other branches of the management sciences, too, can benefit from recent progress in systems thinking. Organization theory's love affair with the systems approach, abandoned in the retreat from functionalism, should be renewed in the light of more recent developments. About accounting, economics, and the rest I know too little to comment; nevertheless, I offer this book on systems methodology to the whole of the management sciences.

I have made use of the social sciences in developing a critique of the different systems methodologies and in arguing for complementarism. The relationship between management science and the social sciences has traditionally been difficult. Management science tried to set itself up on natural scientific foundations and was wary of the apparent lack of rigor and the contentiousness of the debates that took up time in the social sciences. More recently, the importance of some social scientific concerns has become clearer to operational researchers and systems practitioners, and some interchange of ideas has taken place (e.g., Jackson, Keys, and Cropper, 1989). It is hoped that this book has provided management scientists with a relatively easy introduction to some relevant issues in the social sciences and will further stimulate their interest in that area. From the other side, social scientists have tended to write off management scientists as wedded to functionalism and as devoted to the service of one powerful group in society—managers. At least in the case of aware systems practitioners, it is no longer possible for social scientists to do this. Rather, they should see in systems methodologies a means of translating a whole range of social scientific ideas into practical application. This book offers to social scientists an introduction to contemporary systems thinking and a means of making their work usable and useful to all sections of society. Systems methodologies, therefore, are a possible bridge between the management sciences and the social sciences, and my hope is that this book will encourage a fruitful cross-fertilization of ideas.

We are left with the issue of human well-being and emancipation, and how this can be promoted by critical systems thinking. It is as well to acknowledge the difficulty of this matter in today's complex societies and complex world. I would be the first to admit that this book has failed to deal adequately with a possible feminist critique of systems thinking, a critique based on non-European thought, or an ecologically oriented critique. Following Habermas, however, let it just be said that there is the necessity to balance the requirements to develop the productive forces and the steering capacities of societies against the equally pressing need to further mutual understanding. The realm of the practical interest must be protected from the incursions of instrumental reason, and rationalization within that sphere seen as an independent concern resting upon the promulgation of communicative competence. Those are emancipatory necessities. Faced with the complexity of these matters, critical systems thinking cannot hope to offer a solution. More than any other development in the management sciences, however, it is able to recognize the questions being asked and is not afraid to start preparing its answers. Of profound importance to all is the initial critical systems conclusion that adherence to emancipation is not a matter of individual commitment but a logical necessity of the human species, identified as such through the intellectual development of systems thinking.

The reader deserves an easier means of deciding whether he or she is convinced by these ideas. To that end, I offer two quotations that reasonably capture the message of the book. The first comes from a famous 1937 article by Horkheimer (1976) that was the original programmatic statement for the Institute of Social Research, a body from which the social science version of critical thinking was formulated. Horkheimer wrote:

> However extensive the interaction between the critical theory and the special sciences whose progress the theory must respect and on which it has for decades exercised a liberating and stimulating influence, the theory never aims simply at an increase in knowledge as such. Its goal is man's emancipation from slavery.

The second, which stands as a warning to systems thinkers, comes from Scene 14 of Brecht's 1947 play *The Life of Galileo* (Brecht, 1963). I used this quotation to preface my first attempt at unraveling the assumptions underlying systems methodologies almost exactly 13 years ago (Jackson, 1978); I find it just as inspiring today. In the play, Galileo says:

> The movements of the stars have become clearer; but to the mass of the people the movements of their masters are still incalculable. . . . What are you working for! I maintain that the only purpose of science is to ease the hardship of human existence. If scientists, intimidated by self-seeking people in power, are content to amass knowledge for the sake of knowledge, then science can become crippled, and your new machines will represent nothing but new means of oppression. With time you may discover all that is to be discovered, and your progression will only be a progression away from mankind. The gulf between you and them can one day become so great that your cry of jubilation over some new achievement may be answered by a universal cry of horror.

References

Ackoff, R. L., 1970, A black ghetto's research on a university, *Op. Res.* 18:761.

Ackoff, R. L., 1974a, The systems revolution, *Long Range Planning* 7:2.

Ackoff, R. L., 1974b, The social responsibility of OR, *ORQ* 25:361.

Ackoff, R. L., 1974c, *Redesigning the Future*, Wiley, New York.

Ackoff, R. L., 1975, A reply to the comments of Chesterton, Goodsman, Rosenhead and Thunhurst, *ORQ* 26:96.

Ackoff, R. L., 1977, Optimization + objectivity = opt out, *Eur. J. Opl. Res.* 1:1.

Ackoff, R. L., 1979a, The future of operational research is past, *J. Opl. Res. Soc.* 30:93.

Ackoff, R. L., 1979b, Resurrecting the future of operational research, *J. Opl. Res. Soc.* 30:189.

Ackoff, R. L., 1981a, *Creating the Corporate Future*, Wiley, New York.

Ackoff, R. L., 1981b, The art and science of mess management, *Interfaces* 11:20.

Ackoff, R. L., 1982, On the hard headedness and soft heartedness of M. C. Jackson, *J. Appl. Sys. Anal.* 9:31.

Ackoff, R. L., 1983, Beyond prediction and preparation, *J. Mgt. Stud.* 20:59.

Ackoff, R. L., 1986, On conceptions of professions, *Sys. Res.* 3:273.

Ackoff, R. L., 1989, Ackoff's fables, *Sys. Pract.* 2:375.

Ackoff, R. L., and Sasieni, M. W., 1968, *Fundamentals of Operations Research*, Wiley, New York.

Adams, J., 1973, Chile: everything under control, *Science for People* 21:4.

Argyris, C., 1964, *Integrating the Individual and the Organization*, Wiley, New York.

Argyris, C., and Schon, D., 1974, *Theory in Practice*, Jossey-Bass, San Francisco.

Argyris, C., and Schon, D., 1978, *Organizational Learning: A Theory of Action Perspective*, Addison Wesley, Reading, MA.

Ashby, W. R., 1956, *An Introduction to Cybernetics*, Methuen, London.

Atkinson, C. J., 1984, "Metaphor and Systemic Praxis," Doctoral dissertation, Department of Systems, University of Lancaster.

Atkinson, C. J., 1986, Towards a plurality of soft systems methodology, *J. Appl. Sys. Anal.* 13:19.

Atkinson, C. J., and Checkland, P. B., 1988, Extending the metaphor "system," *Human Relations* 41:709.

Bahro, R., 1978, *The Alternative in Eastern Europe*, NLB, London.

Baker, W., Elias, R., and Griggs, D., 1977, Managerial involvement in the design of adaptive systems, in: *Management Handbook for Public Administrators* (J. W. Sutherland, ed.), Van Nostrand Reinhold, New York, pp. 817–842.

Banathy, B. H., 1984, *Systems Design in the Context of Human Activity Systems*, International Systems Institute, California.

Banathy, B. H., 1987, Choosing design methods, in: *Proceedings of the 31st Annual Meeting of the ISGSR*, Budapest, Hungary, pp. 54–63.

Banathy, B. H., 1988, Matching design methods to system type, *Sys. Res.* 5:27.

Barnard, C., 1938, *The Functions of the Executive*, Harvard University Press, Cambridge, MA.

Beer, S., 1959a, *Cybernetics and Management,* EUP, Oxford.

Beer, S., 1959b, What has cybernetics to do with OR, *ORQ,* 10:1.

Beer, S., 1966, *Decision and Control,* Wiley, Chichester.

Beer, S., 1972, *Brain of the Firm,* Allen Lane, London.

Beer, S., 1974, *The Integration of Government Planning,* study for the Government of Alberta.

Beer, S., 1975, Fanfare for effective freedom, in: *Platform for Change* (S. Beer, ed.), Wiley, Chichester, pp. 423–457.

Beer, S., 1979, *The Heart of Enterprise,* Wiley, Chichester.

Beer, S., 1981a, *Brain of the Firm,* 2nd ed., Wiley, Chichester.

Beer, S., 1981b, On heaping our science together, in: *Systems Thinking,* Volume 2 (F. E. Emery, ed.), Penguin, Harmondsworth, pp. 409–428.

Beer, S., 1983a, The will of the people, *J. Opl. Res. Soc.* 34:797.

Beer, S., 1983b, A reply to Ulrich's "Critique of Pure Cybernetic Reason," *J. Appl. Sys. Anal.* 10:115.

Beer, S., 1984, The viable system model: Its provenance, development, methodology and pathology, *J. Opl. Res. Soc.* 35:7.

Beer, S., 1985, *Diagnosing the System for Organizations,* Wiley, Chichester.

Beer, S., 1990, Recursion zero: Metamanagement, *Sys. Pract.* 3:315.

Berlinski, D., 1976, *On Systems Analysis,* MIT Press, Cambridge, MA.

Bevan, R. G., 1980, Social limits to planning, *J. Opl. Res. Soc.* 31:867.

Blackler, F. H. M., and Brown, C. A., 1980, *Whatever Happened to Shell's New Philosophy of Management?,* Saxon House, London.

Blauner, R., 1964, *Alienation and Freedom,* University of Chicago Press, Chicago.

Bolweg, J. F., 1976, *Job Design and Industrial Democracy,* Martinus Nijhoff, Leiden, The Netherlands.

Boothroyd, H., 1978, *Articulate Intervention: The Interface of Science, Mathematics and Administration,* Taylor and Francis, London.

Braverman, H., 1974, *Labor and Monopoly Capital,* Monthly Review Press, New York.

Brecht, B., 1963, *The Life of Galileo,* Eyre Methuen, London.

Britton, G. A., and McCallion, H. J., 1985, A case study demonstrating use of Beer's cybernetic model of viable systems, *Cybernetics and Systems* 16:229.

Brodheim, E., and Prastacos, G., 1979, The Long Island blood distribution system as a prototype for regional blood management, *Interfaces* 9:3.

Bryer, R. A., 1979, The status of the systems approach, *Omega* 7:219.

Buckley, W., 1967, *Sociology and Modern Systems Theory,* Prentice-Hall, Englewood Cliffs, NJ.

Burns, T., and Stalker, G. M., 1961, *The Management of Innovation,* Tavistock, London.

Burrell, G., 1983, "Systems Thinking, Systems Practice": A Review, *J. Appl. Sys. Anal.* 10:121.

Burrell, G., 1989, Postmodernism: Threat or opportunity, in: *Operational Research and the Social Sciences* (M. C. Jackson, P. Keys, and S. Cropper, eds.), Plenum, New York, pp. 59–64.

Burrell, G., and Morgan, G., 1979, *Sociological Paradigms and Organizational Analysis,* Heinemann, London.

Carter, P., Jackson, M. C., Jackson, N., and Keys, P., 1987, Community OR at Hull University, *Dragon* 2(2), special issue.

Checkland, P. B., 1971, A systems map of the universe, *J. of Sys. Eng.* 2:2.

Checkland, P. B., 1976, Towards a systems-based methodology for real-world problem-solving, in: *Systems Behaviour,* 2nd ed. (J. Beishon and G. Peters, eds.), Harper and Row, London, pp. 51–77.

Checkland, P. B., 1978, The origins and nature of "hard" systems thinking, *J. Appl. Sys. Anal.* 5(2):99.

Checkland, P. B., 1980, Are organizations machines?, *Futures* 12:421.

Flood, R. L., 1989b, Archaeology of (systems) inquiry, *Sys. Pract.* 2:117.

Flood, R. L., 1990a, *Liberating Systems Theory,* Plenum, New York.

Flood, R. L., 1990b, Liberating systems theory: Toward critical systems thinking, *Human Relations* 43:49.

Flood, R. L., 1990c, Critical systems thinking and the systems sciences, in: *Toward a Just Society for Future Generations* (B. A. Banathy and B. H. Banathy, eds.), ISSS, Portland, pp. 15–33.

Flood, R. L., and Carson, E. R., 1988, *Dealing with Complexity: An Introduction to the Theory and Application of Systems Science,* Plenum, New York.

Flood, R. L., and Gregory, W., 1989, Systems: past, present and future, in: *Systems Prospects* (R. L. Flood, M. C. Jackson, and P. Keys, eds.), Plenum, New York, pp. 55–60.

Flood, R. L., and Jackson, M. C., 1988, Cybernetics and organization theory: A critical review, *Cybernetics and Systems* 19:13.

Flood, R. L., and Jackson, M. C., 1991a, *Creative Problem Solving: Total Systems Intervention,* Wiley, Chichester.

Flood, R. L., and Jackson, M. C. (eds.), 1991b, *Critical Systems Thinking: Directed Readings,* Wiley, Chichester.

Flood, R. L., and Robinson, S. A., 1989, Whatever happened to general systems theory? in: *Systems Prospects* (R. L. Flood, M. C. Jackson, and P. Keys, eds.), Plenum, New York, pp. 61–66.

Flood, R. L., and Ulrich, W., 1990, Testament to conversations on critical systems thinking between two systems practitioners, *Sys. Pract.* 3:7.

Forrester, J. W., 1961, *Industrial Dynamics,* MIT Press, Cambridge, MA.

Forrester, J. W., 1969, *Principles of Systems,* Wright-Allen Press, Cambridge, MA.

Fuenmayor, R. L., 1985, The Ontology and Epistemology of a Systems Approach, Doctoral dissertation, Department of Systems, University of Lancaster.

Fuenmayor, R. L., 1989, Interpretive systemology: Its theoretical and practical development in a university school of systems in Venezuela, *Department of Management Systems and Sciences Working Paper* 22, University of Hull, Hull, England.

Fuenmayor, R. L., 1991, Between systems thinking and systems practice, in: *Critical Systems Thinking: Directed Readings* (R. L. Flood and M. C. Jackson, eds.), Wiley, Chichester.

Galbraith, J. R., 1977, *Organizational Design,* Addison-Wesley, Reading, MA.

Gerth, H. H., and Mills, C. W. (eds.), 1970, *From Max Weber,* Routledge and Kegan Paul, London.

Giddens, A., 1976, *New Rules of Sociological Method,* Hutchinson, London.

Gouldner, A., 1959, Organizational Analysis, in: *Sociology Today,* (R. K. Merton, L. Broom, and L. S. Cottrell, Jr., eds.), Basic Books, New York, pp. 400–428.

Gyllenhammer, P., 1977, *People at Work,* Addison-Wesley, Reading, MA.

Habermas, J., 1970, Knowledge and interest, in: *Sociological Theory and Philosophical Analysis,* (D. Emmet and A. MacIntyre, eds.), Macmillan, London, pp. 36–54.

Habermas, J., 1974, *Theory and Practice,* Heinemann, London.

Habermas, J., 1975, *Legitimation Crisis,* Beacon Press, Boston.

Habermas, J., 1976a, quoted in: *The Positivist Dispute in German Sociology* (D. Frisby, ed.), Heinemann, London.

Habermas, J., 1976b, The analytical theory of science and dialectics, in: *The Positivist Dispute in German Sociology* (D. Frisby, ed.), Heinemann, London, pp. 131–162.

Habermas, J., 1984, *Reason and the Rationalization of Society,* Beacon Press, Boston.

Hales, M., 1974, Management science and the "second industrial revolution," *Radical Science Journal* 1:5.

Hall, A. D., 1962, *A Methodology for Systems Engineering,* D. Van Nostrand Co., Princeton, NJ.

Harnden, R. J., 1989, Outside and then: An interpretive approach to the VSM, in: *The Viable System Model* (R. Espejo and R. J. Harnden, eds.), Wiley, Chichester, pp. 383–404.

Harnden, R. J., 1990, The languaging of models: The understanding and communication of models with particular reference to Stafford Beer's cybernetic model of organization structure, *Sys. Pract.* 3:289.

Hickson, D. J., Pugh, D. S., and Pheysey, D. C., 1969, Operations technology and organization structure: An empirical reappraisal, *ASQ* 14:378.

Hill, P., 1971, *Towards a New Philosophy of Management*, Gower Press, Epping.

Hitch, C. J., 1955, An appreciation of systems analysis, in: *Systems Analysis* (S. L. Optner, ed., 1973), Penguin, Harmondsworth, pp. 19–36.

Ho, J. K. K., and Jackson, M. C., 1987, Building a "rich picture" and assessing a "quality management" program at Thornton Printing Company, *Cybernetics and Systems* 18:381.

Hoos, I., 1972, *Systems Analysis in Public Policy: A Critique*, University of California Press, Berkeley.

Hoos, I., 1976, Engineers as analysts of social systems: A critical enquiry, *J. of Sys. Eng.* 4(2):81.

Horkheimer, M., 1976, Traditional and critical theory, in: *Critical Sociology* (P. Connerton, ed.), Penguin, Harmondsworth, pp. 206–224.

Jackson, M. C., 1978, *Considerations on Method*, M.A. dissertation, Department of Systems, University of Lancaster.

Jackson, M. C., 1982, The nature of soft systems thinking: The work of Churchman, Ackoff and Checkland, *J. Appl. Sys. Anal.* 9:17.

Jackson, M. C., 1983, The nature of soft systems thinking: Comments on the three replies, *J. Appl. Sys. Anal.* 10:109.

Jackson, M. C., 1985a, The itinerary of a critical approach, review of Ulrich's "Critical Heuristics of Social Planning," *J. Opl. Res. Soc.* 36:878.

Jackson, M. C., 1985b, Systems inquiring competence and organizational analysis, in: *Proceeding of the 1985 Meeting of the SGSR*, SGSR, Louisville, pp. 522–530.

Jackson, M. C., 1985c, A cybernetic approach to management, in: *Managing Transport Systems* (P. Keys and M. C. Jackson, eds.), Gower, Aldershot, pp. 25–52.

Jackson, M. C., 1985d, Social systems theory and practice: The need for a critical approach, *Int. J. of Gen. Sys.* 10:135.

Jackson, M. C., 1986, The cybernetic model of the organization: An assessment, in: *Cybernetics and Systems '86* (R. Trappl, ed.), D. Reidel, Dordrecht, pp. 189–196.

Jackson, M. C., 1987a, Systems strategies for information management in organizations which are not machines, *Int. J. of Inf. Mgt.* 7:185.

Jackson, M. C., 1987b, Present positions and future prospects in management science, *Omega* 15:455.

Jackson, M. C., 1987c, New directions in management science, in: *New Directions in Management Science* (M. C. Jackson and P. Keys, eds.), Gower, Aldershot, pp. 133–164.

Jackson, M. C., 1987d, Community operational research: Purposes, theory and practice, in: Community Operational Research at Hull University (P. Carter, M. C. Jackson, N. V. Jackson, and P. Keys, eds.), *Dragon* 2(2), special issue, pp. 47–73.

Jackson, M. C., 1988a, An appreciation of Stafford Beer's "viable system" viewpoint on managerial practice, *J. Mgt. Stud.* 25:557.

Jackson, M. C., 1988b, Some methodologies for community OR, *J. Opl. Res. Soc.* 39:715.

Jackson, M. C., 1988c, Systems methods for organizational analysis and design, *Sys. Res.* 5:201.

Jackson, M. C., 1989a, Evaluating the managerial significance of the VSM, in: *The Viable System Model* (R. Espejo and R. J. Harnden, eds.), Wiley, Chichester, pp. 407–439.

Jackson, M. C., 1989b, Assumptional analysis: An eludication and appraisal for systems practitioners, *Sys. Prac.* 2:11.

Jackson, M. C., 1990a, Beyond a system of systems methodologies, *J. Opl. Res. Soc.* 41:657.

Jackson, M. C., 1990b, Which systems methodology when?: Initial results from a research programme, in: *Systems Prospects* (R. L. Flood, M. C. Jackson, and P. Keys, eds.), Plenum, New York, pp. 235–241.

Jackson, M. C., 1990c, The critical kernel in modern systems thinking, *Sys. Prac.* 3:357.

Jackson, M. C., and Alabi, B. O., 1986, Viable systems all!: A diagnosis for XY Entertainments, *Department of Management Systems and Sciences Working Paper* 9, University of Hull, Hull, England.

Jackson, M. C., and Keys, P., 1984, Towards a system of systems methodologies, *J. Opl. Res. Soc.* 35:473.

Jackson, M. C., and Medjedoub, S., 1988, Designing evaluation systems: Theoretical groundings and a practical intervention, in: *Cybernetics and Systems '88* (R. Trappl, ed.), Kluwer Academic, The Netherlands, pp. 165–171.

Jackson, M. C., Keys, P., and Cropper, S. (eds.), 1989, *Operational Research and the Social Sciences*, Plenum, New York.

Jackson, N. V., and Carter, P., 1984, The attenuating function of myth in human understanding, *Human Relations* 37:515.

Jacques, R., 1989, Post-industrialism, post-modernity and OR: Towards a "custom and practice" of responsibility and possibility, in: *Operational Research and the Social Sciences* (M. C. Jackson, P. Keys, and S. Cropper, eds.), Plenum, New York, pp. 703–708.

Janes, F. R., 1988, Interpretive structural modelling: A methodology for structuring complex issues, *Trans. IMC* 10:145.

Jenkins, G. M., 1969, A systems study of a petrochemical plant, *J. of Sys. Eng.* 1:90.

Jenkins, G. M., 1972, The systems approach, in: *Systems Behaviour* (J. Beishon and G. Peters, eds.), OUP, London, pp. 78–104.

Jones, S., and Eden, C., 1981, OR in the community, *J. Opl. Res. Soc.* 32:335.

Journal of Applied Behavioural Science, 1986, special issue on "Socio-technical systems: Innovations in designing high performing systems," Volume 22(3).

Kast, F. E., and Rosenzweig, J. E., 1981, *Organization and Management: A Systems and Contingency Approach*, 3rd ed., McGraw-Hill, New York.

Katz, D., and Kahn, R. L., 1966, *The Social Psychology of Organizations*, Wiley, New York.

Keat, R., and Urry, J., 1975, *Social Theory as Science*, Routledge and Kegan Paul, London.

Keys, P., 1987, Traditional management science and the emerging critique, in: *New Directions in Management Science* (M. C. Jackson and P. Keys, eds.), Gower, Aldershot, pp. 1–25.

Keys, P., 1988, A methodology for methodology choice, *Sys. Res.* 5:65.

Keys, P., and Jackson, M. C. (eds.), 1985, *Managing Transport Systems: A Cybernetic Perspective*, Gower, Aldershot.

Kijima, K., and Mackness, J., 1987, Analysis of soft trends in systems thinking, *Sys. Res.* 4:235.

Kilmann, R. H., 1983, A dialectical approach to formulating and testing social science theories: Assumptional analysis, *Human Relations* 36:1.

Klir, G., 1985, *Architecture of Systems Problem Solving*, Plenum, New York.

Knights, D., 1989, Intervention and change, in: *Operational Research and the Social Sciences* (M. C. Jackson, P. Keys, and S. Cropper, eds.), Plenum, New York, pp. 287–292.

Kuhn, T., 1970, *The Structure of Scientific Revolutions*, 2nd ed., University of Chicago Press, Chicago.

Lawrence, P. R., and Lorsch, J. W., 1967, Differentiation and integration in complex organizations, *ASQ* 12:1.

Lawrence, P. R., and Lorsch, J. W., 1969, *Developing Organizations: Diagnosis and Action,* Addison-Wesley, Reading, MA.

Levi-Strauss, C., 1968, *Structural Anthropology,* Penguin, Harmondsworth.

Lilienfeld, R., 1975, Systems theory as ideology, *Social Research* 42:637.

Lilienfeld, R., 1978, *The Rise of Systems Theory: An Ideological Analysis,* Wiley, New York.

Lockwood, D., 1956, Some remarks on "The Social System," *BJS* 7:134.

Luck, M., 1984, Working with inner city community organizations, in: *The Writings of Steve Cook* (K. Bowen, A. Cook, and M. Luck, eds.), Operational Research Society, Birmingham.

Luhmann, N., 1976, A general theory of organized social systems, in: *European Contributions to Organization Theory* (G. Hofstede and M. Sami Kassem, eds.), Van Gorcum, The Netherlands, pp. 96–113.

Luhmann, N., 1986, The autopoiesis of social systems, in: *Sociocybernetic Paradoxes* (F. Geyer and J. van der Zouwen, eds.), Sage, London, pp. 172–192.

Lukes, S., 1974, *Power: A Radical View,* Macmillan, London.

Lyotard, J.-F., 1984, *The Postmodern Condition: A Report on Knowledge,* Manchester University Press, Manchester.

Marcuse, H., 1968, *One Dimensional Man,* Sphere Books, London.

Marx, K., 1961, *Capital,* Volume 1, Foreign Languages Publishing House, Moscow.

Mason, R. O., 1969, A dialectical approach to strategic planning, *Man. Sci.* 15:B403.

Mason, R. O., and Mitroff, I. I., 1981, *Challenging Strategic Planning Assumptions,* Wiley, New York.

Maturana, H. R., and Varela, F. J., 1980, *Autopoiesis and Cognition: The Realization of the Living,* D. Reidel, Dordrecht.

McCarthy, T. A., 1973, A theory of communicative competence, *Philosophy of the Social Sciences* 3:135.

McGregor, D., 1960, *The Human Side of Enterprise,* McGraw-Hill, New York.

Meadows, D. H., Meadows, D. L., Randers, J., and Behrens, W. W., III, 1972, *The Limits to Growth,* Universe Books, New York.

Merker, S. L., 1985, Living systems theory: A framework for management, *Behavioural Science* 30:187.

Miller, J. G., 1978, *Living Systems,* McGraw-Hill, New York.

Mingers, J. C., 1980, Towards an appropriate social theory for applied systems thinking: Critical theory and soft systems methodology, *J. Appl. Sys. Anal.* 7:41.

Mingers, J. C., 1984, Subjectivism and soft systems methodology—a critique, *J. Appl. Sys. Anal.* 11:85.

Mingers, J. C., 1989, An introduction to autopoiesis—implications and applications, *Sys. Pract.* 2:159.

Miser, H. J., and Quade, E. S. (eds.), 1985, *Handbook of Systems Analysis: Overview of Uses, Procedures, Applications and Practice,* North Holland, New York.

Miser, H. J., and Quade, E. S. (eds.), 1988, *Handbook of Systems Analysis: Craft Issues and Procedural Choices,* Wiley, New York.

Mitroff, I. I., and Emshoff, J. R., 1979, On strategic assumption-making: A dialectical approach to policy and planning, *Academy of Management Review* 4:1.

Mitroff, I. I., and Mason, R. O., 1981, The metaphysics of policy and planning: A reply to Cosier, *Academy of Management Review* 6:649.

Mitroff, I. I., Barabba, C. P., and Kilmann, R. H., 1977, The application of behavioural and philosophical techniques to strategic planning: A case study of a large federal agency, *Man. Sci.* 25:583.

Mitroff, I. I., Emshoff, J. R., and Kilmann, R. H., 1979, Assumptional analysis: A methodology for strategic problem-solving, *Man. Sci.* 25:583.

Molloy, K. J., and Best, D. P., 1980, The Checkland methodology considered as a theory building methodology, in: *Proceedings of the 5th European Meeting on Cybernetics and Systems Research* (R. Trappl, ed.), Hemisphere, Washington, p. 17.

Morgan, G., 1983a, Cybernetics and organization theory: Epistemology or technique?, *Human Relations* 35:345.

Morgan, G. (ed.), 1983b, *Beyond Method: Strategies for Social Research,* Sage, Beverly Hills, CA.

Morgan, G., 1986, *Images of Organization,* Sage, Beverly Hills, CA.

Morris, J., 1983, The brain, the heart and the big toe, *Creativity and Innovation Network* 9:25.

Müller-Merbach, H., 1984, Interdisciplinarity in OR—in the past and in the future, *J. Opl. Res. Soc.* 35:83.

Mumford, E., 1983, *Designing Participatively,* Manchester Business School, Manchester.

Naughton, J., 1979, *Anti-GST: An Evolutionary Manifesto,* paper for the Silver Anniversary Meeting of SGSR, London.

Oliga, J. C., 1986, Methodology in systems research: The need for a self-reflective commitment, in: *Mental Images, Values and Reality* (J. A. Dillon, Jr., ed.), SGSR, Louisville, KY, pp. B11–31.

Oliga, J. C., 1988, Methodological foundations of systems methodologies, *Sys. Pract.* 1:87.

Oliga, J. C., 1989a, Towards thematic consolidation in critical management science, in: *Systems Prospects* (R. L. Flood, M. C. Jackson, and P. Keys, eds.), Plenum, New York, pp. 109–114.

Oliga, J. C., 1989b, *Power and Interests in Organizations: A Contingent Relational View,* paper for the 33rd Annual Meeting of the ISSS, Edinburgh, Scotland.

Oliga, J. C., 1989c, *Ideology and Systems Emancipation,* paper for the 33rd Annual Meeting of the ISSS, Edinburgh, Scotland.

Oliga, J. C., 1990, Power-ideology matrix in social systems control, *Sys. Pract.* 3:31.

Pareto, V., 1919, *Traité de Sociologie Generale,* Volume 2, Librarie Payot, Lausanne.

Parsons, T., 1956, Suggestions for a sociological approach to the theory of organizations—1, *ASQ* 1:63.

Parsons, T., 1957, Suggestions for a sociological approach to the theory of organizations—2, *ASQ* 2:225.

Parsons, T., 1960, *Structure and Process in Modern Society,* Free Press, New York.

Parsons, T., and Smelser, N. J., 1956, *Economy and Society,* Routledge and Kegan Paul, London.

Pasmore, W., Francis, C., Haldeman, J., and Shani, A., 1982, Socio-technical systems: A North American reflection on empirical studies of the seventies, *Human Relations,* 35:1179–1204.

Perrow, C., 1961, The analysis of goals in complex organisations, *ASR,* 26:854.

Perrow, C., 1967, A framework for the comparative analysis of organizations, *ASR* 32:194.

Perrow, C., 1972, *Complex Organizations: A Critical Essay,* Scott, Foresman and Co., Glenview, IL.

Peters, T. J., and Waterman, R. H., Jr., 1982, *In Search of Excellence,* Harper and Row, New York.

Piaget, J., 1973, *Main Trends in Interdisciplinary Research,* George Allen and Unwin, London.

Prastacos, G., 1980, Blood management systems: An overview of theory and practice, *IIASA Papers,* Laxenburg, Austria, pp. 80–81.

Pugh, D., and Hickson, D. J., 1976, *Organizational Structure in Its Context,* Saxon House and Lexington Books, Farnborough.

Quade, E. S., 1963, Military systems analysis, in: *Systems Analysis* (S. L. Optner, ed., 1965), Penguin, Harmondsworth, pp. 121–139.

Rapoport, A., 1986, *General System Theory,* Abacus, Tunbridge Wells.

Reed, M., 1985, *Redirections in Organizational Analysis,* Tavistock, London.

Rescher, N., 1979, *Cognitive Systematization,* Basil Blackwell, Oxford.

Rice, A. K., 1958, *Productivity and Social Organization,* Tavistock, London.

Rice, A. K., 1963, *The Enterprise and Its Environment,* Tavistock, London.

Rivett, P., 1977, The case for cybernetics, *Eur. J. Opl. Res.* 1:3.

Roethlisberger, F. J., and Dickson, W. J., 1939, *Management and the Worker,* Harvard University Press, Cambridge, MA.

Rosenhead, J., 1976, Some further comments on "The Social Responsibility of OR," *ORQ* 17:265.

Rosenhead, J., 1981, OR in urban planning, *Omega* 9:345.

Rosenhead, J., 1982, Why does management need management science?, in: *A General Survey of Systems Methodology* (L. Troncale, ed.), SGSR, Washington, pp. 834–839.

Rosenhead, J., 1984, Debating systems methodology: Conflicting ideas about conflict and ideas, *J. Appl. Sys. Anal.* 11:79.

Rosenhead, J., 1986, Custom and practice, *J. Opl. Res. Soc.* 37:335.

Rosenhead, J., 1987, From management science to workers' science, in: *New Directions in Management Science* (M. C. Jackson and P. Keys, eds.), Gower, Aldershot, pp. 109–131.

Rosenhead, J., 1989, Introduction: Old and new paradigms of analysis, in: *Rational Analysis for a Problematic World* (J. Rosenhead, ed.), Wiley, Chichester, pp. 1–20.

Rosenhead, J. (ed.), 1989, *Rational Analysis for a Problematic World,* Wiley, Chichester.

Rosenhead, J., and Thunhurst, C., 1982, A materialist analysis of operational research, *J. Opl. Res. Soc.* 33:111.

Salah, M., 1989, Structural Prerequisites for the Design of Information Systems: A Cybernetic Diagnosis of a Steel Distribution Organization, Doctoral dissertation, Department of Management Systems and Sciences, University of Hull, Hull, England.

Schecter, D., 1990, Critical systems thinking and democratic organizational structure, in: *Toward a Just Society for Future Generations* (B. H. Banathy and B. A. Banathy, eds.), ISSS, Portland, pp. 126–137.

Schecter, D., 1991, Critical systems thinking in the 1980s: A connective summary, in: *Critical Systems Thinking: Directed Readings* (R. L. Flood and M. C. Jackson, eds.), Wiley, Chichester.

Schein, E. A., 1970, *Organizational Psychology,* 2nd ed., Prentice-Hall, Englewood Cliffs, NJ.

Schoderbek, P. P., Schoderbek, C. G., and Kefalas, A. G., 1985, *Management Systems: Conceptual Considerations,* 3rd ed., Business Publications, Dallas.

Schumann, W., 1990, Strategy for information systems in the Film Division of Hoechst, A. G., *Sys. Pract.* 3:265.

Selznick, P., 1948, Foundations of the theory of organization, *ASR* 13:25.

Shannon, C. E., and Weaver, W., 1949, *The Mathematical Theory of Communication,* University of Illinois Press, Urbana.

Sica, A., 1981, Review of "The Systems Approach and Its Enemies," *AJS* 87:208.

Silverman, D., 1970, *The Theory of Organizations,* Heinemann, London.

Simon, H. A., 1947, *Administrative Behaviour,* Macmillan, New York.

Sims, D., and Smithin, T., 1982, Voluntary OR, *J. Opl. Res. Soc.* 33:21.

Spear, R., 1987, *Towards a Critical Systems Approach,* paper for the 31st Annual Meeting of the ISGSR, Budapest, Hungary.

Spencer, H., 1969, *Principles of Sociology* (S. Andreski, ed.), Macmillan, London.

Steering Group for the Community OR Initiative, 1986, *Community OR: Notes for Those Submitting Proposals,* Operational Research Society, Birmingham.

Stowell, F. A., 1989, Organizational power and the metaphor commodity, in: *Systems Prospects* (R. L. Flood, M. C. Jackson, and P. Keys, eds.), Plenum, New York, pp. 147–153.

Strank, R. H. D., 1982, *Management Principles and Practice: A Cybernetic Analysis*, Gordon and Breach, London.

Taylor, F. W., 1947, *Scientific Management*, Harper and Row, London.

Thomas, A., 1980, Generating tension for constructive change: The use and abuse of systems models, *Cybernetics and Systems* 11:339.

Thomas, A., and Lockett, M., 1979, Marxism and systems research: Values in practical action, in: *Improving the Human Condition* (R. F. Ericson, ed.), SGSR, Louisville, pp. 284–293.

Thompson, J. D., 1967, *Organizations in Action*, McGraw-Hill, New York.

Thompson, J. D., and McEwan, W. J., 1958, Organizational goals and environment: Goal-setting as an interaction process, *ASR* 23:23.

Tinker, T., and Lowe, T., 1984, One dimensional management science: The making of a technocratic consciousness, *Interfaces* 14:40.

Tomlinson, R., 1984, Rethinking the process of systems analysis and operational research: From practice to precept and back again, in: *Rethinking the Process of Operational Research and Systems Analysis* (R. Tomlinson and I. Kiss, eds.), Pergamon, Oxford, pp. 205–221.

Tomlinson, R., 1987, Operational research and systems analysis—science in action, applicable mathematics, or social engineering, in: *New Directions in Management Science* (M. C. Jackson and P. Keys, eds.), Gower, Aldershot, pp. 27–41.

Tomlinson, R., and Kiss, I. (eds.), 1984, *Rethinking the Process of Operational Research and Systems Analysis*, Pergamon, Oxford.

Trist, E. L., and Bamforth, K. W., 1951, Some social and psychological consequences of the long wall method of coal-getting, *Human Relations* 4:3.

Trist, E. L., Higgin, G. W., Murray, H., and Pollock, A. B., 1963, *Organizational Choice*, Tavistock, London.

Ulrich, H., and Probst, G. J. B., 1984, *Self-Organization and Management of Social Systems*, Springer-Verlag, Berlin.

Ulrich, W., 1981a, A critique of pure cybernetic reason: The Chilean experience with cybernetics, *J. Appl. Sys. Anal.* 8:33.

Ulrich, W., 1981b, On blaming the messenger for the bad news: Reply to Bryer's "Comments," *Omega* 9:7.

Ulrich, W., 1983, *Critical Heuristics of Social Planning: A New Approach to Practical Philosophy*, Haupt, Bern.

Ulrich, W., 1985, The way of inquiring systems, review of Churchman's "The Design of Inquiring Systems," *J. Opl. Res. Soc.* 36:873.

Ulrich, W., 1987, Critical heuristics of social systems design, *Eur. J. Opl. Res.* 31:276.

Ulrich, W., 1988, Systems thinking, systems practice, and practical philosophy: A program of research, *Sys. Pract.* 1:137.

van Gigch, J. P., 1978, *Applied General Systems Theory*, 2nd ed., Harper and Row, New York.

Varela, F. J., 1984, Two principles of self-organization, in: *Self Organization and Management of Social Systems* (H. Ulrich and G. J. B. Probst, eds.), Springer-Verlag, Berlin, pp. 25–32.

Vickers, G., 1965, *The Art of Judgement*, Chapman and Hall, London.

Vickers, G., 1970, *Freedom in a Rocking Boat*, Allen Lane, London.

Vickers, G., 1973, *Making Institutions Work*, Associated Business Programmes, London.

Vickers, G., 1978, Practice and research in managing human systems—four problems of relationship, *Policy Science* 9:1.

Vickers, G., 1983, *Human Systems are Different*, Harper and Row, London.

von Bertalanffy, L., 1950, The theory of open systems in physics and biology, in: *Systems Thinking* (F. E. Emery, ed.), Penguin, Harmondsworth, pp. 70–85.

von Bertalanffy, L., 1968, *General System Theory*, Penguin, Harmondsworth.

Warfield, J., 1976, *Societal Systems: Planning, Policy and Complexity*, Wiley, New York.

Weinberg, G. M., 1975, *An Introduction to General System Theory*, Wiley, New York.

Wiener, N., 1948, *Cybernetics*, Wiley, New York.

Wiener, N., 1950, *The Human Use of Human Beings*, Eyre and Spottiswoode, London.

Willmott, H., 1989, OR as a problem situation: From soft systems methodology to critical science, in: *Operational Research and the Social Sciences* (M. C. Jackson, P. Keys, and S. A. Cropper, eds.), Plenum, New York, pp. 65–78.

Wilson, B., 1984, *Systems: Concepts, Methodologies and Applications*, Wiley, New York.

Wood, S., and Kelly, J., 1978, Towards a critical management science, *J. Mgt. Stud.* 15:1.

Woodward, J., 1964, *Industrial Organizations: Theory and Practice*, OUP, London.

Index

DATE DUE

The Library Store   #47-0103 Pre-Gummed